Cary Nelson and the
Struggle for the University

Cary Nelson and the Struggle for the University

Poetry, Politics, and the Profession

Edited by
Michael Rothberg
and
Peter K. Garrett

State University of New York Press

Credit: Violet Kazue de Cristoforo (trans.), selections from *May Sky: There is Always Tomorrow*. Copyright © 1997 by Violet Kazue de Cristoforo. Reprinted with the permission of Green Integer Books, Los Angeles, www.greeninteger.com.

Cover photo: Cary Nelson at Yale University, April 2007. Photo by Maris Zivarts.

Published by State University of New York Press, Albany

© 2009 State University of New York

For information, contact State University of New York Press, Albany, NY
www.sunypress.edu

Production by Diane Ganeles
Marketing by Michael Campochiaro

Library of Congress Cataloging-in-Publication Data

Cary Nelson and the struggle for the university : poetry, politics, and the profession / edited by Michael Rothberg and Peter K. Garrett.
    p. cm.
  A collection of essays that examine Cary Nelson's career and the politics of the academy.
  Includes bibliographical references and index.
  ISBN 978-0-7914-7679-6 (hardcover : alk. paper) — ISBN 978-0-7914-7680-2 (pbk. : alk. paper) 1. Nelson, Cary. 2. Critics—United States—Biography. 3. Scholars—United States—Biography. 4. College teachers—United States— Biography. 5. Criticism—United States—History—20th century. 6. Education, Humanistic. 7. Education, Higher—Political aspects—United States. 8. Universities and colleges—Political aspects—United States. 9. United States—Intellectual life— 20th century. 10. Culture—Philosophy. I. Rothberg, Michael. II. Garrett, Peter K.
  PS29.N46C37 2009
  378'.012—dc22
                                        2008005669

10 9 8 7 6 5 4 3 2 1

CONTENTS

ACKNOWLEDGMENTS

This volume began as a conference called "Poetry, Politics, and the Profession: A Tribute to Cary Nelson," which was jointly sponsored by the Unit for Criticism and Interpretive Theory and the Department of English at the University of Illinois at Urbana-Champaign. We are grateful to Martin Camargo, the head of the English Department, for supporting the idea of this event enthusiastically from the beginning. The able department staff, Deb Stauffer, Terri Davis, and Becky Moss, took care of many of the logistical issues for the conference. In the Unit for Criticism office, we were helped immensely by Elizabeth Hoiem and Jennifer Lieberman; Jenni in particular has been actively involved all the way through the production of the book. Paula Treichler was central to this endeavor from the beginning; without her hard-earned skills in managing Cary, the event might never have happened.

A number of additional people helped make the conference a success: Stacy Alaimo, Anne Balsamo, Kathryn Benzel, Jane Buck, Lee Furey, René Garcia, Larry Hanley, Jefferson Hendricks, Constance Penley, William Plater, Mark Van Wienen, Alan Wald, and Dan Vukovich.

Several organizations, offices, and individuals on and off campus were extremely generous in providing funds for the conference. We are grateful to Interim Provost Jesse Delia, the LAS State-of-the-Art Conference Fund, the American Association of University Professors (AAUP), the Illinois State Conference of AAUP Chapters, the University of Illinois at Urbana-Champaign AAUP chapter, the Trowbridge Office for American Literature, Culture, and Society, the University of Illinois Press, the Center for Advanced Study, the Center on Democracy in a Multiracial Society, the Illinois Program for Research in the Humanities, and Richard Powers.

We are grateful to our editors, James Peltz and Larin McLaughlin, for helping make this book possible.

∴ 1 ∾

An Exemplary Career

Cary Nelson and the
Struggle for the University

Michael Rothberg and Peter K. Garrett

> *You cannot be a Union Man,*
> *No matter how you try,*
> *Unless you think in terms of "We,"*
> *Instead of terms of "I."*
>
> —J. P. Thompson, "Union Poem"

> *[P]oetry's political apotheosis comes in the form of collective knowledge and*
> *collective action.*
>
> —Cary Nelson[1]

It is well known that the humanities are currently in dire straits. Funding is stagnating or being cut, and the humanities' position of authority relative to the disciplines that make up the contemporary university continues to erode as market forces increasingly penetrate the so-called Ivory Tower, and business and techno-science replace humanistic learning with respect to resources and, perhaps more importantly, prestige or symbolic capital. This situation is not new, but in the current context it is being exacerbated by the almost uncontested doctrine of neoliberalism, a doctrine that would like to submit all realms of human existence to the exigencies of the market. Yet as necessary as it is to offer such dark assessments of the conditions of humanities research—and, indeed, of fundamental research and public education more generally—such assessments only capture part of the story. Indeed, the situation of the humanities today, as for much of the last few decades, is paradoxical: while, on the one hand, the humanities exist in precarious material conditions and with waning intellectual prestige, it is equally true, on the other hand, that humanities research remains vibrant and humanities teachers remain essential to educating a democratic citizenry.

1

The problem is not one of humanists' irrelevance or obscurity, although that is most often the judgment that emerges from the centers of corporate management and the right-wing media; to the contrary, the insights humanists have to offer are dangerously relevant to a society that would like to banish critical, historical thinking in a time of war and untrammeled market dominance. If scholars and teachers in the humanities are to avoid despair and collaboration in our own demise, then it is crucial to address both sides of the paradoxical situation in which we find ourselves—a task that *Cary Nelson and the Struggle for the University: Poetry, Politics, and the Profession* sets out to accomplish. Accounts are needed of the material constraints that limit possibilities for creative, challenging research and stunt the careers of too many humanities students and colleagues. The humanities must, nonetheless, persist in the production of new, critical knowledge, keeping in mind that the cost of giving up our pursuits would be too high, the end of democratic possibility itself. With these stakes in mind, this book assesses and builds on the contributions of one exemplary scholar-activist—Cary Nelson—whose writings, actions, and vision consistently draw our attention to the varied, if often inhospitable, terrain of twentieth- and twenty-first-century cultural and intellectual life.

A self-confessed "tenured radical," Nelson is probably best known by a general audience for his uncompromising and brutally honest contributions to understanding the first side of the humanities' paradoxical situation—the immiseration of the humanities and the destruction of the conditions necessary to any kind of humanistic education. Consider, for instance, "It Might as Well Be a Conspiracy," the ironically titled introduction to Nelson's most recent book on the academy, *Office Hours*, coauthored with Stephen Watt. Nelson and Watt waste no time saying that "[h]igher education as we have known it for nearly a half century is in the process of unraveling," and they do not hesitate to catalogue the ills that currently beset "disciplines unable to generate their own revenue": "Increased class sizes, increased teaching loads, decreased library resources, decreased research funding, declining real salaries in less entrepreneurial disciplines, increasingly centralized curricular control, steadily increasing reliance on contingent labor, decreasing job security, increasing political threats to academic freedom," and so on (1, 3). There are, in short, more than enough reasons to despair.

But despite such necessary and clear-eyed assessments of real decline, Nelson's career actually provides one of the best illustrations of the importance of addressing both sides of this condition: his career combines field-changing work on modern American poetry, on the one hand, and activist and discursive interventions into the organization and working conditions of the university, on the other. Nelson—and the other colleagues and former students gathered here—is no less passionate when producing new knowledge about apparently esoteric subjects than he is when attempting to change the conditions of possibility for that production. The distinction is not between the political and the nonpolitical: especially in Nelson's hands, work on modern poetry is as political as writing essays on contingent labor and the increasing corporatization of the university or, indeed, as sitting down in the middle of traffic in support of graduate student unionization, as Nelson recently did in order to use his new position as president of the American Association of University Professors (AAUP) to draw attention to a strike at New York University (NYU). To be sure, these interventions work at somewhat different levels and temporalities and come with divergent risks and stakes, yet they are all potentially political—and Nelson's career suggests that we in the humanities should do a lot more of all of them.

The essays and reflections collected in this book make a strong case that Nelson's career is *exemplary*: it simultaneously sets a very high bar for scholarship and activism and yet can and should serve as a model for the engaged academic.[2] Nelson's career is worth exploring in depth both because of the extensive and influential scholarship he has produced and because of the highly visible work he has done as an activist in the academy. Like Nelson's output, the essays collected here may at first glance seem eclectic. But the career, like the book, is held together by overarching commitments that gain in power when they resonate together. The unifying node of Nelson's career is a commitment to the radical democratization of American culture and a recognition of the many progressive projects and energies that have been forgotten or repressed. The major lesson of Nelson's engagement is that the democratization of American cultural history will remain an unfinished project as long as we fail to democratize the *institutions* of American culture—and that means, first and foremost, the university.

In an effort to make Nelson's multifaceted career available for further reflection and revision, *Cary Nelson and the Struggle for the University* brings together well-known and up-and-coming literary and cultural studies scholars to explore an exemplary career in which scholarship and activism have been united. Neither a Festschrift nor a tribute, this book uses Nelson's career as a focal point for a consideration of the politics of the academy. It is organized around the three key roles Nelson has taken on throughout his four decades in the academy: innovative scholar, tireless public intellectual and activist, and dedicated mentor.

Among Nelson's contributions on the scholarly side are six authored, two coauthored, and sixteen edited books, plus more than one hundred essays. As several essays included here demonstrate, his studies of modern American poetry, including *Our First Last Poets* (1981), *Repression and Recovery* (1989), and *Revolutionary Memory* (2001), have energetically recovered, analyzed, and celebrated the cultural work of writers on the Left, and his radically innovative Oxford *Anthology of Modern American Poetry* (2000), accompanied by an extensive and growing Web site, has dramatically expanded the canon. Nelson's long-running, successful efforts to diversify the canon of American poetry dovetail with his more general contributions to ethnic studies and feminist studies. While focused especially on the US context, Nelson's commitment to excavating a pluralist Left also opens up obvious links to internationalism. These links are especially evident in his long-term project to recover the poetry and artifacts of the Spanish Civil War—a project that has resulted in the publication of volumes such as *Madrid 1937: Letters of the Abraham Lincoln Brigade from the Spanish Civil War* (edited with Jefferson Hendricks, 1996), *The Aura of the Cause: A Photo Album for North American Volunteers in the Spanish Civil War* (1997), and *The Wound and the Dream: Sixty Years of American Poems about the Spanish Civil War* (2002).

As Nelson's studies of modern American poetry have led him back into its forgotten past and outward into its international affiliations, he has increasingly articulated the many connections between poetry and politics, both in the work of politically engaged poets he has brought back to our attention and in the ideologically restricted conception of modernism that long excluded them. One of the things that makes his career exemplary is the way it springs from a passionate belief in the value of poetry itself.

> Poetry has had a very long cultural history, as prayer, as chant, as curse, as the song of the subject and the song of the chorus. Nothing poetry has become was foreordained. History might have gone differently. But as things have worked out poetry's inscaped language registers a culture's idealizations and its traumas with unique compression and power. There's nothing else quite like it. Save for technology and science, poetry embodies all you need to know on earth. (Bousquet)

Here, with Nelson's characteristic touch of hyperbole, we can recognize a vital source of his achievement. Just as poetry's history might have gone differently, so might the literary and cultural interests of a critic on the Left have gone into the more typical study of fiction or the media, his or her radical energy into ideological critique. Instead, Nelson's dedication to recovering forgotten poets and critiquing the forces that repressed their memory has dramatically extended our sense of both poetry's recent history and its possibilities. The 161 "poet companion sites" on the Modern American Poetry Site testify to this extension, while their growing network of commentaries and contexts shows the many ways poetry can indeed register culture's idealizations and traumas. Nelson has recently extended this expansive democratizing impulse even farther in his study of poem postcards, rescuing ephemera whose claim on readers' attention is less their intrinsic aesthetic interest than the individual and cultural uses they served, especially in times of war. In paying serious, careful attention to these mass-produced texts, Nelson has found yet another surprising way of celebrating poetry's long cultural history.

As another set of essays suggests, Nelson is also a trenchant analyst of the problems and prospects of the academy. In books such as *Manifesto of a Tenured Radical* (1997), *Academic Keywords* (1999), and *Office Hours* (2004), as well as in the edited volumes *Higher Education Under Fire* (1994) and *Will Teach for Food* (1997), and in dozens of occasional pieces, he has established a reputation as one of the most forthright critics of the status quo in the academy. His biting, but often hilarious, accounts of the strange and destructive customs of the profession have angered many, especially those who occupy the upper reaches of academic privilege, but at the same time they have made him a hero to those toiling at the bottom of the pyramid. Nelson's engagement with such issues as academic freedom and the working conditions of graduate students and adjunct faculty has also informed his lengthy service in the Modern Language Association (MLA) and AAUP, service that has culminated in his current presidency of the latter organization. As AAUP president, Nelson has helped bring into public focus controversial issues concerning academic freedom and politics in the classroom and has generated a necessary, lively—and sometimes contentious—debate. Here too there is much to be learned from Nelson's example. As in his scholarship, so in his "service" (typically the least honored and rewarded of the three categories of expected academic activities), he has found remarkably effective ways to advance his expansive, democratic agenda. He shows how the solitary work of a researcher in the archive and the collective work of committees and policy debates can become joined in a continuum of underlying values.

While ever productive and always engaged with forces at the institutional level, Nelson's ultimate influence may be felt through the younger scholars he has inspired and helped spur on to further projects. His legacy is a direct result of his dedicated work as a mentor, especially for graduate students. He has directed more than two dozen dissertations, of which ten have already been published as books. His students occupy important positions in the profession and have already made major contributions to scholarship; these students, many of whom are represented in this book, make up what Nelson calls in his afterword a "research community" dedicated to working on various sides of a common project. This aspect of his career is exemplary precisely in suggesting the necessity of considering intellectual work a collective endeavor, involving tasks greater than any one scholar—even one as prolific as Nelson himself—can or should accomplish alone. Nelson's persistent and generous attention to mentoring is reflected in the essays that close this book, attesting to the formation of a community of scholars united—although not without tension or difficulty—by common intellectual, political, and personal commitments. Attentive to the poetics as well as the politics of mentoring, these final reflections suggest that the struggle for the university will continue as new generations of scholars and students revise and rework the lessons of their teachers and mentors. Seen in objective terms, the present and future of the profession may look grim. But if there is to be hope for radical change—or even significant reform—in the institutions of higher learning, then it is going to come because of the kinds of collective projects that Nelson has played such a key role in inaugurating.

Divided into three parts—"The Canon and the Politics of Poetry," "Corporatization and the Politics of the Academy," and "Pedagogy and the Politics of Mentoring"—the essays collected here are accessibly written, lively, and funny, as is only fitting for a volume that considers the Nelsonian legacy! They are also passionate in their commitments to politically informed scholarship and pedagogy. That most of the scholars here have long-standing affiliations with Nelson—either as colleagues or former students—does not mean that these essays all toe a common line. Far from it. Rather, the interest of this book lies in the intellectual energy of engagement that is common to the contributions: some essays survey Nelson's contributions to particular areas (poetry, activism, mentoring), while others engage quite critically with some of his ideas, and yet others recognize the need to extend his contributions into fields he has not yet weighed in on.

Thus in the poetry section, part 1, Edward Brunner and Walter Kalaidjian take up Nelson's work on modern American poetry, but they come to rather different conclusions about the nature of his critical career, with Brunner arguing for long-term continuities and Kalaidjian locating a significant break between Nelson's first two books. Meanwhile, Grant Farred develops some unexpected affinities between Nelson's archival activism and Derrida's theory of archive fever, and Karen Jackson Ford and Michael Thurston take inspiration from Nelson in order to develop their own particular projects in poetics.

Marc Bousquet opens the section on the politics of the academy, part 2, with a detailed account of different notions of corporatization. He stresses Nelson's contributions to the critique of the corporate university and seeks to extend Nelson's engaged cultural studies model through his own original research on the dominance of administrative logic. Michael Bérubé turns to Nelson the "organization man." He makes a strong connection between Nelson's work on marginal poetry and his defense of marginalized teachers in the academy; just as *Repression and Recovery* was dedicated to uncovering "modern poems we have wanted to forget," Nelson's work at the institutional level is, Bérubé suggests, dedicated to "uncovering and redressing academic realities we have wanted to forget." Stephen Watt's essay demonstrates just why we need more "organization men"; he tracks some of the internal limits to activist organization in the self-defeating tendencies of some humanities professors. Once again there are some disagreements about Nelson's model—here with respect primarily to activism. While Lisa Duggan finds inspiration for contemporary political engagement in the model of cultural studies developed by Nelson and others at Illinois in the 1980s and 1990s, Jane Juffer's provocative essay on how to respond to the corporate academy takes issue with central aspects of Nelson's approach to the politics of the academy. At the same time that Bousquet and Andrew Ross acknowledge Nelson's critique of corporatization, they nonetheless suggest the need to attend to new avenues for such political engagement. Ross's timely and original essay calls for a new account of the global university.

In the section on mentoring, part 3, former students highlight not only what they learned from Nelson as a teacher but also how they have continued to develop and transform what they have learned. Marsha Bryant's essay on the "poetics of mentoring" opens this section by laying out the ways she has developed Nelson's practices into a full-fledged program for mentoring. James Finnegan, Brady Harrison, John Marsh, James D. Sullivan, and Jeff Sychterz take a productively direct approach in their reflections on Nelson's professional personae; they employ bracingly honest voices that assess the brutalities and purposes of working in the humanities, and they track the influence of Nelson's pedagogy and research into the diverse locations of higher education, including community colleges and even the US Naval Academy. It is in these essays especially that the themes of this book coalesce; Nelson's former students demonstrate how thoroughly intertwined teaching, research, and service actually are in practice, but also how difficult it remains for the profession to recognize this basic fact. In addition to testifying to Nelson's personal as well as professional influence, these pieces indicate how the political purposes informing his scholarship and activism can extend into the training of the next generation: political activism and intellectual commitments come together in Nelson's graduate mentoring to form an exemplary pedagogy.

If a name can be given that would unite the many sides of Nelson's career, it would probably have to be cultural studies, as Bousquet also suggests. Taking inspiration especially from the British cultural studies of Raymond Williams and Stuart Hall, although giving it a decidedly American spin, Nelson has remained true to what Hall called the "presentist" moment of cultural studies—its insistence that the political stakes of all scholarship are in the contemporary world, even when that scholarship is dedicated to a mutually enlightening dialogue between the past and the present. Cultural studies, Nelson has wittily remarked in a controversial sixteen-point manifesto, might be thought of as something like a rat among the disciplines: "a largely urban animal who is wary, focused on local conditions, and willing to eat almost anything. [. . .] [a] political animal attuned to assuring the survival of his or her interests" (*Manifesto* 73). This image of Machiavellian omnivorousness nicely captures the tactically minded, necessarily eclectic intellectual and political commitments that define the best of cultural studies and Nelson's own work.

Nelson himself has played a galvanizing role in the emergence of cultural studies as an intellectual and political force in the US academy, a story Duggan's and Harrison's essays vividly narrate. His contribution to interdisciplinary research in the humanities and social sciences is manifested especially in his leading role in organizing and editing the proceedings of two major international conferences, *Marxism and the Interpretation of Culture* (1988) and *Cultural Studies* (1992), monumental collections that remain unsurpassed in their scope and ambition. These works are, without the slightest exaggeration, legitimately called landmarks, and they testify to the brilliance of Nelson, as well as his coeditors, Lawrence Grossberg and Paula Treichler, in identifying the right contributors, the right essays, and the right moment to make the intellectual intervention. Indeed, it is difficult to imagine the contemporary theoretical landscape without some of the essays published in those volumes, such as Gayatri Spivak's "Can the Subaltern Speak?" and Fredric Jameson's "Cognitive Mapping," from the Marxism volume, or Constance Penley's and Donna Haraway's innovative explorations from the cultural studies volume, among many other highly influential essays in those collections.

Those two mega-conferences were organized under the auspices of the Unit for Criticism and Interpretive Theory, a unique program Nelson cofounded in the early 1980s. Under Nelson's early leadership and ongoing involvement, "the Unit"—as it is known in Urbana-Champaign— served as a portal throughout the 1980s for the introduction of cultural studies to the American academy. Today, in a moment sometimes facilely defined as "posttheoretical," the Unit continues to promote intellectual community among theoretically minded faculty and graduate students by providing a base for interdisciplinary scholarship with a progressive political edge. If, as Nelson remarks in his manifesto, "the work of theorizing [. . .] is inescapably grounded in contemporary life and current politics," and it thus becomes impossible "to theorize for all times and places," the work of theory is not rendered dispensable (*Manifesto* 68). Rather, it remains an ongoing commitment, a necessary component of humanities scholarship and political activism. Furthermore, as Nelson recognizes (and discusses in his afterword), ongoing commitments—to theory, cultural studies, and activism—require habitable institutions and communities. The Unit's persistence well into its third decade owes much to Nelson's belief in the importance of institution building—and his institutional savvy.

This book derives from the most recent in the Unit's tradition of simultaneously scholarly and politically committed conferences. It seeks to learn from Nelson's exemplary career in order to set out a multifaceted (if necessarily partial) program for recognizing the radical potential of American culture and for facing up to the ideological and institutional limits that often block that potential or render it invisible. Like the book itself, this program comprises three parts: an exploration of the politics and political potentialities of culture (here charted in exemplary fashion via the ongoing reconsideration of modern American poetry and the problem of the canon); a critical interrogation of the academy itself as the macro-context of intellectual production (with a special focus on the neoliberal corporate academy in both its domestic and increasingly global guises); and the excavation of the micro-politics of intellectual inquiry through a textured, personal consideration of pedagogy and mentoring that reveals the importance of cohorts and communities of scholars in enabling innovative research. Thus although organized through intensive focus on an individual career, the "argument" of this book maintains that intellectual projects are most likely to succeed when pursued with awareness of their larger enabling and limiting institutional contexts, and when understood as oriented toward the creation of and participation in communities and collective structures. This is, of course, an argument that owes a large debt to Nelson's own work; as Nelson and Watt write, "There is [. . .] but one way to resist all the forces at work to disempower and degrade the professoriate and instrumentalize education—collective action" (*Office Hours* 2). In a moment of budget cuts, war, and wiretaps, the essays collected here advance a project for collective action: a cultural politics dedicated to free inquiry, workplace solidarity, creative scholarship, and a deep sense of the relevance of the struggles and legacies of the past.

Notes

1. J. P. Thompson's poem, published by the Vancouver Branch of the Industrial Workers of the World on a folded red card, circa 1909, is reproduced in Nelson, *Revolutionary Memory* 30. The card comes from Nelson's personal collection. The quotation from Nelson is from the same book, p. 9.

2. For a related view of the exemplary status of Nelson's career, see the tribute by Alan Wald.

Works Cited

Bousquet, Marc. "An Intellectual of the Movement: An Interview with Cary Nelson." *Workplace: A Journal for Academic Labor.* 5.1 (2002). 4 Dec. 2007 <http://www.louisville.edu/journal/workplace/issue5p1/bousquetnelson.html>.

Nelson, Cary. *Manifesto of a Tenured Radical.* New York: New York UP, 1997.

————. *Revolutionary Memory: Recovering the Poetry of the American Left.* New York: Routledge, 2001.

Nelson, Cary, and Stephen Watt. *Office Hours: Activism and Change in the Academy.* New York: Routledge, 2004.

Wald, Alan. "Il Miglior Fabbro." *Workplace: A Journal for Academic Labor.* 5.1 (2002). 4 Dec. 2007 <http://www.cust.educ.ubc.ca/workplace/issue5p1/wald.html>.

PART 1

THE CANON AND THE POLITICS OF POETRY

⌒ 2 ⌒

PRESERVING THRESHOLDS

THE SCHOLAR IN THE MUSEUM,
JUNK SHOP, AND LIBRARY

Edward Brunner

> *Criticism is [. . .] a special way of projecting individual experience through the medium of preexistent texts. Both the critic and the texts [. . .] will be transformed in the process of creating a critical language. [. . .] This dialectic between self and other, embedded in the critic's language and method, is really what criticism is "about." There is no way a critic can simply talk about history without trying to engage and co-opt it.*
>
> —Cary Nelson, "Reading Criticism"

That Cary Nelson has something of an archivist's sensibility may be one of the few uncontroversial statements that can be made about him. The signature Nelson essay of the last twenty years places such unusual material on display as the back cover of a first edition, a limited-printing pamphlet, a poster salvaged from a far-off corner of the world, a family member's scrapbook, an obscure advertisement from a yellowing page in a newspaper or magazine, or a scrap of paper with a handwritten note. More recently, the range of this material has expanded well beyond material ordinarily found within library walls to include the versified texts that appear on commercial postcards in various languages, on regional trading cards once printed to advertise local businesses, and on custom-designed memorial envelopes.

The introduction of such material bears considerably on what Nelson set out to do, on what he has achieved and how those achievements invite building upon. In this essay, I consider the career of a scholar of twentieth-century poetry who developed into a cultural critic in part through his willingness to enter the archive at points that are increasingly messy and open to dispute. I hope to suggest what positive effects might follow from such disruption, especially since Nelson has been in recent years deliberately,

even aggressively, superseding presentations that were startling enough
when they first appeared in his influential 1989 book-length study, *Repression and Recovery*. Accordingly, I examine his collections of Spanish Civil
War documents and his editing of ten volumes in the American Poetry Recovery series as two projects that constellate unusual material in provocative ways. I end with a recent project that radically expands into strange
territory that taxes the descriptive terminology of either a historian or literary interpreter or theorist: a study of the industrialized art of the versified postcard—a study that is also an examination of private voices in
relation to the most brutal of public events, the twentieth century's
immersion in a sequence of worldwide wars.

1

The collector, as Walter Benjamin noted in a 1931 essay in which he considered the books on his own shelves, is less interested in the collected object itself and more interested in the object as "the scene, the stage" of its
"fate" (60). For Nelson, what it means to recover the object's "fate" has expanded and deepened over the years, even as it has also remained fixed on
the reader's complex relation to writing that exists in relation to a visual
display that is itself already complexly mediated by professional designers,
illustrators, and editors. Restrictions on printing illustrations almost certainly handicapped the original essay that established the groundwork and
methodology for what would become the breakthrough study *Repression
and Recovery*. "The Diversity of American Poetry" appeared under a deceptively generic title, innocently commissioned as it was by Emory Elliott, editor of the 1988 *Columbia History of American Literature*. But the essay is quick
to describe such unusual matters as the look of the large-scale typeface in
Wyndham Lewis's *Blast*, the discordant typefaces in Charles Henri Ford's
View, and the page from a 1931 issue of *Contempo* where Langston Hughes
published "Christ in Alabama." This essay's boldness was to propose that
modern poetry, exactly because it was so innovative, was not only diverse
but ubiquitous. Pervading the first half of the twentieth century, the poetry
envisioned in this essay was not limited to a handful of rare expressions in
a fine group of scarce publications. Instead, the innovative techniques that
poets employed to "alter the role language and poetry are expected to play
in the culture" were the very qualities, it was proposed, that gave them "a
strongly material existence by insisting they can be part of our physical and
visual environment" (Nelson 930).

Of course the fifty-one illustrations central to the greatly expanded
version of the essay that became *Repression and Recovery* and that ranged
from broadside printings to first-edition endpapers to designs in magazines and newspapers were quick to reveal just how much of modern

poetry's material history has been forgotten, if not virtually erased. It is one thing to be reminded that libraries discarded dust jackets or that publishers designed omnibus collections that abandoned clever designs in order to convey newly won respectability (Nelson 97, 279–80), but it is another thing actually to view the items or presentations that institutions judged negligible. It is one thing to read a description of "Christ in Alabama" and another thing to witness the poem's accompanying image of a black man holding up hands with stigmata formed by bullet holes.[1] The surprise, shock, and intensity of the poetry of the first half of the twentieth century were on display in examples whose inventiveness and provocation and transgression were immediately present for inspection. The sharp colors, the dramatic postures, and the astonishingly questionable taste of much of this collaborative artwork of modernity were brought home as Nelson introduced a visual dimension that, not coincidentally, often focused on the first publications of numerous modern poems.

Such alertness to the visual had been in fact a predicate of Nelson's first book, theoretically grounded in a phenomenology that portrayed an absolute reading experience that, as it unfolds, surrounds words with an accumulative scaffold of meaning. *The Incarnate Word: Literature as Verbal Space* (1973) shows an attraction for the visual not just in its sixteen illustrations for the chapter on Blake's *Jerusalem* but in its twelve additional illustrations (one appearing in a footnote) that function in effect as epigraphs to individual chapters and that range from an anonymous drawing to sketches by Klee to photographs taken by the author. Such abundance was also featured in a structural design that embraces physical crowding, as if the book itself were eager to escape the restraints imposed by words. No blank space occurs between chapters. Instead, each chapter has an "interchapter," two or three pages that offer a cascade of *Arcades Project*-like quotations, subsumed under a general concept. A final chapter gathers fourteen sets of conceptual categories, aggregated as an intersecting field, leaving the reader of *The Incarnate Word* with a tenth chapter that not so much fuses the book's interchapters with the nine text-based chapters so much as it surrounds the entire process and calls for a reexamination of the whole as a process.

If *The Incarnate Word* is characterized by its readiness to generate an abundance of meaning—itself becoming a field as it pieces together intersections of the temporal and the spatial—then *Our Last First Poets: Vision and History in Contemporary American Poetry* (1981), in keeping with its ominous title, dramatizes and investigates an American poetry that has come to be bereft. Void of all illustrations, with even the footnotes that appear at the bottom of every other page in a type size only minimally different from that in the main text, the book proposes that the concept of "open form" in the 1960s and 1970s no longer can be associated, as it had been in previous generations, with pioneerlike innovation. Open form has become instead the mark of our emptiness, our exhaustion, our confusion, as if poetry in the last decades had used up or discarded all its tactics, degrading what had been a field of possibility into a site strewn with ruins. *The Incarnate Word* had moved, with something akin to boundless delight, from the *Pearl* poet to William Burroughs, traversing separate chapters on *The Tempest, Paradise Regained, Jerusalem, The Prelude,* and *Paterson.* But this mobility actually belongs to the past; at the moment, poetry is symptomatically constrained. *Our Last First Poets* uncovers an American poetry no longer able to provide the interactive recognitions, the supportive social presence, that once generated powerful conceptual frameworks. If the idea of "first poets"—whether associated with American exceptionalism or breakthroughs that developed fresh readings—is no longer viable, then the necessary alternative is to consider the unthinkable, that "perhaps contemporary poems that are convincingly American will be about the failure of poetry" (10). Indeed, the powerful poems in this study are those that, with an honesty that is rigorous and unbearable, acknowledge themselves as overwhelmed by the devastating and corrosive effect of the Vietnam War. To dramatize that devastation, this study moves relentlessly toward W. S. Merwin's desiccated and fragmentary verse of the 1970s, underscoring the self-analytic vacuity of this starkly verbal poetry. The blank space that surrounds and suspends Merwin's brief lines, establishing them in a spatial blankness by extracting them from a temporal flow, also recognizes that the visual field in which they appear is simply vacant. The study's final chapter regards Merwin's 1970s' poetry as "a single enterprise [. . .] all one book" whose minimalist phrasing depletes any and all attempts at the affirmative.

    In this respect, the "illustrative turn" that leads to foregrounding the poem as a material object in *Repression and Recovery* arises in response to a crisis, to doubts concerning poetry's future. To find a turning point requires in this case a turning back, a realization that at an earlier time the modernist American poem occupied a "verbal space" that also included history. In the decades before the ruinous war in Vietnam, there did exist interlocking, overlapping, collaborative communities whose ability and eagerness to work together began to be erased after the shortsighted triumphalism of the years following World War II. Here, in this near past, is a restorative flood of visual evidence, evident in newspaper arrangements, in pamphlets and book covers, in posters and broadsides, all of which confirm the existence of communities in which interest groups spontaneously intermingled, mixing politics with aesthetics and associating visual design with verbal texts. These intersections become evident in the study's numerous close-up examinations of the modernist poem as a presentation in its time. The poem's interactive arrangement with other design elements is more than simply the mark of a presentational strategy. Rather, the material arrangement is a trace of how others imagined using the text, positioning it in relation to their desires. Inaugurating a series of readings that probes the relationships between the verbal and the visual, the evocative and the material, the past moment of tentative arrangement and the present experience of dense comprehension, *Repression and Recovery* emphasizes the interplay between the poem and factors of design such as suggestively framing, amplifying, undercutting, or paralleling it. The poem is inseparable from a constellation of activities that will dramatically, meaningfully, respectfully, or disruptively interpellate one another.

To bring to a poem such expectations was not only to challenge the assumption, current at the time, that modernist poetry should be approached primarily as an "oppressive burden" that always takes shape as an "intimidating and attenuated form" (Nelson, *Repression* 35, 38) but to conjecture an alternate history that would provide a new direction for literary studies. Nelson's modernism was certainly not the Pound era. For that matter, it was not anyone's era. It was an "era" that had no ruler establishing a regime, but a time that was open to one and all. *Repression and Recovery* formed an invaluable bridge between poststructural theory and critical exegesis. It shifted focus off the poem as a stage in a single poet's career and transferred attention to the poem as it appeared in a historical moment. It offered a model for interpreting modernist poetry that directed interest away from the poem's creator to its audience, from the poem's display value to its use value.

The role of the archivist in such a procedure, needless to say, extends considerably beyond the careful preservation of an artifact whose value is without question. This procedure invites just the opposite. Instead of positioning the poem as an artifact in a privileged position within the pages of a hefty anthology where it is framed by such "objective" structures as chronological placement and discretionary annotation, the poem is now returned to a thick-textured site, one of its originative public moments. What is recovered is the immense potential that surrounds any initial appearance. The designs that surround the poem—as a vernacular visual "commentary"—become inventive interactions helping to generate the occasion's multiple possibilities. Since this surrounding material exists in a register parallel to but different from the text, it encourages further responses from its audience. Just as the audience of the poem engages with the poet's work through resolving why the poem's form is appropriate for its content—a calculus that can never be wholly resolved and, invaluably, is factored distinctively by each reader—so the audience's resolving the "gap" that opens between surrounding material and central object engages them directly, endlessly, and individually with the poem in a moment of history.

2

The antipreservationist stance so distinctive to *Repression and Recovery* is amplified in later projects that focus on usage that extends well beyond the disciplined audience of the literary text. Nelson's publications documenting the Spanish Civil War are extensive enough to vie with his writings on academia and labor politics as the other area beyond poetry most central to his thinking. Indeed, his scholarship on the Spanish Civil War may not just be adjacent to his workplace essays as instrumental to them. These documentary publications are ambitious collaborations that cross disciplinary lines and appeal to diverse audiences. They include a massive edition of private and unpublished letters of Americans who served in the Abraham Lincoln Brigade (Nelson and Hendricks, *Madrid 1937* [1996]); an exhibit of the posters, broadsides, and paintings that comprised the visual artwork of the war (*Shouts from the Wall* [1996]); a collection of the photographs, both private and public, from the casual snapshot to the official portrait, that constitutes a record of the daily life among people and volunteers (*The Aura of the Cause* [1997]); and an anthology of the verse produced in response to the war both during and after it, in a collection that extends from the 1930s to the present (*The Wound and the Dream* [2002]). At the core of this research is Edwin Rolfe, the left-wing poet introduced and examined in publications that include an extended biographical essay presenting material acquired by the University of Illinois's rare book room (1990); an annotated volume offering corrected versions of all Rolfe's poems (1993); a reader's edition of selected poems (1995); and a detailed chapter in *Revolutionary Memory* (2001).

     To accord centrality to the Spanish Civil War is to propose a significant reorientation of the cultural history of modernism. "No other conflict in this century," Nelson has written, "has combined the drama, the historical importance, and the ethical clarity of the struggle between democracy and fascism" (*Shouts* 7). What made this conflict unique was the volunteerism it elicited. Those who committed themselves freely to the struggle "had a deep understanding of why they were there." Refusing to be caught up in history as ingredients, these volunteers sought to shape history through their activism. They willingly intended "to risk everything in pursuit of a better world" (*Shouts* 7). Rolfe's poems reflect this most powerfully. His Spanish Civil War poems perform transformations in which nobility and strength emerge from a testing situation. They are his first mature work, even as they still show strands that attach it to his earlier political work. The phrase used to title the reader's edition of selected poems, *Trees Became Torches,* is drawn from a description of a bombing raid that instead of shattering morale only motivates a greater resolve, as "the trees became torches / lighting the avenues / where lovers huddled in terror / who would be lovers no longer" (50). As Rolfe witnesses actual bombing raids, it is as though the slogans that had previously existed in 1930s' revolutionary poetry turn into objective correlatives right before his eyes. But Nelson also extends consideration to those volunteers who found more modest ways of expressing their relation to history. Examining a series of snapshots that often shows only "tiny figures" engaged in simple tasks, he writes: "From time to time, often repeatedly on any given day, the ordinary activities of cleaning a rifle or loading a truck or practicing advancing under fire would be recast imaginatively and politically as events on a world historical stage. [. . .] In a very real sense, then, these photographic ephemera are actively monumental in scale and meaning" (*The Aura* 20–21).

The ability to conceive of artwork as an interactive event was central to *Repression and Recovery,* but there it served to challenge scholars of poetry to reorient their reading practice. There the investigative work called for searches in obscure corners of institutional archives and special collections, in overlooked pages of fugitive or popular publications, and in design elements of everything from deluxe editions to pamphlets. But these documentary histories of the Spanish Civil War reveal a literal model of interactivity, one that existed in the world. Interactivity is no longer just a delicate, elusive process of textual exploration; remarkably broadened, now interactivity is at the center of historical change—it is effectively the defining action of the war. To battle against a highly organized, repressive enemy, American partisans, in tandem with allies from countries around the world, developed ingenious tactics that depended upon people working together, a spirit reflected within the artworks they interactively produced, and responded to, and then developed even further.

Here Nelson is assembling, organizing, and introducing material in volatile mixes of the usual with the extraordinary, the everyday with the exceptional, the vernacular with the stylized. Inventive mixing is a hallmark of a war supported by the populace. In it, sophisticated and elaborate poster art jostled for attention with amateur snapshots and casual photos, just as letters home and journal entries similarly contended with sonnets and extended lyrical sequences. Poems stepped away from the pages of well-designed books and erupted on broadsides that circulated in the marketplace. Graphic art vied with poetry for the attentions of a vast audience. At least once, a poem existed on banners one hundred feet high, requiring the side of a city building to display them—a display that, at it is recorded on film and distributed in cinemas, also captures people in numbers pausing and squinting up to follow the lines. In none of these examples, moreover, is it possible to assign clear dominance to one mode over another. The evidence of these innovative collaborative energies, reacting against and striving to commandeer a moment of crisis, throws into strong relief one of the cardinal tenets of cultural studies, the conviction that, as Nelson writes, it is "the relational nature of meaning" that should hold our attention as we pursue "how meaning was materially realized in actual practices" ("Politics and Labor" 288).

If the Spanish Civil War recalls a moment when the individual tactics associated with a communal effort—a selfless gathering of volunteers from all nations—temporarily confounded the strategic plans of dominant regimes, then it is also to be valued for its latent energy. That war could exemplify, Nelson writes in a recent evaluation, "a whole history of regularly thwarted or co-opted left-wing social agendas." But the point of reconstructing this particular history in such detail is to demonstrate how clearly it "also resonates among the choices available to us in the present day" ("The Letters" 307, 309). At numerous points in these documentary editions, Nelson sets forth the claim that he is not initiating a process but taking up what had once been interrupted. "Had the war continued or the war been won by the Republic," he writes, describing photographs that show volunteers in retreat during the disastrous last months of 1938, when democratic nations withheld their help, "no doubt some of these images would have been published in 1939 or thereafter" (*The Aura* 42, 43). Describing the letters from Abraham Lincoln Brigade volunteers as exceptionally valuable, because "the only mementoes volunteers had were often the things they sent home, like their letters or their diaries," Nelson adds that after the war the brigade veterans "planned to gather letters for publication, but World War II intervened, and the long night of McCarthyism descended" (Nelson and Hendricks, *Madrid 1937* 7, 14). Even a publication as invaluable as Rolfe's eyewitness history, *The Lincoln Battalion: The Story of the Americans Who Fought in Spain in the International Brigades* (1939), is rendered unfinished when Nelson recovers and publishes Rolfe's dedicatory note in a presentation copy to friends: "This is not the book, you know; I've pulled too many of the accurate and universal punches. But it has taken care of the superstructure and now the work on the fundamentals begins" (*Revolutionary Memory* 115).

Writing about literary history in 1992 and implicitly looking back to his own two-volume *History of Modern Poetry* (1976, 1987), David Perkins described the literary historian as a specialist who imaginatively inhabits another time and place and is thus a "citizen of two ages" who "can bring one [age] to bear critically on the other" (185–86). But this genial formula overlooks the complications that occur when one "age" has been abruptly curtailed, its maturation frustrated. Formulating a different kind of question in a 1994 essay for *American Literature*—"What does it mean to recover a past that might have had a public life but never did?"—Nelson centers on what Perkins evades: not just the peculiar gaps but also the productive possibilities that crowd forward when one of the "two ages" in which Perkins's specialist-citizen chooses to live is not quite finished, half developed, and as a result, unkempt, unruly, and clamoring to exert its lost influence ("What Happens" 132). If the ten volumes selected for the American Poetry Recovery series between 1993 and 2004 exhibit fewer family resemblances than most publications in an edited series, then it is because together they mark a collective judgment against the body of work that has come to represent twentieth-century poetry.[2] Rather than arriving with the idea of presenting material that will find, at last, its own true place in literary history, they come to question the idea of "progress" in literary history.

These editions, then, are strange constellations that deliberately clog literary history at key points. The series inserts into the Harlem Renaissance an immigrant from the Caribbean, Claude McKay, writing as a Red formalist, all cool judgment and fiery anger, then promotes Chicagoan Frank Marshall Davis who disburses phrasings from 1930s swing and 1940s bebop that celebrate lyrical matters in a setting of terrifying violence. Sarah Piatt steps out of the supportive matrix of women poets who dominated newspaper and magazine verse in the late nineteenth century to write with coruscating irony on the fate of the poor and the powerless in America and Ireland. Vincent Ferrini appears as a poet engaged with and attentive to his region, quite unlike the scarred role he plays as a footnote in *The Maximus Poems* through Charles Olson's contemptuous dismissal. While hard-Left poet Don Gordon employs literary form in only the sketchiest of ways, writing a free verse so loose that its most commanding formal attribute is the stanza, Nelson produces an exact contemporary, Aaron Kramer, who is equally on the Left but who welcomes any and all formal limitations, from rhymed metrical verse to nonce stanza arrangements, writing them all in virtuosic fashion. Several volumes in the series place the Spanish Civil War close to their center. In the final work of the series, in the anthology entitled *The Wound and the Dream,* war emerges as the spectacular secret that has provided a hidden source of radical power from one generation to the next, from Robinson Jeffers (born 1887) and Genevieve Taggard (1894), to Edwin Rolfe (1909) and Muriel Rukeyser (1913), to James Wright (1927) and Philip Levine (1928), to Leslie Ullman (1947) and David Wojahn (1953).

If poems turn invisible when the tradition out of which they were written exists as secret or erased knowledge, then a once-invisible poem, as it takes shape again, may also revitalize elements within that tradition. Like life-support machinery that hovers benignly nearby, copious annotations are needed to surround many texts in this series, as in Mark Van Wienen's revelation of the body of American poetry that engaged with, questioned, and undermined the brutal realities of the Great War. Vachel Lindsay's "The Jazz Bird" (1918) invites admiration for the brio of its opening stanzas' slangy phrasing:

> The jazz Bird sings a barnyard song,
>   A cock-a-doodle bray,
> A jingle-bells, a boiler works,
>   A he-man's roundelay.
>
> The eagle said: "Son Jazz Bird,
>   I send you out to fight."
> And the Jazz Bird spread his sunflower wings,
>   And roared with all his might. (229)

Until Van Wienen's *Rendezvous with Death: American Poems of the Great War* (2002), this poem by Lindsay had effectively ceased to exist. It was not among the *Collected Poems* published after Lindsay's untimely death, nor was it in a 1963 selection from his work. A version published in *Poetry* in 1918 was, as its reconfigured title suggests ("The Modest Jazz Birds"), a sanitized abridgment that omitted the poem's climactic three stanzas. In the poem's crucial last lines, Lindsay's descriptions turn disturbing, once Van Wienen's notes confirm that "jazz birds" are African Americans. These troops take revenge on the Kaiser's troops with gestures that are specific and all-too familiar:

> [The troops'] necks are broken by the hemp,
>   They goose-step in a line,
> Their stripped bones strutting in the wind
>   Swinging as a sign
>
> That Jazz Birds come on sunflower wings
>   When loathsome tyrants rise . . .
> The Jazz Bird guards the gallows,
>   He lights it with his eyes. (229, ellipses in original)

The triumphal violence unleashed at the end is ominously inflected, deeply fraught with the fear that power, as always, may be complexly reversed. Tapping unnervingly into white anxieties about past injustices toward African Americans, the poem admires the strength of black troops even as it recoils from those same troops' homecoming possibilities. Van Wienen's notes recuperate forgotten slang ("'sunflower' is argot for black America" [327]), and at the same time they reveal a publishing record that implies suppression and explain the national controversy over the role of African American troops. While citing important and little-known statistics—370,000 African Americans were drafted for the Great War—Van Wienen also speculates on the poem's occasion: the arrival of the first black troops on the Western Front in May 1918 where their valor produced citations from the French for three of the four regiments but nothing comparable from the Americans. And an idealized poster that Van Wienen reproduces from 1918 shows a well-dressed black woman bidding a stately farewell to a smartly uniformed black soldier about to join a vast rank of similar figures, marching behind an American flag, all bearing rifles.

To glimpse how poetry might once have been used of course brings into prominence audiences that have too often been discounted, that have been kept invisible and sidelined by the reputation of experts. Examining the scrapbook maintained from 1916 to 1918 by twenty-year-old Pittsburgh socialist Rudolph Blum reveals not a haphazard arrangement but a careful layering, page by page, in which several poems are collected, with the clipping that is one poem placed carefully in relation to another: "Things done and things believed are yoked together, rhymed, in the conceptual agency granted one reader by the poems he collected" (Nelson, *Revolutionary* 43).[3] Blum's scrapbook clearly resists "the modern idea about the primacy of form and the linking of art to other artworks" that Rita Felski associates with the belief that "art is often defined as the province of specialists." For Felski, this nonprofessional audience broadens the idea of "aesthetic response" to include "emotion, excitement, escapism" and such other responses that "cannot be evaluated, graded, and ranked" (35). But Blum's scrapbook, as it shows its engagement with poetry, also registers a "conceptual agency" that is clearly involved with evaluation and ranking.

It is not a coherent alternate history of modern poetry that these ten volumes together propose. Each volume even stands apart from its companions, as together they form an affront to literary history as currently constituted. At the same time, few collections of poetry more strikingly reveal that the value that appears to emanate from the poem is dependent on information we bring to it in the form of the history we remember, the cultural narratives we share, and the facts we deem significant.

3

These editions of poetry, interpretive essays, and documentary collections extend remarkable care to that which was rescued from the past. The past, of course, can never be wholly revisited. Yet much of that past is so evocative that it is tempting to dream of repossessing it, as Nelson first acknowledged in *Repression and Recovery:* "And yet there have been moments—especially when I take pleasure in a book or magazine that most people now writing

about modern poetry have never seen—when I feel I have broken through
the interested forgetfulness of decades, divested myself of present interests,
and established an authentic relationship with a discourse from the past"
(10–11). This thought is no sooner uttered than dismissed in a lengthy footnote, as well as in a following sentence that explicitly derides the idea as a
"fantasy." Like all fantasies, though, it has a way of returning. An explana-
tory passage in one of the sections that provides historical background to
the Spanish Civil War in *Madrid 1937* suddenly and remarkably shifts, and
we are no longer in the discursive reality of historical fact—we are walking
down the street in Barcelona in March 1938:

> [. . .] the city was beautiful. One could walk from the wide cen-
> tral Plaza de Cataluña, down the tree-lined Rambla with its cafes
> and flower stalls, all the way to the harbor's edge where Colum-
> bus's statue stands. On some days, however, the flower stalls were
> empty. Funerals for bombing victims had taken all the flowers
> that Catalonia had to offer. (Nelson and Hendricks 418)

In one of many haunting moments in *Revolutionary Memory,* Nelson offers
the example of graphic artists who so vividly registered the power of the
enormous "*No Pasaran!*" banner strung above a street in Madrid that they
duplicated the very feel of the moment of its creation: "They wanted to
feel the words enacted in the sinews of their drawing hand," he writes,
"so they redrew the photograph in a variety of styles, illustrating books or
articles" (*Revolutionary* 243; *The Wound* 54). Nelson has almost gone this
far himself: the "Poetry Chorus" that he has twice assembled from lines
written by others in the 1930s or written in homage to Lorca trespasses in
that very direction (*Revolutionary* 166–73; 229–31; "Modern" 94–98; *The
Wound* 41–43).[4]

Longing for a return to an originative moment is if not fulfilled is at
least legitimated in recent work where Nelson centers on postcard poems
and the personal messages that accompanied them. By taking up not only
the poem that is on the postcard but the writing on its other side, what suddenly emerges is an "other side" that had previously hovered on the edge
of inaudibility and invisibility. The postcard poem is not only a remnant
of a time that seems quite lost to us, an era when words that were compressed into rhyme circulated widely as a means by which persons could
begin to think through their situations, but it also affords us a glimpse of
how that poetry may once have been used. Writing on the collector whose
interests have radically expanded, Susan Stewart has suggested that "the
souvenir still bears a trace of use value in its instrumentality" while adding
that the collection, as an aggregate of souvenirs, can threaten to aestheti-
cize use value, to become "a form of art as play" (151). But to introduce the

words written by the postcard's user as part of a larger script that includes the postcard's poetic discourse and its visual iconography begins a process by which the use value of the cultural artifact takes on a sharper, though still arguable, legibility. The manufactured word and image may alternately function to shelter, offset, contextualize, or even threaten the user's presence, in a fantastic moment that is fraught with unreality, confusion, and contradiction.

So fiercely antagonist a differential was not characteristic of visual and verbal interchanges that Nelson had examined earlier. As reprinted in *Repression and Recovery* (212–13) and the Oxford *Anthology* (1230–31), a two-page spread from a December 1931 issue of the *New Masses* shows an elaborate arrangement that surrounds the shifting stanzas of Langston Hughes's "Waldorf Astoria" poem with gestures of mutual respect. Walter Steinhilber's sketches of the wealthy cavorting at various windows, pleasurably filling up luxury space, rise vertically the length of the page, in contrast to foreshortened images of the less advantaged, many of them staring faces without bodies, placed horizontally at the bottom. The arrangement interpretively amplifies such formal aspects in Hughes's poem as parenthetical comments in a sharply ironic voice designed to pierce any illusion that the wealthy even glance at the poor. From the typography that headlines the titles of each section to the voices that appear in lines functioning like poetic word balloons for the cartoon-like figures, the overall arrangement extends and deepens both drawing and poem.[5]

A nation's postcards, however, when printed during wartime, always ventriloquize for the state, their semiotics designed to amplify the state's voice. Modernized nations such as Germany in World War I were engines of efficiency quick to appropriate advanced weaponry such as the U-boat as metonyms of the state, sleekly elegant, focused on victory, and gliding dangerously in and out of sight. German postcard poems celebrating the exploits of submarine commander Otto Weddingen ("The Heroic Deed of the U-9," "Hail, U9"), whose U-9 sank three British cruisers on one day in 1914, evolved (after Weddingen's death in combat prompted elegiac tributes) into narrative poems centered both on victory and sacrifice, producing images and songs, including elaborately staged and attractively designed death scenes, that would be recycled two decades later. But the advantages of producing war as a stage setting, within which a citizen would be invited, coaxed, or coerced to take a distinct role, were already in development in US Civil War preprinted letter sheets in verse that left a space to insert an addressee's name and in envelopes with cartoon drawings and snippets of verse (in the South, brutally racialized caricatures and doggerel in black dialect, while in the North, traditional images of eagles or flags with metrical lines in poetic diction), which turned the simple act of mailing into a patriotic sentiment.

This is industrial art, and not surprisingly almost everything about it endangers the individual. Yet the confidence with which a regime, working spectacularly on one side of the postcard, goes about insisting simply, commandingly, and threateningly just how a good citizen is exposed for her or his coercion is disrupted the moment a single voice begins to make a personal space out of the postcard's other side. While offering postcards that recapitulate a history of America's modern wars, from the Civil War to the Second World War, Nelson also presents a microhistory of people whose voices do not usually get recorded. These are people who may not even know they lack a voice—or perhaps even what it would mean to want or have "a voice"—and yet who persist in addressing others with words that may collapse into truisms or sentiments but that remarkably convey their desire for claiming or passing on a message to another, even when that is a strain.

Acts of scholarship that refuse to erase the user's presence promote a view of history more encompassing than selective. While Derrida's *The Post Card* examines the ultimately uncommunicative aspect of fragmentary messages whose strangeness is only magnified when one is not an addressee, Nelson aims not only to register inevitable gaps and lost significance but also to recover as much as possible of a message that was once to be delivered ("Only Death" 29). Lost voices, voices that had been eaten by history, can be temporarily, astonishingly revived as if they could be in a poem of their making instead of on the other side of what someone else has defined as a poem. We are at once thrust into a sense of the smallness of anyone's voice as it sounds within the vast arenas of history, and at the same time made to feel that the voice is not small, that it has imagined a way to convey its presence to those it longed to address. Small details and intimate gestures contend for attention against the brash imagery and bold rhetoric of the postcard's industrialized art. Perhaps just as important, this approach allows a space for the critic's own subjectivity, and perhaps even a glimpse of what has driven him or her as a scholar, in an admission that occurs—in a sentence whose openness would unlikely be found in any other scholar's essay—at the close of a discussion of poems that Soviets printed on lightweight paper, airdropped over German troops: "I have some of the cards themselves, feeling eerily as if I almost reached out and caught them in the air before they fluttered to the ground 60 years ago" (Nelson, "Martial Lyrics" 278).

In a lengthy footnote to the first chapter in *Revolutionary Memory* ("Modern Poems We Have Wanted to Forget"), Nelson set forward the kind of "specialized library collection" that might include forgotten poems, especially those with such "wildly varied publication histories" that no common thread could explain "their relative erasure from our cultural memory" (55). A collection so strange, he conceded, might be one that "few librarians are altogether ready for"—a combination "mixed museum, junk shop, and library" (247). The archivist of such a strange place—at once curator, trash collector, and scholar—would have to be able to recognize that, depending on their use, any artifacts might be transposed from one category to another, from historical item to discarded trash to valued artwork. But have not Nelson's findings always sustained just such uncertainty? What some see as trash others see as a broken promise, as what is yet to be done. What is the debris that piles up around us if not a mark of the random flow of history and a sign that history, as it is written, now might also be reconsidered, reinvented, and even redeemed?

Notes

1. It is appropriate to introduce this page by Langston Hughes early in this essay and give it prominence since the 1931 "Christ in Alabama" is the single illustration that has most often accompanied Nelson's essays on modern poetry. It is reproduced in *Repression and Recovery,* as well as in *Revolutionary Memory* (74), the Oxford *Anthology of Modern American Poetry* (1232), and *The Cambridge Companion to American Modernism* (90). If Nelson has a touchstone visual, it may be this page with its Hughes poem that dramatically overlays the terror of Southern mob injustice with the Christian narrative of the Crucifixion.

2. That "body of work," at least when represented in the several-hundred-page poetry anthology, edited for classroom assignments, is likely to appear marred to the editor and the editorial board that have negotiated reprint fees with publishers. What may appear to outsiders who see the table of contents as a rich harvest of luminaries appears to insiders as a ruined landscape scattered with capricious fragments. To expose the mystified practice of choosing and editing among poets and poems, Nelson has written confessionally about the actual compromises involved in negotiating reprint rights in the process of editing the Oxford *Anthology of Modern American Poetry* ("Economics" 165–80). The essay questions how many anthologies resist becoming assemblages that largely reflect the struggles of publishers attempting to restrict the circulation of poems to which they own exclusive rights.

3. Three of the pages from Blum's scrapbook are reproduced in *Revolutionary Memory,* figures 13–15 (40–42) and another page reproduced to illustrate "Politics of Labor in the Fin de Siècle and Beyond" in *Modernism, Inc.,* figure 13.6 (282). Nelson often adds new and subtracts previous illustrations from essays that are moving from journals or anthologies to books, underscoring the abundance of the unreported archive. One example is the introduction to *The Wound and the Dream,* which draws heavily on all of the material in the final chapter of *Revolutionary Memory,* but which has an abundance of illustrations not in the chapter.

4. More controversial is Nelson's gathering together of haiku by Japanese Americans incarcerated in American concentration camps in World War II, identified by the writer's name only in the table of contents in the Oxford *Anthology of Modern American Poetry* (xvii) but arranged by Nelson in a sequence and printed

as a sequential set of twenty-nine haiku (718–20). In "Relativism, Politics, and Ethics," Nelson recalls experimenting with an essay on 1930s' poetry that eliminated all authors' names but that friends found "intolerable to read" because of "large numbers of quotes unmoored to any writers' identity" (46–47). "For a critic to withhold a writer's name is," he concluded, "in any case, clearly an affront, one for which I have not yet found a way to gain a hearing" (47).

5. The turn-of-the-century trade card that advertises as it rhymes is treated by Nelson as a relatively accessible entry to a lost past, and in that sense it resembles most closely the arrangements between poets and artists and editors and designers that provoke exceptionally careful readings that balance the verbal with the visual. Examining a single trade card from 1903, for which barber Henry Eisenhauer composed original verse advertising his services ("With razor keen and water hot / You always find me on the spot." [. . .] "And give my bath rooms a fair trial, / By bathing there once in a while" ["Boom Town Barber" 13), prompts an extended consideration of poems on other trade cards by merchants that in turn evokes a detailed history of Moberly, Missouri, from 1870s to the early twentieth century.

Works Cited

Benjamin, Walter. "Unpacking My Library: A Talk about Book Collecting." *Illuminations*. Trans. Harry Zohn. New York: Schocken, 1969. 59–67.

Felski, Rita. "The Role of Aesthetics in Cultural Studies." *The Aesthetics of Cultural Studies*. Ed. Michael Bérubé. Malden: Blackwell, 2005. 28–43.

Lindsay, Vachel. "The Jazz Bird." *Rendezvous with Death: American Poems of the Great War*. Ed. Mark Van Wienen. Urbana: U of Illinois P, 2002. 229.

Nelson, Cary. *The Aura of the Cause: A Photo Album for North American Volunteers in the Spanish Civil War*. Waltham: Abraham Lincoln Brigades, 1997.

———. *The Incarnate Word: Literature as Verbal Space*. Urbana: U of Illinois P, 1993.

———. "Boom Town Barber: The Biography of a Trade Card." *The Advertising Trade Card Quarterly* 9.4 (Winter 2002): 12–16.

———. "The Diversity of American Poetry." *Columbia Literary History of the United States*. Ed. Emory Elliott. New York: Columbia UP, 1988. 913–36.

———. "The Economics of Textbook Reform." *Office Hours: Activism and Change in the Academy*. New York: Routledge, 2004. 165–80.

———. "The Letters the Presidents Did Not Release: Radical Scholarship and the Legacy of the American Volunteers in Spain." *Left of the Color Line: Race, Radicalism, and Twentieth-Century Literature of the United States*. Ed. Bill V. Mullen and James Smethurst. Chapel Hill: U of North Carolina P, 2003. 299–314.

———. "Martial Lyrics: The Vexed History of the Wartime Poetry Card." *American Literary History* 16.2 (Summer 2004): 263–89.

———. "Modern American Poetry." *The Cambridge Companion to American Modernism*. Ed. Walter Kalaidjian. Cambridge: Cambridge UP, 2005. 68–101.

———. "Only Death Can Part Us: Messages on Wartime Cards." *Iowa Journal of Cultural Studies* 8–9 (Spring/Fall 2006): 25–43.

————. *Our Last First Poets: Vision and History in Contemporary American Poetry.* Urbana: U of Illinois P, 1981.

————, ed. *Anthology of Modern American Poetry.* New York: Oxford UP, 2000.

————. "Politics and Labor in Poetry of the Fin de Siècle and Beyond: Fragments of an Unwritable History." *Modernism, Inc.: Body, Memory, Capital.* Ed. Jani Scandura and Michael Thurston. New York: New York UP, 2001. 268–88.

————. "Reading Criticism." *PMLA* 91.5 (October 1976): 801–15.

————. "Relativism, Politics, and Ethics: Writing Literary History in the Shadow of Postculturalism." *Manifesto of a Tenured Radical.* New York: New York UP, 1997. 39–51.

————. *Repression and Recovery: Modern American Poetry and the Politics of Cultural Memory, 1910–1945.* Madison: U of Wisconsin P, 1989.

————. *Revolutionary Memory: Recovering the Poetry of the American Left.* New York: Routledge, 2001.

————. *Shouts from the Wall: Posters and Photographs Brought Home from the Spanish Civil War by American Volunteers.* Waltham: Abraham Lincoln Brigades, 1996.

————. "What Happens When We Put the Left at the Center?" 1994. *Manifesto of a Tenured Radical.* New York: New York UP, 1997. 126–36.

————, ed. *The Wound and the Dream: Sixty Years of American Poems about the Spanish Civil War.* Urbana: U of Illinois P, 2002.

Nelson, Cary, and Jefferson Hendricks, eds. *Madrid 1937: Letters of the Abraham Lincoln Brigade from the Spanish Civil War.* New York: Routledge, 1996.

Perkins, David. *Is Literary History Possible?* Baltimore: Johns Hopkins UP, 1991.

Rolfe, Edwin. *Trees Became Torches: Selected Poems.* Ed. Cary Nelson and Jefferson Hendricks. Urbana: U of Illinois P, 1995.

Stewart, Susan. *On Longing: Narratives of the Miniature, the Gigantic, the Souvenir, the Collection.* Durham: Duke UP, 1993.

∽ 3 ∽

CARY NELSON

EXPANDING THE CANON OF AMERICAN POETRY

Walter Kalaidjian

In accounting for Cary Nelson's role in "expanding the canon of American poetry," I begin by briefly unpacking the article of this topic's key term—expanding *the* canon of American poetry. "Where was it," Wallace Stevens, famously asks in "The Man on the Dump" that "one first heard of the truth? The the" (Stevens 203). From that thoroughly worldly vantage point there is, of course, no such thing as "*the* canon." Canon law—constituting the traditional body of statues and decrees laid down by the Pope and his ecclesiastical councils—can be read as a material but compensatory supplement whose legislative corpus would stand in for the ideal of transcendental signified meaning. That is, the canonical authority of "the the" is always already an idealization but one whose ideological force nevertheless adjudicates matters of political struggle, social antagonism, and cultural distinction in the name of universal truth. Such idealization, as we know, led T. S. Eliot to argue that the peculiar "historical sense" of the canon never devolves into a contingent temporality but remains essentially spatial and, above all, "timeless"—upheld by the author's "feeling that the whole of the literature of Europe from Homer and within it the whole of the literature of his own country has a simultaneous existence and composes a simultaneous order." If it must be expanded, the canon—whose "existing order is complete before the new work arrives"—incorporates the new into the ideal regime of the same, reconfiguring itself to achieve a "conformity between the old and the new" (28).

Eliot's idealization of "the canon" rests on an imaginary fantasy of the literary purged of historical contingency, social antagonism, and linguistic difference whose lack otherwise haunts the canon's symbolic order with what Jacques Derrida called "archive fever." Indeed, the constitutive role of the archive's techniques and institutional practices of preservation, as

31

Derrida argued, "determines the structure of the archivable content even
in its very coming into existence and in its relationship to the future"
(*Archive Fever* 17). Such archival practices do not just record but actively
frame the terms of literary and cultural discourse: what Michel Foucault
characterized as "the general system of the formation and transformation
of statements" (130). Similarly, arguing against simply expanding the idealized and largely conservative "order" of Eliot's Anglo-European canon,
"the major issue," as Paul Lauter recognized long ago, "is not assimilating
some long-forgotten works or authors into the existing categories; rather,
it is reconstructing historical understanding" (40). As we shall see, Nelson's career traverses the literary fantasy of "the the" of canonicity working
its uncanny circuit of imaginary repression through archival trauma toward a negotiated conjuncture among the forces of cultural recovery, disciplinarity, and historical change.

This journey begins in 1973 with Cary's first book *The Incarnate Word:
Literature as Verbal Space* whose visionary phenomenology imagines verbal
form "as an author's projection of a self-projective and self-generative
space that transcends or escapes historical time" (4). Cary's early attention to the corporeal space of verbal incarnation has the virtue of deter-
ritorializing the disciplinary boundaries of narrow nationalisms and
conventional periodicity across a range of texts extending from the Middle English *Pearl* poem through Shakespeare's *The Tempest*, Milton's *Paradise Regained*, Swift's *A Tale of a Tub*, Blake's *Jerusalem*, Wordsworth's *The
Prelude*, Williams's *Paterson*, the fictional labyrinths of Borges and Burroughs, and Sontag's *Death Kit*. These readings, in turn, engage in a dialogue with striking visual plates and interchapters of textual collage.
However unsettling the disciplinary protocols of post-New Critical reading practices, and while understanding the limits of verbal space to lie in
historical repression, the book invests more often than not in a literary
hermeneutics of faith rather than suspicion. It subscribes to visionary
embodiments that are archetypal, transcendent, and endlessly self-
renewing: the "posture," say, of "Christ standing at the still center of the
turning world—a stone phallus in the womb of nature" (Nelson 100), or
of Prospero, who similarly "stands at the center of his island [. . .] at the
center of his world. [. . .] as his imagination embraces the heavens" (75).
Indeed, *The Incarnate Word* performs a certain mastery of its constituting
metaphor—literary space as verbal field—as its final lines end with the
figure of Theodore Roethke streaking clean out of sight intoning, "The
field is mine! Is mine!" (274).

However decisively *The Incarnate Word* ventriloquizes and thereby
claims literary canonicity, Cary's career nevertheless quickly comes to disavow that fantasy as itself an oppressive symptom of disciplinary containment. Not insignificantly, in his retrospective preface to *Disciplinarity and*

Dissent in Cultural Studies (1996), Cary recalled the inspiring example of his early Illinois colleague Nuel Pharr Davis and the troubling departmental resistance that greeted his groundbreaking cultural study *Lawrence and Oppenheimer* (1968). This encounter with the provincial limits of disciplinary judgment, coupled with the traumatic legacy of Vietnam, leads in Cary's subsequent 1981 volume *Our Last First Poets* to his gradual withdrawal from *The Incarnate Word*'s phenomenological field of literary reading. The visionary optimism celebrated there becomes unsustainable in the face of Vietnam's traumatic historicity. Simply put, "The faith," Cary writes, "that an exemplary dialogue between poetic vision and historical actuality could persist and perhaps even be beneficial—did not survive the events of the period" (x). The tradition of the long poem in the United States since Whitman had once held out the promise of an Adamic innocence. After Vietnam, however, that national myth tellingly belied and even enabled America's otherwise unspeakable history of violent imperial aggression. In *Our Last First Poets*, the poetics of field composition and its visionary compact with literature's remove from history began to unravel decisively with Roethke—reaching a nadir of diminishing returns in Galway Kinnell, Robert Duncan, and Adrienne Rich, finally suffering a radical reversal of poetry's escape from history in the linguistic effacements and deconstructive ironies of W. S. Merwin's radically pessimistic poetics. In Merwin, the fantasy of a self-sufficient literary vision suffers a double loss as the trauma of Vietnam "permeates" the verse, even as the poet comes to occupy the Derridean role of an "anonymous American figure who announces the harmonizing dissolution of language" as such (178). In *The Incarnate Word*, Cary could still imagine the writer and reader entering into a pact of mutual relationship "both sharing a desire to enact the work" (4). But in the wake of Vietnam, *Our Last First Poets* attends to terminal expressions of loss, reflecting "the poet's defeated confession that a receptive audience simply does not exist" (3). Cary's identification with Merwin's deconstructive poetics would extend beyond *Our Last First Poets* throughout the two collections of mid-1980s *W. S. Merwin: Essays on the Poetry* (1987) and *Regions of Memory* (1987). By then, not unlike Merwin, Cary would irrevocably abandon the literary idealism that had otherwise sustained the phenomenological hermeneutics of *The Incarnate Word*. Strangely, it is at this moment that—as if scripted by David Lynch—the lost highway of Cary's career makes a quantum detour into a narrative reversal of literature's canonical logic. Taking, perhaps, Merwin's gnomic advice in "A Scale in May," that "If you find you no longer believe, / Enlarge the Temple" (111–12), Cary made the commitment to the material possibilities of communal agency asserted by means of—not despite—temporal change, the contingency of literary valuation, not to mention social and linguistic difference as such. Abandoning the fantasy of literary plenitude—tied as it is to canonical empowerment, historical repression, and disciplinary containment—Cary would avow in his 1989 field-changing *Repression and Recovery*, that "it is the problem of history at its most intractable that I need to confront" (3). Rereading canonicity now as a material practice driven by social desire, not fantasies of the literary, this magnum opus is chastened by the knowledge that "Nothing that we can say or think about a poem is free of social construction" (10). This key recognition, coupled with the book's neo-Gramscian critical methodology, would decisively recast poetic modernism as a discourse not just of literary canoncity but of repressed social desire.

Cary's recoveries of poetic modernism coincided with the new social movements that shaped African American, feminist, postcolonial, gay and lesbian, and cultural studies. These newer developments not only changed the complexion of contemporary literary canonicity but also had certain recombinatory side effects on the makeup of canonical modernism. The older and more conservative story of high modernism's emergence between the world wars had pitted the period's genteel anthologies against the New Critical campaign to move T. S. Eliot and Ezra Pound from the intellectual margins of the modern canon to its center.[1] In retrospect, this traditional take on high modernism's displacement of the genteel tradition, as Cary argued, not only failed to account for the full diversity of modernist aesthetic production but served politically as a strategy of cultural containment. "Once our image of the period," writes Cary, "is contained and structured this way—once our sense of the discourses at work is limited to these choices—it is easy to feel that experimental modernism deserved to win this battle, for it is difficult to recapture the knowledge that these were not the only forces in play. But in fact they were not" (21). By now in the twenty-first century, Eurocentric high modernism is read—thanks to Cary and many others—in relation to, not transcendence of, the diverse social text of the interbellum public sphere.[2]

As Cary shows, the interface between literary experiment and the new economic, cultural, and social energies of American modernism likewise shapes the rich rhetorical inventiveness of modern American poetry. As he demonstrates in his overview of the verse genre, modern American poetry's creative breadth, its variety of forms, and its diversity of voices exceed any single or monolithic account of the period. Indeed, the dominant story of the modern image—promoted by Ezra Pound, T. S. Eliot, F. S. Flint, and H. D. (Hilda Doolittle)—is no longer considered *the* defining template for modern American poetry. Moreover, as he argues in 2005, literary Imagism, as a "founding movement in modern American poetry [. . .] is richer and more diverse than we have been inclined to think" (72). To take one example, image-text traditions in the arts, popular culture, and advertising discourse influence the collage techniques of such *291 Gallery* talents as Agnes Ernst Meyer and Marius De Zayas in experimental works like "Mental

Reactions." As a vehicle of poetic innovation, modern collage, as Nelson shows, encompasses a remarkable presentational range of forms and techniques in the poetry of T. S. Eliot, Ezra Pound, and Mina Loy. Similarly, Nelson surveys the verbal experimentalism of Gertrude Stein, Marianne Moore, and Hart Crane. Equally important, as Nelson notes, such otherwise distinctive poets as Robert Frost, Claude McKay, and Edna St. Vincent Millay share a common agenda of masterfully appropriating traditional verse forms such as the sonnet, ballad stanza, and dramatic monologue, in powerfully original modes of new social expression.

Beyond literary formalism and the compositional strictures of the Imagist moment in American verse, Nelson's recovery project demonstrates how the new social discourses of race, empire, class, and gender—not to mention the period's defining historical events such as the Spanish Civil War—complicate and enrich the literary heritage of modern American poetry. That recovered diversity of American poetries is nowhere more available to general and scholarly readers alike than in Cary's definitively edited collection for the new millennium, the Oxford *Anthology of Modern American Poetry* (2000). "With perhaps as much catholicity of taste as one editor can muster, I have tried," Cary has written, "to present twentieth-century American poetry in its astonishing and endlessly energetic variety" (xxix). That variety embraces not only the familiar offerings of the modern American poetry canon but a chorus of recently recovered poets writing out of the otherwise repressed social contexts of the American labor and women's movements, the black power, Chicano, and Native American movements, and other scenes of historical oppression such as Japanese and Chinese internment and concentration camp experiences. Here Nelson surveys the expansive field of modern American poetics ranging from the formal mastery of the haiku, sonnet, and villanelle through open free-verse and long encyclopedic poems.

In remapping the terrain of modernist literary reception, the revolutionary culture wars of our own moment also have unearthed certain specters of modernism long repressed at the heart of the key social antagonisms of the interbellum period. Whether emanating from the Old Left or Agrarian Right, such modernist revenants return in figures of social agency that are not just historical—not, that is, safely consigned to the past—but, more radically, "out of joint" in time. The "untimely" return of such hauntings, according to Derrida in *Specters of Marx*, involves, precisely, "a question of repetition: a specter is always a *revenant*. One cannot control its comings and goings because it *begins by coming back*. [. . .] [N]o one can be sure if by returning it testifies to a living past or a living future, for the *revenant* may already mark the promised return of living being" (11, 99). The "ghostlier demarcations" (130) of modernism—to borrow from the lexicon of Wallace Stevens—are doubly uncanny: they not only

anticipate present aesthetic debate as itself a repetition of forgotten political clash but, more enigmatically, they invoke a future whose utopia we
have not yet grasped.[3] The present task of imagining new possibilities for
revolutionary, literary representation necessarily conjures the specters
that haunt modernism's repressed cultural politics.[4] One exemplary figure, no doubt, of this kind of spectral recovery—for which we have to
thank Cary—remains Edwin Rolfe.

As a *nom de plume*, Edwin Rolfe describes an imaginary figure for the
enabling cultural history that empowered the poet with a class-specific,
social identity. A counterpart to Fitzgerald's Jay Gatsby—who "sprang
from his Platonic conception of himself" (99)—Rolfe, as a cultural sig-
nifier, is the poetic emanation of America's immigrant, working-class
community. Even before he became Edwin Rolfe, Solomon Fishman was
a homegrown product of the American Left. Time does not allow here
for a close reading of Rolfe's work but, as we know, the particular historicity witnessed in his verse has crucial cultural value now precisely as a
usable countermemory to the ahistoricism that has dominated the postwar containment of twentieth-century verse, first through the formal constraints of American New Criticism and later in the solipsistic impulses
shaping academic verse traditions from the 1960s onward.

Against that better-known version of American poetry, Rolfe's career
preserves three definitive moments of a quite different literary history
that is now seldom seen. His three published volumes, *To My Contempo-
raries* (1936), *First Love, and Other Poems* (1951), and *Permit Me Refuge*
(1955), give voice to a democratic tradition of international socialism
that evolves, respectively, through the Popular Front years of the Depression era, the Spanish Civil War, and the postwar Red Scare. That judg-
ments of poetic taste involve social, not universal, acts of valuation is
something Thomas McGrath's 1955 foreword to *Permit Me Refuge* foregrounds in accounting for the formal transitions Rolfe's poetry under-
went, particularly in his successful efforts during the Red Scare "to name
the new thing that a degenerate age had created" (207). Some four
decades later, Nelson's cogent preface to the definitive *The Collected Poems
of Edwin Rolfe* (1993) underscores that historicizing recognition. Trans-
coding the reception of Rolfe's formative stances for a very different cultural moment and a very changed readership, Nelson acknowledges that
"[n]o effort to make Rolfe's poetry an appropriate subject of historical
inquiry can avoid asking whether his work represents a past that remains
usable now" (Rolfe 3).

Nelson's recovery of Rolfe's verse, I would argue, remains eminently
usable precisely insofar as it restores a set of literary coordinates by which
we can plot a progressively American aesthetic legacy not only as the
forerunner of the feminist, antiwar, and black aesthetic movements

of the Vietnam era but, equally important, as the harbinger of a cultural poetics beyond the triumph of multinational capitalism, whose social barbarism dominates our moment. The poems themselves, as Cary says, "urge us to reexamine our national past if we are to have any chance of acting responsibly and progressively in the present" (12). Thus to read Rolfe now is also to reread the very much unfinished business of classism, racism, sexism, and fascism that the poet struggled against throughout his career. Across the great divide of history that separates Rolfe's moment from our own, his verse nevertheless makes pressing claims not only on our habits as readers of American poetry but on our present political reflexivity as such, for it is cultural memory that is supremely at stake both in the repressive 1950s—the decade that decisively censored Rolfe's publication—and in the reactionary resurgences of the contemporary period. Rolfe is an uncanny figure in modern American poetry, for through him we begin to recognize just how far the same sociocultural agenda that repressed his poetics persists even now in the received disciplinary protocols shaping our own naturalized habits of reading.

Recovering Rolfe in the era of advanced capitalism is thus imbricated in a broader cultural task, whose politics entail, as Alexander Kluge and Oscar Negt have theorized, an active remembering, a "working through of the suppressed experience of the entire labor movement that has been mutilated by the bourgeois public sphere" (95). Witnessed in Rolfe's writing is the erasure of the progressive counterpublic sphere that his generation conceived out of the Great Depression and sought to defend in the Spanish Civil War and later during the postwar inquisitions of the McCarthy era. Reading Rolfe now recalls troubling historical defeats: defeats that are hardly over and done with but live on as they "exert pressure," according to Kluge and Negt, "on the ability to remember" (95). Part of the trouble in our cultural recall of modern American poetics is politically determined by the culture wars of the 1930s, where the formal innovations and social representations of proletarian poetics were countered by a conservative wave of critical reception. The clashing ideologies of the Great Depression pitted cultural workers of the American Left against the Southern Agrarians. Contrary to the Agrarian, Fugitive, and New Critical campaign to silence proletarian verse—to dismiss it as agitprop doggerel—the poetry of Edwin Rolfe testifies to the rich, working-class aesthetic that flourished throughout the interbellum decades.[5] As an organic intellectual in Antonio Gramsci's sense, Rolfe in the 1930s voices the lived experience of urban starvation in "Season of Death," industrial disease in "Asbestos," political martyrdom in "Witness at Leipzig," local activism in "Unit Assignment," collective labor unrest in "Not Men Alone," and international solidarity in "Winds of Another Sphere." Inscribed in these works is not just the defining social poetics of the Great Depression but the structure of feeling of what it was to be alive and active in the class struggle against global capital and international fascism.

Space does not permit here a detailed discussion of the kind of group anthology projects and choral poetics that Nelson has put in productive tension with the careers of individual talents. Nevertheless, the example of Rolfe's retrieval from cultural oblivion stands as an exemplary model of the extensive field of recovery projects that Nelson has advanced and overseen, both in the work of his students and colleagues and in subsequent volumes such as his recent 2001 study *Revolutionary Memory: Recovering the Poetry of the American Left*, as well as the several edited volumes of verse in the American Poetry Recovery series: *Palace-burner: The Selected Poetry of Sarah Piatt* (2005), *The Whole Song: Selected Poems of Vincent Ferrini* (2004), *Wicked Times: Selected Poems of Aaron Kramer* (2004), *The Collected Poems of Don Gordon* (2003), *The Complete Poems of Claude McKay* (2003), *Black Moods: Collected Poems of Frank Marshall Davis* (2002), *Rendezvous with Death: American Poems of the Great War* (2002), and *The Wound and the Dream* (2002).

Advancing the spirit of Cary's recovery work, my own recent book project—*The Edge of Modernism: American Poetry and the Traumatic Past* (2005)—has explored modes of involuntary, traumatic memory inscribed in the modernist archive as witnessings to the legacies of, among other things, the Middle Passage, total war, and genocide. Seldom in the theories of social, cultural, and aesthetic modernisms has the trauma of genocide featured prominently in what defines the modern condition. It is curiously elided in the critical reception of modernism. Amidst the wears and tears of postmodernism, the reigning discourses of the state, the media, and the academy have served arguably to repress, deny, and normalize the extreme experiences of total war and industrial mass murder.[6] Not a phenomenon, however, that belongs to the distant past, genocide first happens within the turbulent forces of social modernism with its emerging systems of technology and rapid information exchange. Accompanying these sophisticated advances, genocide persists as the underside to the progress of modernity otherwise witnessed in the twentieth century. Repressed for the most part in the modern public sphere, the legacy of genocide troubles the closure of modernist periodization with the repetition of its event. Returning in Cambodia, Rwanda, Bosnia, Guatemala, and Kosovo, the genocidal edge of modernism cuts through the social fabric of postmodernism. But equally important, the unfinished business of genocide's revisionist historicism and political denial bleeds into our own moment. Thus in discerning literary modernism anew, we might begin with asking, "What was the uniquely traumatic force of genocide in dissociating the modernist sensibility"?

On the one hand, the risk in writing trauma lies in succumbing to a melancholic acting out of its original event. On the other hand, as Judith Butler, David Eng, and others have argued, melancholic attachment to traumatic loss also can produce new modes of aesthetic and cultural representation, social identity, and political agency. Analyzing the unique conditions and effects of trauma, Sigmund Freud theorized a key difference between traumatic events and traumatic memory. Only the latter's deferred action (*nachtraglichkeit*), he insists, constitutes psychical trauma proper insofar as its memory "acts like a foreign body which long after its entry must be continued to be regarded as an agent that is still at work" (6). What does it mean, however, for traumatic memory to have agency— "to act like a foreign body at work" in the modern archive? What are the consequences for civic subjectivity of that psychic labor, inflected as it is by the disjointed temporality of deferred action? Can one assume a civic voice prior to, or apart from, the psychic agency of such archived "foreign bodies," or must the former always already be worked through the latter? Such questions of how archived, traumatic memory bears on civic identification, nation formation, and other social modes of class, racial, gender, and ethnic orientation become further complicated, as Michael Rothberg has argued, by today's postmodern condition—a world increasingly defined by the mechanical reproduction and circulation of sign exchange in photojournalism, film, museum and gallery culture, academic and literary discourses, and the popular entertainment industry.

The return of trauma's enigma further ruptures the historical sense of time as such by intruding upon the normative continuities of linear temporality underwriting conventional narration. "The event," as Giles Deleuze has written, "[. . .] is always already in the past and yet to come" (143). Insofar as secondary witnessing is defined by an encounter with extremity's unfinished business, it has to deal with a temporality marked by the future anterior of trauma's "after-effects" of time "out of joint." Thus as Derrida has it in "Passages," "memory is not just the opposite of forgetting [. . .] to think memory or to think anamnesis, here, is to think things as paradoxical as the memory of a past that has not been present, the memory of the future—the movement of memory as tied to the future and not only to the past, memory turned toward the promise, toward what is coming, what is arriving, what is happening tomorrow" (383). Beyond an encounter with radical loss, the unique temporal structure of trauma encompasses not just the period of latency between the event and its present return in memory but, equally important, the promise of an anticipated futurity of difference.

The expanded temporal frame of traumatic latency opens important avenues for redefining the disciplinary boundaries dividing literary modernism and postmodernism and for rethinking modernist periodicity.

Instead of foreclosing modernity, say, at the end of the Second World War in 1945, the temporal rhythms that I have explored recently afford a much more dynamic view of literary periodicity. Specifically, in my latest book, I discern the "edge" of modernism's definitive scenes of extremity in terms of their punctuation of the present and their future returns. Thus across several comparative contexts of traumatic historicity, I examine modernism's unfinished business as its "edge" cuts through the literary representations, themes, and formal techniques of contemporary poetics. Not insignificantly, this close attention to traumatic temporality opens up utopian possibilities for imagining transformative cultural identity, political agency, and social change. The project I engage in *The Edge of Modernism* would glean the shock of difference that trauma insinuates into the otherwise foreclosed reproduction of postmodern historicity. Throughout this book, whether reading the radically open forms of Rachel Blau du Plessis or fixed forms such as Anthony Hecht's sestina "The Book of Yolek," I demonstrate the ways in which the formal resources of poetry—in its figurative language, its reliance on catachresis, aposiopesis, anacoluthon, its grammatological techniques and the spatial arrangement on the page—offer a salutary medium for staging traumatic histories in ways that resist the banal spectacle of the image world otherwise governing contemporary consumer society.

The event of the traumatic past, paradoxically enough, calls for new modes of being in the world and new models of community. "What is new, newness itself," writes Judith Butler, "is founded upon the loss of original place" (*Loss* 468). That loss calls for new modes and communities, and a new attention to modernist forms of mourning is also an implicit assumption, I would argue, animating Cary's new book. Throughout his career, Cary has authored works that create the discursive possibilities for opening fresh directions in contemporary scholarship. Not just a work of comprehensive and careful scholarship, *When Death Rhymed: Poem Cards of the Great Wars* is canny in its conception and far-reaching in its implications. In his former works—most notably *Repression and Recovery* but also his edited volumes on *Marxism and the Interpretation of Culture* (1988) and *Cultural Studies* (1992), not to mention his writing on the English profession and his recovery of notable poets such as Edwin Rolfe—Cary has not been satisfied with the typical functions of academic authorship. *When Death Rhymed* is no exception. In it, Cary attends to what was once a popular mode of witness to modernity's "Great Wars" precisely through the recovery and reframing of the poem card: a mass-mediated artifact. The poem card emerges, in Cary's account, not merely as an ephemera of modern everyday life but, more importantly, as a significant new object of disciplinary analysis and as a recoverable mode of social agency. "The kind of agency poem cards offered," Nelson insists, "is also complex and multiple. And poem cards demonstrate that poetry is not universally quite the transcendent art form that has been urged on us since the early nineteenth century" (274). *When Death Rhymed* provides a theoretically sophisticated and readable account of the ephemeral limits on the postcard as a mass-mediated mode of communication. At the same time, however, the book also pays sustained attention to audience analysis and offers detailed case studies of specific correspondences gleaned from exhaustive detective work into the obscure subgenre of the war postcard. "These small poem cards," Nelson writes, "offer us a unique—and largely unstudied—access to how ordinary people actually used poetry over nearly two centuries. They thus, for the first time, give us detailed information about popular poetry and human agency."

Nelson continues:

> What a study of poem cards makes clear is that neither frontline or domestic users of poetry appear to have sought out antiwar poetry. A selective canon of ironic poems has come to stand in for the whole history of modern wartime poetry. At that point the exceptional antiwar ironic poem is falsely constructed as characteristic. Poetry played several different roles in these events, but they cannot be recognized from canonical literature alone. Reading widely in the poems soldiers and civilians actually used during these wars can begin to correct the story of the paper wars of the last century. There is, importantly, a difference in some of the messages people write at various points in war, most notably after a victory for their side. There is also a widespread increase in weariness and the desire for peace in World War I messages in the autumn of 1916 and thereafter. But the poems ordinary people used most frequently, it turns out, were often printed on cards or envelopes, and they generally support the war at issue. Neither our understanding of these poems nor our evaluation of them, finally, can be firmly grounded unless we gather evidence of how they were actually used. For that, the poem card with its holograph messages offers a unique archive. (273)

When Death Rhymed provocatively broadens the intersection of modern literary studies and modern cultural studies by inflecting both through an expansive transnational register of social exchange. Cary offers nuanced readings of the formal relations between image and text that govern the discursive conventions of illustrated poem cards. But equally important, he considers the cultural work these cards performed as persuasive rhetoric in mobilizing national and international consensus about what exactly was at stake in modern warfare. In this vein, he provides discerning analysis of the particular codes and iconography of national, class, gender, and racial identification that the postcard urged on its many constituencies in and among the United States, England, France, Russia, Finland, Germany, Italy, and Japan. Not just a book of modern scholarship, however, *When Death Rhymed* is an expansive, discursive reference project tied to the larger textual archive of actual cards that Cary has retrieved and that the book elegantly showcases in its visual impact. One cannot emphasize enough the custodial service Cary has provided in assembling, preserving, and disseminating the war postcard. Some of these cards are elegant aesthetic objects; others, as Cary explains, are ugly and offensive pieces of xenophobic, militaristic, and racist propaganda. All of them, however, deserve the archival representation that Cary presents in this book. *When Death Rhymed* is destined to be a field-changing book, one that in time will be every bit as significant as Frederick Hoffman's 1946 publication *The Little Magazine: A History and Bibliography*. Taking Hoffman as a guide, Cary's scholarship abides as a powerful example for a whole generation of recovery projects undertaken in the field of American modernism. More than anyone else, Cary has opened the field of modern American poetry to new disciplinary objects and ephemera, to long-forgotten flows of subcultural exchange, and to new modes and methodologies of interpretive reading. In this way, he continues to lead the way in expanding—and, equally important, unsettling—the literary canon.

Notes

1. For a discussion of the anthology market between the wars and its relation to the high modern canon, see Abbott.

2. See Foley, Denning, Kalaidjian, Lauter, Nelson, Rabinowitz, and Wald.

3. Michael Davidson takes Stevens's phrasing from "The Idea of Order at Key West" for his book *Ghostlier Demarcations: Modern Poetry and the Material World.*

4. Through their own clinical experience and readings of Freud's well-known case study of the Wolf Man, Nicolas Abraham and Maria Torok have marked the discursive crypts of phantom signifiers in terms of narrative "gaps left within us by the secrets of others" (Abraham 171). For an extended analysis of cryptonyms, see Abraham and Torok, *The Wolf Man's Magic Word: A Cryptonymy.* Building on the work of Abraham and Torok, Derrida has adapted his discussion of the "hauntology" of cryptonyms to the philosophy of political economy in *Specters of Marx: The State of the Debt, the Work of Mourning, and the New International.*

5. See, for example, Robert Penn Warren, "The Present State of Poetry in the United States."

6. For a critique of the normalizing denial of global catastrophe in the "end of history" rhetoric of Francis Fukiyama, see Jacques Derrida, *Specters of Marx: The State of the Debt, the Work of Mourning, and the New International.*

Works Cited

Abbott, Craig S. "Modern American Poetry: Anthologies, Classrooms, and Canons." *College Literature* 17 (1990): 209–22.

Abraham, Nicolas. "Notes on the Phantom: A Complement to Freud's Metapsychology." *The Shell and the Kernel: Renewals of Psychoanalysis.* Vol. 1. Trans. and ed. Nicholas T. Rand. Chicago: U of Chicago P, 1994. 171–76.

Abraham, Nicolas, and Maria Torok. *The Wolf Man's Magic Word: A Cryptonymy.* Trans. Nicholas Rand. Minneapolis: U of Minnesota P, 1986.

Butler, Judith. "Afterward: After Loss, What Then?" *Loss: The Politics of Mourning.* Ed. David L. Eng and David Kazanjian. Berkeley: U of California P, 2003. 467–74.

———. *The Psychic Life of Power: Theories in Subjection.* Stanford: Stanford UP, 1997.

Davidson, Michael. *Ghostlier Demarcations: Modern Poetry and the Material World.* Berkeley: U of California P, 1997.

Deleuze, Giles. *Cinema 2: The Time-Image.* Trans. Hugh Tomlinson and Robert Galeta. Minneapolis: U of Minnesota P, 1989.

Denning, Michael. *The Cultural Front.* New York: Verso, 1996.

Derrida, Jacques. *Archive Fever: A Freudian Impression.* Trans. Eric Prenowitz. Chicago: U of Chicago P, 1996.

———. "Passages—From Traumatism to Promise." *Points . . . Interviews, 1974–1994.* Ed. Elisabeth Weber. Trans. Peggy Kamuf et al. Stanford: Stanford UP, 1995. 372–98.

———. *Specters of Marx: The State of the Debt, the Work of Mourning, and the New International.* Trans. Peggy Kamuf. New York: Routledge, 1994.

Eliot, T. S. "Tradition and the Individual Talent." *The Sacred Wood.* London: Methune, 1920; rpt. in *The Sacred Wood and Major Early Essays.* New York: Dover, 2000. 27–33.

Eng, David L., and David Kazanjian, eds. *Loss: The Politics of Mourning.* Berkeley: U of California P, 2003.

Fitzgerald, F. Scott. *The Great Gatsby.* New York: Simon, 1992.

Foley, Barbara. *Radical Representations.* Durham: Duke UP, 1993.

Foucault, Michel. *The Archaeology of Knowledge.* Trans. A. M. Sheridan Smith. New York: Pantheon, 1972.

Freud, Sigmund. *Studies in Hysteria. The Standard Edition of the Complete Psychological Works of Sigmund Freud.* Vol. 2. Trans. James Strachey. London: Hogarth and the Institute of Psycho-analysis, 1955.

Kalaidjian, Walter. *American Culture between the Wars.* New York: Columbia UP, 1994.

———. *The Edge of Modernism: American Poetry and the Traumatic Past.* Baltimore: Johns Hopkins UP, 2005.

Kluge, Alexander, and Oscar Negt. *Public Sphere and Experience: Toward an Analysis of the Bourgeois and Proletarian Public Sphere.* Trans. Peter Labanyi, Jamie Owen Daniel, and Assenka Oksiloff. Minneapolis: U of Minnesota P, 1993.

Lauter, Paul. *Canons and Contexts.* New York: Oxford UP, 1991.

McGrath, Thomas. "Foreword." *Permit Me Refuge,* rpt. in Edwin Rolfe, *The Collected Poems of Edwin Rolfe.* 207.

Merwin, W. S. "A Scale in May." *The Lice* (1967), rpt. in *The First Four Books of Poems.* Port Townsend: Copper Canyon, 1993.

Nelson, Cary. *The Incarnate Word: Literature as Verbal Space.* Champaign: U of Illinois P, 1973.

———. "Martial Lyrics: The Vexed History of the Wartime Poem Card." *American Literary History* 16.2 (2004): 263–89.

———. "Modern American Poetry." *The Cambridge Companion to American Modernism.* Ed. Walter Kalaidjian. New York: Cambridge UP, 2005. 68–101.

———. *Our Last First Poets.* Champaign: U of Illinois P, 1981.

———, ed. *Anthology of Modern American Poetry.* New York: Oxford UP, 2000.

———. *Repression and Recovery: Modern American Poetry and the Politics of Cultural Memory, 1910–1945.* Madison: U of Wisconsin P, 1989.

———. *Revolutionary Memory: Recovering the Poetry of the American Left.* New York: Routledge, 2001.

———. *When Death Rhymed: Poem Cards and Poetry Panics of the Great Wars.* Urbana: U of Illinois P, forthcoming.

———, and Ed Folsom, eds. *W. S. Merwin: Essays on the Poetry.* Urbana: U of Illinois P, 1987.

———, and Ed Folsom, eds. *W. S. Merwin, Regions of Memory: Uncollected Prose, 1949–82.* Urbana: U of Illinois P, 1987.

———, and Dilip Parameshwar Gaonkar, eds. *Disciplinarity and Dissent in Cultural Studies.* New York: Routledge, 1996.

Rabinowitz, Paula. *Labor and Desire.* Chapel Hill: U of North Carolina P, 1991.

———. *They Must Be Represented.* New York: Verso, 1994.

Rolfe, Edwin. *The Collected Poems of Edwin Rolfe.* Ed. Cary Nelson and Jefferson Hendricks. Champaign: U of Illinois P, 1993.

Rothberg, Michael. *Traumatic Realism: The Demands of Holocaust Representation.* Minneapolis: U of Minnesota P, 2000.

Stevens, Wallace. *The Collected Poems of Wallace Stevens.* New York: Vintage, 1990.

Wald, Alan. *Exiles From a Future Time.* Chapel Hill: U of North Carolina P, 2002.

———. *The Revolutionary Imagination.* Chapel Hill: U of North Carolina P, 1983.

Warren, Robert Penn. "The Present State of Poetry in the United States." *The Kenyon Review* 1 (August 1939): 384–98.

❖ 4 ❖

"WE SHOULD ALWAYS READ WHAT
OTHER PEOPLE ASSURE US IS NO GOOD"

THE GOOD OF THE NO GOOD

Grant Farred

*Without the irrepressible, that is to say, only suppressible and repressible, force
and authority of this transgenerational memory, the problems of which we
speak would be dissolved and resolved in advance.*

> —Jacques Derrida, *Archive Fever: A Freudian Impression*

*The received notion of literary history is here the object of a deliberate deconstruc-
tion; it is the false promise of an objectivity I have done what I can to disallow.*

> —Cary Nelson, *Repression and Recovery: Modern American
> Poetry and the Politics of Cultural Memory, 1910–1945*

Cary Nelson's *Repression and Recovery* is, as he says late in this text, a work
of "deliberate deconstruction." However, *Repression and Recovery* constitutes less the critical undoing of the canon of American modernist literature, though it is that too, than the identification, through the archival
work of literary history, of the aporias within the canon. As Nelson phrases
it, "The challenge in thinking [. . .] the interpenetration of present and
past in literary history is not to master the problem, or even to identify all
its components—for neither goal is achievable—but rather to decide how
to proceed in the midst of problems that can be acknowledged and clarified but not fully resolved" (3). In order to work through aporetic interrogation, *Repression and Recovery* casts the canon as a "problem not to be
mastered." So one cannot, tempting as it is, remain focused solely on solv-
ing the problem of history or reconciling conflicting temporalities, that
always difficult relationship between the time of articulation or production and the time of critique. *Repression and Recovery* is, as a mode of anti-
mastery (so that any claim to "mastery" is, a priori, itself the subject of
suspicion; so that those named, by the history of criticism, "masters," have

their work drawn, perforce, into question), a work saturated with the spirit of "impossibility": the impossibility of determining, with any sustainable authority, what constitutes "literature," "good" or "bad," the impossibility of "resolution," of pronouncing finally, definitively on a body of literature. Or, more precisely, the impossibility of evaluating for all time those bodies of American modernist literature that exist firmly either inside or antihegemonically outside the canon. *Repression and Recovery* critiques, with a resonant equivocation, the canonized, the uncanonized, the Communist Party poets and the Southern agrarians, the Harlem Renaissance bards, and the unrecognized homoerotic verses produced by the likes of Angelina Weld Grimké, bodies of modernist literature that function in a complex proximity to each other.

After all, how does one think recovery, the politics of recovery after repression, the act of bringing back into critical life the literature of the substratum, that body of work upon which the canon rests so uneasily, those poems and novels published in obscure or even not-so-obscure places, all those works excluded by the ordering of the canon into a single hermeneutic, except as a recurring "problem"? We might ask, following W. E. B. DuBois's historic invocation of the precarious condition of "Negro life" in the antebellum South in *The Souls of Black Folk*, "how does it feel to be a problem" poem or novel (7)? To be "a problem," the problem of the inhospitality of the canon, if you will, to the canon? Why would a Countee Cullen sonnet such as "Yet Do I Marvel" present itself as a "problem" to the canon? Given that the Harlem Renaissance's Cullen was at once writing to and from within the deepest enclaves of the European literary canon—the Romantic poet protesting injustice, the metaphysical poet performing his erudite pyrotechnics—and against that self-same canon's exclusion of, say, a Phyllis Wheatley, Nelson compels us to ask: How, precisely, could it be a problem? What is, as it were, the nature of the problem? And, moreover, *Repression and Recovery* insists that the only political critique of the canon worth making is the determination to think the canon from the view of— following Jameson's and Žižek's thinking—the "parallax": to alter, either radically or subtly, the location from which the canon is thought—in Nelson's instance, the substrate, the repressed, the historically im-pressed text that is recovered through a radical literary politics—and, in so doing, is made, either slightly or drastically, unfamiliar to itself. The canon, then, as a "parallactic" problem, becomes not a fixed—always, of course, an unfulfillable, phantasmatic desire—body of work but a historically precarious assemblage—and ordering—of texts. The only true value of the canon, in this parallactic conception, becomes its capacity to generate "problems."

To name a canon, its formation, its maintenance, an "irresolvability" or a concatenation of "problems" is not only to argue against the impossibility of definition but to demand modernism's thinking as an "irrepressible" series of "parallactic" questions: its dynamic, "dialectical" (because the parallax is inconceivable without the Marxist dialectic) thinking of its own constitution, the moment of its making, its relationship to the future, the possibility of its thinking against itself, and to think against what Derrida names the "radical finitude" (of the archive, or, for our purposes, the canon [19]). These are all "questions" that, as Nelson says, "are not decidable" (*Repression* 240). These questions, all of which are inscribed with their own varying import, are therefore perpetually in circulation, functioning as the ghostly unspeakable, and thus all too articulate, the spirit of both the non-canonical and the anticanonical; and, always, that which lies beyond both, that which is, as yet, unnamed but will, surely, compel its own parallactic encounter in the not-too-distant future. Because these questions are "not decidable," certainly "not decidable" in advance, they articulate, from the very outset of *Repression and Recovery*, a conflict with the law, that set of rules that proposes the canon as a defined body of texts, a collection of critical works, resolved or resolvable according to established, unchangeable protocols. What, we might inquire, is the canon if not the law of the discipline? Through *Repression and Recovery* (and, the order of those terms in the title should give us pause, should demand its own reflection because we can only "recover" that which has been "repressed"; "recovery" is necessary in order to understand the full extent of canonical "repression," which, of course, again provokes the ghostly matter of that which has been repressed but has not yet, cannot yet, be recovered), Nelson draws the Law into question. The power of the Law, the (precarious) constitution of the canon, is subjected to the "undecidable questions." The canon is where, in literary-political terms, the law lives: the canon is constituted through the Law; the canon is how the Law of literature lives itself. The texts that compose the canon have, in Derrida's phrasing, the "power to interpret the archives [. . .] these documents in effect speak the law: they recall the law and call on or impose the law" (2).

The Law, however, invariably draws attention to what we might name the "extrajudicial," to those texts outside the Law (are these, then, also of pure rhetorical necessity, also "Law-less" texts?), which the Law excludes but over which it only has a tenuous authority. These anticanonical texts live, according to the Law, singularly unruly lives—lives that the Law cannot bring to order, cannot command by itself, because the Law is, as it were, the Law. It is because of the in-finite possibility of recovery, of enabling the repressed ghost to speak—as a form, as a critical essay, as a political tract—that neither the process of canon formation nor the Law of the canon is ever complete. (This is also to recognize that there is always potentially a limit to the number of texts, to exactly which texts, can be recovered; that repression can obscure some things from recovery as much as it can reveal others; the canon reveals the finitude, that is, the vulnerable extremities of the Law; or, the extremities that make the Law susceptible to the literary force of the "unruly." There is inherent in every series of anticanonical or noncanonical texts not only a constitutive vulnerability but also an erasure; the anticanon or noncanon cannot account for all the texts outside the canon. Every recovery, as much as every repression is, per force, an incomplete project, each riddled with its own erasure.)

Because no epistemology, no canon, can absolutely legislate itself or is ever fully knowable to itself, the work of the intellectual—in this instance Nelson as literary historian—is to struggle, however tendentiously, against impossibility in order to make "fully" public the unknowable; it is the intellectual's brief to work within and against the partial tendencies of the aporia. It is the intellectual's responsibility to both work against impossibility and to continually respond to the making public—the revealing of itself—of the unknown or unknowable (or irrecoverable) texts; it is the task of the intellectual to understand the necessary partiality (incompleteness) of intellectual labor and to acknowledge, as *Repression and Recovery* does, the "problematic" value of that work—intellectual work as always originating in the problem of the political, the "literary political," in this instance. Through this impossible intellectual striving against the impossible, the canon is always vulnerable to revision, to rearticulation, to having its very status as "canon" rendered illegitimate, its foundations shaken and possibly even removed—to having its problematic become a DuBoisian "problem."

Thinking the literary canon, the critiques of its formation, plays a key role in this delineation of Nelson as an intellectual, in how he conceives of himself and does his work as an intellectual. As he demonstrates in *Repression and Recovery*, for the intellectual based in a language department "literary thought"—literary criticism, if you will—continues to have considerable purchase. Literary thinking of the *Repression and Recovery* variety shows how crucial political issues, race, gender, sexual orientation, and ideological location are always endemic to any understanding of the canon; literary thinking complicates the relationship of the literary "outside" to the canon, and it demonstrates how thinking the canon, the anticanon, or the noncanon demands a thoroughly reflexive kind of intellectual labor. *Repression and Recovery*'s literary thought is nothing less than a critical engagement with, in varying degrees of simultaneity, history, politics, culture, literature, and temporality.

The Politics of Repetition

> *The beauty of the resolution on this particular level [. . .] is marked as a fragile figure by the very nature of its content.*
>
> —Fredric Jameson, *The Geopolitical Aesthetic*

The project that *Repression and Recovery* undertakes is to interrupt the ceaseless reproduction of the canon through the aporia produced by the text's literary history, its reclaiming of the substrate. As Derrida argues, *"There is no archive without a place of consignation, without a technique of repetition, and without a certain exteriority. No archive without outside"* (11, emphasis in original). There can be no canon without the ceaseless "repetition" of the canon which, paradoxically, is precisely what reveals the aporetic nature of the canon. As Jameson puts it in his work on the "geopolitical aesthetic" (itself a kind of "canonical" problematic), the "beauty of the resolution" resides in its "fragility." The "fragility," moreover, emerges from within, from within the "very nature of its content," from the lapsarian moment, the very act of formation: of "making" the canon, repeating the canon to itself, through itself, of repeating the canon as canon, because without the canon the text, presumably, would have no standing, at worst, and, at best, a precarious sense of its literary self. In the act of repeating itself, the canon, momentarily, unmakes itself and opens the possibility to (and for) that which lies "outside" of itself. It is in the act of canonical repetition that the "exteriority" of, in *Repression and Recovery*'s terms, the Southern agrarian poets or Wallace Stevens's (or William Carlos Williams's) status as previously excluded poet, is revealed. (How does one, indeed, can any literary critic today conceive of an American canon sans either Williams or Stevens? Probably not, and yet these modernists have only very recently come to enjoy this "historic" status. It is this process of canon making that *Repression and Recovery* is, in part, dedicated to revealing.) It is, then, only through repeated reading, both in the speaking again and again of a Williams poem and the hermeneutic work of discovering, repeatedly, the impossible-to-fix "ontological truth" of a Stevens poem, that either of these writers can become canonical. No canon without the repeated speaking of the poet, the memorizing of the lines of the poet's poems (itself the most literary form of repetition), and, as importantly, the saying again and again—as if invoking or iterating a holy word—the name of the poet; especially, of course, favorably, in relation to other canonical names: "Shakespeare," "Wordsworth," "Keats," "Eliot," "T. S." or "George," no matter which, though their differences are no small narcissistic matter.

Constitutive of the act of repetition is the risk of revelation: of the canon revealing not only what is outside it or why it is outside it, but the very struggle to keep the excluded texts outside. Any and every time "literary agents," be they publishing houses or scholarly critics, either produce a new or revised anthology or pronounce on the "merit" or intentionality of a poem, their very actions—which are repeated routinely, if not daily—simultaneously reify the canon and render it vulnerable to those texts and those critical voices that are categorized as noncanonical.

That is, according to Nelson, the rationale for the relentless interrogative. The canon, Nelson argues, "should always [. . .] be questioned, not just defended, though it will resist impulses that undermine its authority" (*Repression* 55). The "authority" in question, the "authority" that girds the canon, turns upon, in Carl Schmitt's terms, a kind of nomos: the order of the canon, the ordering of texts, the relation of filiation (how one text articulates to another), the achievement of order through exclusion. Canonical "authority" makes itself vulnerable to being "undermined," however, not only because of repetition but because it is in the nature of the excluded through either their silent hauntings or their ghostly articulation to create—like the murdered King in *Hamlet*—dis-order, perhaps even chaos. (In *Hamlet*'s case, a simple, albeit nervous, interrogative "Who goes there?" provokes a crisis in a sovereign nation-state. It is a question that addresses itself, more directly than might first be imagined, to Claudius in the sense that it makes imperative anterior knowledge: Who went, as it were, before Claudius? What can the dead king's return signal but, as Derrida might have it, the coming as/into ghostly being the "force of [. . .] transgenerational memory"? The passing of the ghostly father into the troubled, nonsovereign—or, if Claudius is to be believed, not-yet-sovereign—son?)

It is out of what is named, almost certainly improperly, "chaos," that the recovery of repressed literary histories makes, what Nelson implicitly designates, "thinking" possible. It is only in its thinking, in being forced to think again about its constitution, that the canon can be made again, this time possibly made against itself, made against its own (surprisingly, and, according to Jameson, not-so-fragile) order, made against its own laws, made to think itself—its "beautiful," beautifully ordered "content"—rather than continue to practice itself as infinitely ordered—as the nomos of the literary earth. Chaos is what obtains when, as Derrida phrases it, "Order is no longer assured" (5). And if order is usurped, like Claudius usurped the late-King Hamlet's authority, then how can there be a canon, because it is impossible to sustain a canon without literary order? It is for this reason that the canon means so much to Nelson, why it preoccupies him in works as varied as *Repression and Recovery* and *Office Hours*. The canon links these texts in the Nelson oeuvre because for him the canon is the primary site of literary thinking. It constitutes the grounds upon which the critic (of poetry, drama, the novel) intervenes and the terms against which the intellectual thinks; to think the "problem" within the space of repetition (that space opened up by repetition) [1]; to recognize repetition as the (first) bulwark against the "problem"; as the impossible figurative elimination of the "problem."

To think the canon aporetically, as the problem of repetition, is to disrupt the canon's desire to live itself into perpetuity as the order of stasis.

And yet, Nelson cautions, "no one ever actually 'recovers' the thing itself" (*Repression* 8). The work of the literary historian is, because of the impossibility of "full recovery," infinitely incomplete-able: the "recovered" or problematic text, whether it is "admitted" into the canon or not, whether it is now under the protection of the Law or not, remains haunted by its historic status: it emerged, and is always emerging, from the substrate, so that it is forever tinged with the ghostly imprint of otherness—of death, terror, racism, the writing of the difference of the nation. It remains, in Gilles Deleuze's terms, a "minoritarian"[2] literature housed uncomfortably in the canonical mansion of the majoritarian. The "minoritarian" speaks, symbolically, if not literally, a different language—it speaks not only against the canon but in a way that is inimicable to the canon's mode of speech. It is written in the same language as the canon without ever being (fully) recognized, recognizable, as the language of the canon. The desire for an uninimicable belonging is, according to Toni Morrison, the very raison d'etre for writing: "I have always wanted to develop a way of writing that was irrevocably black" (qtd. in Gilroy 181). To write: America: America as "irrevocably black," as "irrevocably" against "blackness." In Morrison's emphatic phrasing is the full deconstructive force, lyrically sung, of the Other, the terrible threat of the minoritarian, a threat only partially identified by Deleuze.

For Nelson, however, the real difference between the minoritarian and majoritarian, between Morrison's "black" and, implicitly, white, resides elsewhere: "The distinction between a major and a minor literature is convincing only because it is unthought" (*Repression* 38). How does one think the condition of "irrevocably black"? The proper distinction between these two Deleuzian modes of literature can only be understood and accounted for when it is "thought"—when the intellectual explicates the relationship of the "minoritarian" to the "majoritarian"; when the status of each, hegemonically white and "irrevocably black," is explained historically. When, as Nelson argues, minor literature is understood as an "epistemological threat to the socially constructed transcendence of literary excellence" (*Repression* 39).

After having employed the order of the Law to exclude, the canon is now subjected to a kind of haunting from within. The canon becomes, in this way, a domicile familiar to Morrison scholars: it has an address to which it addresses itself: "124 Bluestone Road," the most haunted address in contemporary American literature—that metonymic house of American fiction is where the past lives as the phantasm that haunts America, because it, Jim Crowism, the failure of the civil rights movement, and so on can never be settled; the past can never find a new address while the old one is, as it were, still in (perfectly) good working order; a place that is not irrevocably haunted.[3] It is onto and into the very bodies of the inhabitants of Sethe's house that the violence of the past is phantasmatically inscribed. "124 Bluestone Road" is that place from which the past, the canon of (racialized, historic) violence, can never be excised. Following Nelson, we might propose that the "thing" may be irrecuperable except as a haunted incarnation of the thing itself. This is, of course, not to suggest that the historically haunted text cannot be reified, appropriated by both the nomos of the canon and the organs of (literary) capital; it is, rather, to enunciate the haunted novel or poem as *differánce*—the text that remains both literally canonical and antiphonal, while always susceptible to appropriation (and mis-representation), marked by the traces of its otherness, the text whose belonging in the canon is always mediated by its historic, a priori, nonbelonging, by the explicit, and implicit, desire of the author not to succumb to the stasis-inducing hermeneutic of the canon.

In *Repression and Recovery* intellectuality, the politics of thinking the canon, constitutes the act of working against repression toward recovery. It is in the practice of reading the proscribed or dismissed, memorably described by Nelson as "what other people assure us is no good," in reading the noncanonical texts or canonical texts against the canon (reading from within), that the work of thinking occurs. More than anything, it is intellectuality that militates against the canon's propensity for nomos, for the strict guarding against dis-order; intellectuality is what makes impossible the canon's determination to continually imagine itself as capable of a single articulation, as a majoritarian thinking; it is intellectuality that resists the canon's representation of itself as a historically settled archive, a body of knowledge capable of restricting itself to a permanently sedimented collection of not only fictional and critical works but a fixed hermeneutic.

The "history of canonization is pervasively racist, sexist and anti-intellectual," Nelson asserts. The canon, as Literary Law, is thus nothing less than the act of epistemological violence. As Walter Benjamin reminds us, "Violence [. . .] is the origin of the law" (286). Nelson charges that "custodians, of course, concern themselves not only with conserving the past but also with selectively disposing of much of it, though the two impulses become deceptively conflated in the imagination of academic disciplines" (*Repression* 4). It is in the act of "selectively disposing of much of it" that violence—the provocative act of ordering that has not historically always met with the critique such violence demands—is done to both minoritarian and majoritarian literary histories. In Deleuze's terms, the language of canonical violence is audible in more than one language. Within the canon, there is one register, one set of metaphors or tropes, in which violence is spoken. Violence is done to literature through the denial of raced, gendered, and "intellectual" histories: the consigning to the beyond, that place where the literary tenuousness of the DuBoisian "veil" obtains, of the excluded: exiling the uncanonizable to that place, the substratum of the canon, where it is imagined that no order is imposed, that place—we could call it women's literature, ethnic or proletarian fiction, or Harlem Renaissance poetry—where hermeneutic exchange, if it occurs at all, is Hobbesian: mostly volatile and unordered, nasty, brutish, and where valued works of fiction are in short supply. That is, in canonical terms, the only place where the texts about race, gender, sexual orientation, or dissident intellectuality can be countenanced; the place, in canonical terms, that is no place. Because it lives as the substratum, that place beneath the settled archive, the uncanonized has to continually understand and resist its own marginalization, its own "public" silence and silencing. The substratum has to, in its ghostly silencing, comprehend and articulate itself as nothing less than a threat to the sovereignty of the canon. The substratum is the product of violence that derives from the "origin of the law."

The task of canonical violence is, as *Repression and Recovery* recognizes only too well, to conserve. To canonize is, as it were, to confer indisputability, or, more metaphorically, "sainthood" upon a violently selected set of texts. *Repression and Recovery*'s response to this violence is to intellectualize the canon through the retrieval of the unruliness of literary history; Nelson is in the business of "secularizing," in Edward Said's "worldly" sense, with poetic abandon, the process of collecting excluded texts. To "intellectualize" is to not only restore the canon to disorder but to a vigorous hermeneutic life—to an interpretive liveliness. To secularize constitutes the radical breaking up, the deliberate breaking into, the deconstruction for all to see, of the law—secularization constitutes the act of making the Law unworkable for itself, and, unworkable and unreproducible as itself. To secularize or intellectualize is to make possible the public irruption of that hermeneutic propensity and energy that is already there in the unspeakable substratum of the Law—the intensities of raced or gendered or classed lives that articulate vibrantly from beneath, that speak eloquently, angrily but always persistently in the Harlem Renaissance poetry of Langston Hughes (or the noncanonical sonnets of Countee Cullen), in the underengaged erotic verse of H. D. or the brooding, insistently urbanized, Chicago-shaped lines of Carl Sandburg, in the baleful, overwhelming loss that makes *The Souls of Black Folks* such a memorable account of America's spiritual failure.

The texts, repressed, forgotten, ignored, and uncanonized, irrupt, through the literary history that is *Repression and Recovery*, into the Law of America's modernist canon. *Repression and Recovery* instantiates the history that de-forms the canon, forms against the canon, forms and lives—sometimes effervescently, sometimes more mutedly, sometimes barely surviving in a distant literary field—in spite of the canon. And, importantly, Nelson is utterly intolerant of that phenomenon, named, in other contexts, "tokenized inclusion" into the canon—the exceptional black or female or gay author allowed to take up residence in the white,

male-dominated canon. He argues that "recovering forgotten and excluded traditions entails more than a series of individual additions to
the canon" (*Repression* 23). It is not enough, according to Nelson's logic,
for the haunted text to be "accommodated" by the canon. Following Benjamin, "Its purpose is not to punish the infringement of law but to establish
new law" (286). With, we might add, all the fraught possibilities the enunciation that such a "new law" will make possible; the "new law" that will
never be entirely free of the law that it displaced but remains residual to
and resonant within the "new law." The canon must be uncanonized, "deliberately deconstructed," taken (fully) apart, before it becomes possible to
even consider "recanonizing" it, if such a project were even desirable.[4]

The Intellectual and the Canon

The canon cannot be reconceived except through a critical thinking, a
thinking that establishes a reciprocal, umbilical relationship between "intellectuality" and what *Repression and Recovery* designates "anti-intellectuality." In Nelson's engagement with the canon of American modernist
poetry and criticism, there is the implicit recognition that "anti-intellectuality" does not constitute "non-thinking," nor is it against the practice of
thinking. In fact, just the opposite. In doing battle with the canon, there
emerges a keen sense that anti-intellectuality constitutes a very particular
mode of thinking. Anti-intellectuality is, in this signal way, nothing less
than an unfulfillable intellectual project: the grand canonical dream of
making the Law unimpeachable (absolute), the desire to make the canon
unthinkable on terms other than its own. The canon strives toward, however fallaciously, nothing so much as the dream of sovereignty.

In this way, the real work of the canon is to make readers of the canon
forget that it is the canon; to write out of history that the canon is the
product of the original historic violence of the Law. The real desire of the
canon is to make itself onto-theological: the very essence of a series of
sacred texts whose canonization is assumed and respected a priori, ad in-
finitum; it must not be thought about because the prefatory and final
(and finite—to invoke Derrida's notion of "radical finitude") work of
thinking is already completed by the act of canon formation. The first
principle of canon formation is to prohibit the thought of, the thinking
that produced, canon formation—completed, done, never to be revisited.
It is in this problematic way that the canon does stand against thinking—
the thinking that reveals its historic thinking of itself into a canon. The
canon works to make of the practice of anti-intellectuality intellectuality.

What *Repression and Recovery* reveals is that the canon rests upon
something other than only itself: its substrate, the unruly repressed, the
unspeakable, perhaps even the unremarkable or unworthy and, finally,

the unsilence-able, that series of texts, produced by an array of literary constituencies, which the canon would not absorb or allow into itself. That which the canon repressed, that which it denied, that which it will not subject to scrutiny because it is deemed unworthy, is precisely that which makes the ground of its own anti-intellectuality, its own nonthinking, unthinkable. At the very limits of the sanctioned poem or an anthologized critical essay on American modernism (a project, of course, unthinkable without the dark presences and articulate women of Faulkner's peculiarly disturbed, and disturbing, landscape) is that novel or "doggerel" verse that "people assure us is no good," presuming, of course, that the canon alone can decide, and has in fact decided, what is "no good" without having to account now for why a piece of fiction or an essay is "no good."

It is the accomplishment of *Repression and Recovery* that it reveals how it is only on the terrain of the "no good" that thinking, that the robust, uncertain, demeaned, unremarkable, aggressively alternative texts that compose the secular uncanonized, can take place: the antinomos or the chaos of the "no good" demands a critical thinking, an evaluation of all the criticism and poetry that has gone before but is never, ever, gone, precisely because the "no good" is so resistant to—so violently occluded from—the order of the canon. That is why the canon works so diligently against retrieval or recovery. "Custodians," Nelson reminds us, "concern themselves not only with conserving the past but also with selectively disposing of much of it, though the two impulses become deceptively conflated in the imagination of academic disciplines" (*Repression* 4). Because "conservation" is as important as the act of "selectively disposing" that which, by its very literary being, articulates the sovereignty of the canon, that which promises to introduce potentially unstoppable chaos—the wild fecundity of Faulkner's Southern gothic—into the nomos of the canon. It is the recovery of the uncanonized, perhaps even uncanonizable, that threatens, with its own constitutive violence, the sovereignty of the canon. In order, we might argue, to undo sovereignty, only partisanship—which is different from, but not unrelated to, enmity—will suffice. (Following Schmitt, we might say that the canon represents an instance of partisanship: the absolute division: friend or enemy, canonizable or uncanonizable.) The anti-intellectual impulses of canonical conservation must be confronted with, as *Repression and Recovery* demonstrates, the anti-intellectually violent partisanship of literary history.

The canon wants to determine the relationship of Literature to the future: the past must be represented as a single aspect to the future. It is for this reason that what is written directly beneath the canon, that which lies pressed, from below, against the canon, both a set of excluded texts and a temporality that threatens the Law most directly. The "no good" is that force of literary history that will not allow the drive of anti-intellectuality toward conservation to remain unthought beyond preservation. To conserve is to preclude radical transformation. It is a "conservative" force that the "no good" will not, in its *Repression and Recovery* enunciation, countenance.

In *Repression and Recovery* Nelson turns the question of the canon from the rootedness, the immobility of the past, into a question for the present and the future by making it an issue of the politics—"racism, sexism"—of literary history and a question for the innumerable moments to come. Without the future there can be no canon; without the moment to come, the canon has no meaning; because of the future, expectation, the historically freighted looking to, and the past, the time of Faulkner and Morrison that is never "irrevocably" resolved, the canon might be made to collapse under the interrogative pressure of the aporia. But before that happens (and because it might never happen, which is precisely, we might argue, the prospect that a literary historian such as Nelson fears most), *Repression and Recovery* retrieves the canon from its repression, retrieves it for us, gives it to us as the Maussian gift of literary history: the act of giving that creates a political obligation: to critique the aporetic, contested, temporally unstable body of literature that is kept, if not out of circulation, then too routinely out of critical purview (see Mauss). *Repression and Recovery* gives us these texts—Sterling Brown, Claude MacKay, Muriel Rukeyser—so that we might think it again, as if for the first time but fully cognizant of the fact that it will certainly not be for the last time. As Nelson puts it, "A book on modern poetry necessarily engages history as a palimpsest of two durations—then and now, the earlier period that is overly 'under consideration' and the current period, uneasy about its potentially apocalyptic destiny but so far uncertain about its concluding date" (*Repression* 3). The work of thinking, *Repression and Recovery* insists, the work of the intellectual, as well as that of the anti-intellectual, is never done, especially when confronted with the prospect of canonical sovereignty. Or, as a cause for greater political hope, a challenge, perhaps even a threat, to canonical sovereignty.

Nelson is, in this way, a thinker for whom the precise temporal conjuncture matters intensely. It is not only a matter of understanding the history of the time, but it is necessary to know how to think in relation to temporality—to think in relation to more than one temporality simultaneously. What is critical, Nelson insists, is the "uneasy" relation of one temporality to another—the "then" to the "now." This issue achieves its full complexity in the act of decision: to be "under consideration" demands, of historical necessity, a decision. This means that the "then" is never fully revealed in and for the "now"; it is always "under consideration," to be decided upon again (and again) in the ever-changing "now." The ir-resolved relation of one temporality to another is what militates against the Law of the canon, against its absolute, atemporal sovereignty. However, it is precisely because the canon always demands a relation of the "then" to the "now" that it opens the possibility for thinking—for thinking the time of canonical relation, for thinking through temporal relation, for thinking against canonical reason.

The work of the intellectual is, because of the centrality of time, not simply to recover that which has been repressed but to make us think again, yet again, about what kind of labor it takes to recover the past for the future-present, and, to what use we put that which has been recovered, never fully, always only partially. That is precisely the reason we must read, perhaps before all else, that which "people assure us is no good." In canonical terms, there can be no thinking except that which takes place on the ground, in the time, of the "no good." In times of crisis, such as modernism frequently experienced, "Among the lessons to be learned from the fulcrum of events that helped propel us into postmodernity—from the Holocaust to Hiroshima," it is only the "no good" that can argue against, from that precarious, unique pressure point below, the sovereign impulses of the literary nomos (*Repression* 13). It is only through recovering the "no good" that the thinking of the canon's anti-intellectual propensities can at once be revealed, understood, and countered. The canon can, in this way, be thought against itself, simultaneously, on the terms of both anti-intellectuality and intellectuality: these are less two different modes of thinking, though they are that too, than an invitation to think the intellectuality of anti-intellectuality.

What is retrieved through *Repression and Recovery* is not only the repression of the noncanonical but the very way in which the canon thinks thought itself into public life. The "good" of the "no good" is that it makes unsustainable any desire toward stasis that the canon might have, any illusion the canon might have that the matter of thinking is settled at the moment that the canon is announced. That is the space—of and for literature, the political, theory, and culture—that Nelson's work opens up, opens into. In *Repression and Recovery* Nelson makes available to thinkers that terrain where the full interrogative value of the "good," as it were, of thinking the "no good," resides.

Notes

1. That is not to say that Nelson does not engage in other forms of thinking. *Office Hours* and *Academic Keywords* demonstrate another modality of Nelson's thought. However, regarding the canon—in *Repression and Recovery*—Nelson is committed to both struggling against the thinking of the canon and to imagining and producing, through that engagement, a critical mode of canonical thought.

2. I take this phrase from Gilles Deleuze's essay, "He Stuttered," especially his notion of "minorized" literature.

3. There are, of course, several other domiciles in African American literature, from Invisible Man's last, overly well-lit redoubt in Ellison's novel to the New York elevators that speak the history of black postwar migration in Colson Whitehead's *The Intuitionist.*

4. The project of "recanonizing" is, of course, always desirable, not only because the law of the canon is repetition, even if it is repetition with a difference, but because the canon is also lucrative business for those publishing houses—and editors, authors, and critics—who make it available.

Works Cited

Benjamin, Walter. *Reflections: Essays, Aphorisms, Autobiographical Writings.* Trans. Edmund Jephcott. New York: Random, 1978.

Deleuze, Gilles. "He Stuttered." *Essays Critical and Clinical.* Trans. Daniel W. Smith and Michael A. Greco. Minneapolis: U of Minnesota P, 1997.

Derrida, Jacques. *Archive Fever: A Freudian Impression.* Chicago: U of Chicago P, 1996.

Du Bois, W. E. B. *The Souls of Black Folk.* New York: Vintage/Library of America, 1990.

Gilroy, Paul. *Small Acts: Thoughts on the Politics of Black Cultures.* London: Serpent's Tail, 1993.

Jameson, Fredric. *The Geopolitical Aesthetic: Cinema and Space in the World System.* Bloomington: Indiana UP, 1995.

Mauss, Marcel. *The Gift: The Form and Reason for Exchange in Archaic Societies.* Trans. W. D. Halls. New York: Norton, 2000.

Nelson, Cary. *Academic Keywords: A Devil's Dictionary for Higher Education.* New York: Routledge, 1999.

———. *Office Hours: Activism and Change in the Academy.* New York: Routledge, 2004.

———. *Repression and Recovery: Modern American Poetry and the Politics of Cultural Memory, 1910–1945.* Madison: U of Wisconsin P, 1989.

Žižek, Slavoj. *The Parallax View.* Cambridge: MIT, 2006.

∽ 5 ∾

The Lives of Haiku Poetry

Self, Selflessness, and Solidarity
in Concentration Camp Haiku

Karen Jackson Ford

Most literary histories trace the beginnings of haiku in America to modernism when the Imagists investigated its possibilities for making poetry new. Pound's legendary reduction of a thirty-line poem to "In a Station of the Metro" is a parable of modernist formalism. He termed the two-line final version "*hokku-like*" not just because it was brief but because its brevity resulted from promising aesthetic principles (286).[1] Haiku was a form that purportedly used no superfluous word, relied on vivid imagery rather than on sound, took its images from the natural world, and abjured abstractions. But even more important—and underwriting all these techniques— was a *hokku-like* attitude of impersonality, an enviable cultural trait thought to characterize the Japanese. Cultivating impersonality through these formal constraints, it was argued, could relieve Western poets' obsession with the self and thus aid in purging poetry of Victorian and Georgian verbosity, sentimentality, abstraction, and vagueness.

Impersonality was therefore extolled as a corrective to Western poetic excesses.[2] Oscar Wilde, for instance, praised the East's adherence to an art-for-art's-sake aesthetic: "While the Western world has been laying on art an intolerable burden of its own intellectual doubts and the spiritual tragedy of its own sorrows, the East has always kept true to art's primary and pictorial conditions" (134). John Gould Fletcher admonished poets to "sit once more at the feet of the Orient and learn from it how little words can express, how sparingly they should be used, and how much is contained in the meanest natural object" (16). But impersonality was also explicitly racialized and opposed to the West in those terms. Percival Lowell devoted an influential book to the subject in 1888[3]:

59

The peoples inhabiting [the earth's temperate zone] grow steadily more
personal as we go west. So unmistakable is this gradation of spirit,
that one is tempted to ascribe it to cosmic rather than to human
causes. It is as marked as the change in color of the human complexion observable along any meridian, which ranges from black
at the equator to blonde toward the pole. In like manner, the
sense of self grows more intense as we follow in the wake of the
setting sun, and fades steadily as we advance into the dawn.
America, Europe, the Levant, India, Japan, each is less personal
than the one before. We stand at the nearer end of the scale, the
Far Orientals at the other. If with us the *I* seems to be of the very
essence of the soul, then the soul of the Far East may be said to
be Impersonality. (14–15)

Ironically, at about the same time the Imagists were proposing impersonality and haiku as tools of modernist cultural renewal, Japanese poetic
innovators were taking haiku in just the opposite direction. In 1915,
Ippekiro Nakatsuka and Kawahigashi Hekigodo founded a new school of
poetry, freestyle or Kaiko haiku, that elevated the feelings of the poet and
loosened the formal restrictions on the poems. They published an influential journal, and by the 1930s other poets in the Japanese avant-garde
joined in the rejection of what they considered an outdated, genteel style.
Neiji Ozawa and Kyotaro Komuro brought the new style of haiku to North
America when they immigrated to the United States in 1907, founding
freestyle haiku groups in California; these clubs provided Japanese American haiku poets an opportunity to share their work and a forum for discussions of poetry and poetics. Thousands of haiku were composed,
distributed, and read by these poets, and freestyle haiku flourished in the
United States, mostly on the West Coast, where many of the Japanese
immigrants had settled, until the outbreak of World War II.
    "Shortly after the bombing of Pearl Harbor and the United States'
entry into the Second World War," Cary Nelson recounts in his 2000 *Anthology of Modern American Poetry*, President Roosevelt "signed the now infamous Executive Order 9066, which authorized the forced roundup,
relocation, and detention of Japanese Americans. [. . .] More than 120,000
Japanese Americans, most of them American born, were suddenly taken
from their homes and confined in concentration camps set up in the
swamplands of Arkansas or the deserts of Arizona, California, and New
Mexico" (717). Among the internees were members of the Kaiko haiku
clubs, who continued to write poetry during their detention. Even so, the
written record of the Kaiko movement was all but obliterated, both in the
United States and Japan, during and after World War II. Violet Kazue Matsuda de Cristoforo, a poet interned for three years, strove after the war

to gain political reparations for Japanese Americans and to restore their literary record. In 1987 she published a bilingual volume, *Poetic Reflections of the Tule Lake Internment Camp 1944*, which combined her own fifteen surviving haiku and related reflections in memoir form. Ten years later, she published *May Sky: There Is Always Tomorrow: Concentration Camp Kaiko Haiku*, in which she collected and translated 300 poems by dozens of poets written during the internment. Nelson's inclusion of the *May Sky* haiku in his prominent *Anthology* brought them to an even wider readership.

Now de Cristoforo and Nelson obviously share a desire to recover this poetry; however, crucial differences in their editing practices subtly evoke the matter of impersonality, an issue that has become increasingly important in post-World War II haiku in the United States. Nelson prints the poems as a "miniature narrative":

> In order to emphasize the narrative potential that is revealed when the poems are treated as a collective enterprise, we have removed the poets' names from the poems here, though they are listed in the book's contents. (718)

By omitting the poets' names in the text proper and assembling their individual compositions into a single communal narrative, Nelson shifts attention from individual authorship to collective voice, presenting the poetry as a response to shared experience. He explicitly theorizes his rationale for such an editorial move a year later in *Revolutionary Memory: Recovering the Poetry of the American Left* (2001), where he again suppresses individual authorship in order to create a "five-part poetry chorus assembled out of fragmentary quotations" taken, this time, from socialist poetry of the 1930s (166).

Revolutionary Memory proposes two, apparently opposite, methods for approaching forgotten political poetry, both of which bear upon the question of personality and impersonality: analysis of a single author's work and career, and analysis of a community of writers engaged in a collective enterprise. Both methodologies are deeply rooted in history, and Nelson considers them related rather than opposed[4]:

> I see these two models of reading and recovery less as competing approaches than as two sides of the same coin, necessary dimensions of understanding that balance, complement, and challenge one another. The first approach, exemplified in the chapter on Edwin Rolfe, combines biography and history. The second, embodied in two "poetry chorus" chapters, focuses on community and continuity in the collective enterprise of progressive poetry. The two poetry chorus chapters come last in the book to suggest

that in some of the key constitutive moments of political poetry a
collective literature is a destination and an overriding value; it tri-
umphs over the individual voice. (3)

Indeed, when Nelson foregrounds the public commitments of a particular writer over her or his private identity, he follows the poet's own
choice to participate in a collectivity. Thus the choral assemblages in *Revolutionary Memory*—the first orchestrating fragments of revolutionary poetry from the 1930s, the second lines from elegies for Federico García
Lorca—deliver individual voices, the voices of poets we have tended to ignore, to a collaborative cultural and political "intertext" (176) that allows
us to recognize their poetic strategies and value.

And yet, ironically, that very recognition of value, apprehended in
the collective environment, provokes many readers to set each poet apart
as an individual. Though for decades we had ignored the poets Nelson
recovers in his poetry choruses, readers were uncomfortable encounter-
ing lines of poetry without authorial attribution. At the symposium where
I first presented this essay as a paper, Nelson informed us that the poetry
chorus sections of *Revolutionary Memory* were originally presented without
authors' names. However, he included the names when he found that his
readers could not tolerate the omission. Such uneasiness suggests how
dependent we are on a conventional understanding of authorship, an
"understanding" that renders many poems unintelligible or invisible to
us. Nelson navigates these contradictions adroitly in *Revolutionary Memory*: "Although the emphasis is on a discursive formation rather than on
individual achievement," he explains, "the names of the authors are
noted in parenthesis, so that readers can have a sense of authorial participation in the continuing dialogue of the time" (166). Without denying the achievement and distinctiveness of each author, Nelson trains
our attention toward the "mutually responsive contributions" of poets involved in a particular movement and thus toward the historical moment
itself. As we shall see, his editing of the concentration camp poetry in the
Anthology accords with the poets' own complicated sense of their haiku as
simultaneously personal and collective, lyrical and historical.

In contrast, de Cristoforo attempts to preserve each poet's "unique"
experience even as she recovers a record of collective expression (*May Sky*
63).[5] Her editorial commitment to individuality reflects her participation
in the freestyle haiku movement, which, again, had abandoned certain requirements of classical haiku—the syllabic measure, the seasonal reference, the cutting word, and, most of all, the attitude of impersonality—in
favor of an emphasis on a modern self and a modern form. According to
de Cristoforo, the new style enabled them

to express the modern, more descriptive lyrical poetry with passion, rather than the restrictive expression of scenery and objective
subtleness associated with the earlier classical haiku which was considered suitable primarily for the gentle elderly. (*Reflections* E 29)[6]

Clearly, Kaiko's emphasis on subjective expression finds powerful purpose among the poets interned during World War II. "[U]nder those oppressive conditions," de Cristoforo recounts in the earlier volume of her
own poetry, "I became more and more introspective and found solace in
my Haiku as the humble expression of the dejection experienced by a
lonely young mother with small children" (E ix). Her commentaries in
Poetic Reflections ensure that the haiku are understood in the context of
her personal suffering.

Thus the poems consistently represent the external world through
de Cristoforo's emotional states. She glosses "Strong Sunrays Barracks
Are All Low and Dark," for instance, as an image of her discouragement
as well as a representation of "objective" fact: "After the long, gloomy
winter days the intense glare of summer creates a strong contrast and
makes the low, dark, tar-papered barracks seem even more dismal and
disheartening" (E 14). Likewise, many of her poems depart from the traditional concept that haiku must not concern itself with history or personal experience.[7] "Flowers on Tule Reeds and Sandy Flats Brother
Confined over 200 Days" (E 15) or "Harsh Summer Ground Being Ill
Day after Day" (E 16) are poems that register both the terrible historical
circumstances she and others endure and her individual situation within
that history. However, even as her modern Kaiko practice enables individual expression, haiku's classical "expression of scenery and objective
subtleness," that is, haiku's assumed earlier effacement of the self, returns with a new usefulness. Many poems articulate a complex recognition of nature as both a reflection of the self and a consolation to the
suffering individual (that is, as *not* a reflection of the self):

Autumn Grass Not Yet Tall Fall Comes Earlier on the High Plains

AUTUMN GRASS

It is not yet autumn by the calendar yet the fall weather is
here. The stunted Tule reeds already have tassels and we are
heading for another long and gloomy winter of confinement
and uncertainty. Fall comes too soon in captivity. Where do I
turn to lament my fate? (E 25)

The poem and commentary on the following page answer this question. "An Autumn Day Flowers with Thorns a Lump in My Heart" responds to her anguish at the injustice, brutality, and humiliation her brother and mother-in-law endured.[8] The answer to "Where do I turn to lament my fate?" is "How do I express my feeling of repugnance, except to talk to my flowers?" (E 26). Flowers are no longer the archaic possession of the "gentle elderly" but are now vital, external facts that simultaneously represent de Cristoforo's despair and alleviate it. In "Flowers Are Good I Endure a Long Time Raising Flowers," she emphasizes this latter function: "Again, I turn to my flowers for solace so I can endure the indignity, inhumanity, and injustice" (E 27). And in her final poem of the collection, "Death Brings Deep Thoughts No Breeze on the Hilltop Today," contemplation of nature helps de Cristoforo surmount her grief over her friend's suicide and assume a classically objective perspective on the horrors of camp life: "Then I realized we must all die sooner or later, whether today, tomorrow, or later on, and peace came to my tormented soul as I dedicated this Haiku to her memory" (E 28). In *Poetic Reflections* haiku and nature become almost synonymous once again as de Cristoforo orchestrates haiku's ancient detachment with Kaiko's modern "passion."

In the *May Sky* volume, poets likewise respond to their misery and anger with the entire range of haiku's historical possibilities. But in her commentary, de Cristoforo foregrounds only the Kaiko aesthetic of individual expression: "In contrast to the poets' pre-war haiku, what was written in the camps reveals the internees' dejection, the oppressiveness of their lives behind barbed wire, and the sadness caused by this tragedy which daily faced them" (29–30). Yet the poem she offers as evidence of the shift from prewar to wartime haiku, and from which she takes the title of her anthology, suggests something more complicated than a change from "gaiety" to "despair": "From the window of despair / May sky / There is always tomorrow" (30). The poem registers the personal despair of Neiji Ozawa, who was suffering from tuberculosis and living at a sanatorium on the Gila Indian reservation, but juxtaposes it with the spring sky, thus situating his suffering in the natural world and finding hope in that larger context. Again and again the poets collected in the volume leaven their dejection and anger with an assertion of the surpassing beauty, renewal, and continuity of nature, joining Kaiko's attention to the emotions with classical haiku's detachment from those very feelings. Paradoxically, there is always tomorrow because, poetically, there is always yesterday—because the poetic tradition includes a conception of the form that transcends individual hardship in its depiction of natural processes and its attitude of selflessness. The epilogue to the volume affirms the importance of literary tradition: "Through the mist of the surging seas / has emerged a beacon to help us / recall our past and guide us on / our course." Haiku is the beacon that illuminates the past and therefore ensures the future.

The productive tensions inherent in wartime haiku between convention and innovation are felt in the difference between the volume's commentary on the poems and the poems themselves. The numerous prefatory essays all emphasize freestyle haiku's elevation of the subjectivity of the poet. Makoto Ueda's Foreword addresses

> [. . .] those who may wonder how haiku, often considered nature poetry that sings mainly of flowers and birds, could become a vehicle for presenting painful realities of human life, such as those at war-time relocation camps. [But] Haiku poets feel they have vented much emotion and, indeed, they have. (10)

Similarly, in his introduction, Mayumi Nakatsuka refers to the volume as "a diary of the genuine sentiments" of the internees, again stressing the subjective validity of the poems (11). And de Cristoforo's preface echoes the other introductory essays in its focus on individual responses to world history. She conceives of the volume as "the legacy of wartime poets to future generations" and asserts that she wrote her own haiku during the war "to give vent to my feelings while being detained in concentration camps" (17). Her selections, she says, "attempt to portray the individuality of each writer and the atmosphere of the various detention centers, each with its own distinctive features" (18). Photographs of the poets before the war and of the relocation camps during it, like the maps of relocation sites and other documentary illustrations, reinforce the personal and historical specificity of the poems. This is a motive de Cristoforo underscores repeatedly: Kyotaro Komuro's "dedication and initiative" in encouraging internees to write, she says, "inspired the Delta Ginsha poets to express *their* personal perceptions and emotions" (46, emphasis in original), and she remains insistent on each poet's distinct experience even in shared conditions: the internment "gave rise to many unique expressions reflected in the poets' haiku" (63).

Yet as the internment continued, expressing personal emotions and giving vent to unique expressions were not adequate responses to the concentration camp experience, and their haiku once more adapted to new historical circumstances. Komuro's introductions to two volumes of haiku published in the camps reveal the Kaiko aesthetic of individual voice and expression expanding to include the classical aesthetic of detachment and contemplation of nature.[9] Introducing volume 1, which covers the period from their initial incarceration in the Stockton Assembly Center in May 1942 to their relocation to the Rohwer Concentration

Camp in Arkansas through October 1942, Komuro focuses on "those verses which best depict the individuality of each writer, the living conditions in the camp, and the hopes and disappointments of the internees in captivity" (87).[10] A year later, however, his introduction to volume 2 draws attention to nature rather than the camp conditions and to shared rather than individual experience:

> In order for us to transcend our condition we must immerse ourselves in nature, and be grateful to find happiness in the life of haiku poetry. (89)

The poets did not revert from the personal lyric to the impersonal haiku associated with classical times, but they did enlarge the range of their poetry to articulate their individual experiences and perceptions within a vast universe, and their notion of classical haiku aided them in achieving this larger perspective.

Thus the *May Sky* poems record personal events and impressions while simultaneously working to comprehend these events and find consolation despite them: "Friends leave one by one / autumn sun / sets behind forest" or "Someone said / white cabbage miso soup / warms one up—it did" or "Sat alone staring / at dark and dismal wall / spring night" (115, 135, 147). The natural world is the source of both understanding and solace. Nature, therefore, may mirror their circumstances, as when the first chill of winter correlates to a parent's apprehension—"Parents— / whose sons are called to the service / first snow falls"—or may measure their misery by nature's indifference to it—"Autumn foliage / California has now become / a far country," or "Separated a year ago today / Chinese quince / must be blooming in my garden" (113, 139, 145). But nature also reveals the insignificance of human suffering: "Whether one comes or goes / canna flowers / in the planter box"; "For puny individuals / futile to invoke higher powers / winter comes"; "Green forests in time / also bid farewell / to men"; "Cosmos in bloom / as if no war / were taking place"; "Dandelion has bloomed / a moment of bitterness— / of what consequence?" (137, 173, 199, 245, 275).

However, as one particularly provocative poem intimates, nature is not simply landscape and weather; it is a whole order of existence that includes the disorder of war:

> Naturally,
> talk of evacuation
> fall rain continues. (131)

Nature here is freighted with a bitter inevitability, making it as "natural" for people to be gloomy in the camp as it is for the weather to be dreary in the autumn. If nature is the tranquil reference point for traditional haiku, then it receives a painfully ironic treatment in this poem.[11] Ironic in another way, several poets depict nature as warlike rather than as a respite from war: "Summer morning / wind blowing audibly / young leaves warring"; "Black clouds instantly shroud / autumn sky / hail storming against us today also" (183). And nature can also figure forth hopelessness: "At daybreak / stars disappear / where do I discard my dreams?" (221). In this poem, dawn loses its familiar positive connotations and becomes a glare that obliterates the faint stars just as internment has eclipsed the poet's dreams. Even worse, though, dreams do not naturally fade, as stars in daylight, but persist to make disappointment more acute. In such poems as these, attention to nature does not bring transcendence of suffering, since suffering itself is natural.

By the same token, natural occurrences could seem as ominous as historical events, as warring leaves and pelting storms indicate. One of the most unsettling poems in *May Sky* depicts a natural world thoroughly implicated in history:

> Winter night
> pale faced man
> taps my shoulder. (251)

The speaker may merely be describing the snow falling on his shoulder as the white touch of a personified winter, but in this season of decline, he may also mean to represent the night as a "pale" phantom come to take him to his death.[12] Further, the racial connotations of "pale faced man" are unavoidable, and the figure of the white man as a harbinger of death is equally obvious and apt.[13]

As this poem suggests, the internees were forced to feel a heightened sense of racial difference in World War II America, and perhaps this stimulated an increased emphasis on a traditional Japanese poetry. Though we have only a small sample of both prewar and internment haiku by these poets, the poems from the camps give evidence of a concerted assertion of Japanese identity during the incarceration—an identity that is simultaneously individual and collective, personal and impersonal. The prewar haiku included in *May Sky* treat the West Coast seasons, local natural phenomena, and the bustle of daily life (gardening, chatting with neighbors, children playing, working about the house [33–37]) with no explicit mention of Japan, while the haiku written in the camps consistently make reference to being Japanese (103, 121, 149, 195, 219, 235, 241, 273), Japanese cultural occasions (107, 109, 111, 161, 171) and practices (127, 135, 177, 181, 237, 243, 247, 257, 269), nostalgia for the Japanese homeland (139, 215, 231), the contradictions of being

Japanese American (175), and to being alien in the United States (221, 239). This turn toward Japanese cultural references provided a thematic counterpart to the renewal of formal interest in haiku's classical conventions. In one sense, haiku became more self-consciously Japanese in the concentration camps during World War II as poets drew on its traditional powers for consolation and resistance.

At the same time, however, the internment experience exposed the complexities of racial and national identity. In addition to the sense of danger and estrangement from their white captors, poets contemplated their relationship to Italians incarcerated with them (119) and to other people of color brought into their proximity by the relocation. Internees at Rohwer Concentration Camp in Arkansas wrote about African American laborers (127, 153, 154); at Gila Concentration Camp in Arizona and Crystal City Detention Camp in Texas about Native Americans and Mexican Americans (171); and at Tule Lake Segregation Center in Northern California about being situated near the site of "the last battle ground of the Modoc Indians," Castle Rock Mountain (*Poetic Reflections* E 23). These encounters with other dispossessed Americans and their histories were pointed for the Japanese Americans, giving them a sense of solidarity, if not hope. De Cristoforo describes the mountain as her constant "inspiration" during her captivity: "And always my vision and my thoughts were drawn to Castle Rock, comparing our fate to the Modoc Indians' last stand in their Lava Bed Campaign of 1872–73."[14] And others also remark on the painful similarity between the internees' situation and that of the Modocs: "Summer mountain / cross on Castle Rock / pitiful last days of Indians" (249).[15] Relocation prompted a consideration of racial politics and national identity by denying Japanese Americans their rights as citizens on racist grounds and by bringing the struggles of other people of color into close view.

In fact, Castle Rock becomes an emblem of resistance to America's reprehensible policies toward all oppressed peoples and simultaneously a sign of the internees' specific situation: "Looking at summer moon / on Castle Rock / we are living in alien (enemy) land" (239). And again, "Enduring two year submission / in enemy (alien) nation / wife is drying *daikon*" (221).[16] The official wartime view of people of Japanese descent as "resident aliens" and the reclassification of Japanese American servicemen as "enemy aliens" are racist locutions turned back on the government in these poems where the country itself is the enemy land, the source of betrayal and alienation. The Kaiko poets in the internment camps explored America's racial dynamics in poetry even as they simultaneously pressed their haiku to rise above the terrible circumstances racism produced.

The significance of the *May Sky* recovery project extends well beyond de Cristoforo's goal of restoring these Japanese American voices to the literary record and even beyond the broader goal of acknowledging the internment experience in the historical record. The haiku produced by Japanese Americans in concentration camps does not merely fill a void in our account of American literary history but also establishes crucial connections between the formal politics of World War II America and those of the postwar period. Though the *May Sky* poets may not have felt implicated in America's history of colonialism and conquest—as many other US haiku writers do—their significant interest in the "pitiful last days of Indians" strangely presages this curious fact of post-World War II haiku: that it is a form American poets have continued to employ for addressing racialized experience in the United States. Contemporary poets have asserted a persistent association between haiku and Native peoples in particular. Among others, Gary Snyder draws haiku and Native America together in his vision of a Pacific Rim community united by geography, ecosystems, and prehistoric cultural roots; Anishinaabe writer Gerald Vizenor has spent his career resisting the notion that sites of conquest like Castle Rock represent the last days of Indians, and he credits haiku with broadening his perspective beyond US myths about Native America; William Oandasan, whose father was Filipino and mother Yuki Indian, employs haiku to articulate a cross-cultural identity he himself embodies; and Rhoda and Foster Jewell, Anglo authors of the haiku "epic" *Hiawatha's Country*, move almost inevitably from haiku's philosophy of impermanence, to haiku as elegy, to elegizing the "Vanishing Americans." Each marshals haiku's supposed impersonality to the project of representing Native America. The sometimes paradoxical identities evident in the concentration camp haiku—encompassing individual subjectivity, impersonality, a collective Japanese identity, and solidarity with other people of color—help us understand the complexities of American national identity that later poets also struggle to represent.

Poetic Reflections and *May Sky* are already out of print; however, Nelson's inclusion of Japanese American concentration camp haiku in the *Anthology* preserves this poetry and places it where we can continue to confront its meanings for both World War II America and our own time. In that volume, moreover, the haiku come to belong to a continuing tradition of exceptionally concise poems taking up historical and political topics, often with a personal inflection. There they join Sandburg's "Chicago," Grimké's "The Black Finger," Spencer's "White Things," Toomer's "Portrait in Georgia," and Hughes's "Christ in Alabama" and anticipate Knight's prison haiku and Momaday's haiku-like poems about Native America, such as "Plainview," whose very title evokes the haiku aesthetic of directness and clarity. Nelson's anthology also allows comparison between the Angel Island poems by Chinese immigrants and the Japanese American concentration camp haiku, two groups of poets writing concise testimony poems in internment. In the *Anthology*, the Kaiko poets join a number of informing poetry choruses.

As the editors of the legendary *Heath Anthology of American Literature* observe in their fourth edition (2002), "Most anthologies of American literature followed our lead in diversifying the scope of what constituted 'American literature'" (xxxv). And it is true that anthology prefaces and introductions today typically rehearse the truism that American literature is diverse, and that an anthology of American literature must be inclusive of this diversity.[17] Yet it is equally true that most of the major anthologies of American literature, and of American poetry in particular, remain committed to publishing the "best work," works of decided "literary significance," poems that inspire a "genuine response"—that is, to preserving (and therefore prescribing) those elusive qualities of poetic greatness that "diversity" has so thoroughly called into question.[18] Nelson, too, admits his own impulse to judge the value of a work of art, but he characteristically acknowledges this as a matter of individual "taste" and describes his editorial purpose in exuberantly open terms: "I have tried to present twentieth-century American poetry in its astonishing and endlessly energetic variety" (xxix). Significantly, Nelson's anthology alone keeps the internment haiku in print and thus makes it possible to track an extremely popular and surprisingly political development in twentieth-century poetry in the United States, the haiku phenomenon.

His telling interest in creating a *story* of American poetry ("Here and there I invent chronologies" [xxx]), rather than a tradition of individual talents, informs his very apprehension of these poems. "For the Japanese American concentration camp poems, I create a miniature narrative by selecting and arranging these wartime Haikus in a particular order," he explains. A crucial aspect of that "particular order" is its seasonal structure: "This sequence begins with arrest in summer and moves through the experience of internment" (718). In fact, the mininarrative does not just begin in summer but moves systematically, naturally, through the year, from "summer heat" (718) to "Frosty morning" (719) to "hail storming" (719) to "Winter wind" (720), accruing symbolic significance as nature figures forth the loss of hope, the descent into despair, and the literal fact of death. In this seasonal context, the closing poems of Nelson's sequence render concentration camp experience with immense symbolic force: "Doll without a head / lying on desk top / one evening" (720). If Nelson's "choral" editing foregrounds a sense of solidarity and communal identity that the camp poets themselves elaborated, then his seasonal narrative similarly summons classical haiku's reference point for human endeavor and struggle: the natural world. Simultaneously, this is a natural world mediated by the harsh facts of confinement, where camp images frame nature: "barbed wire fence," for instance, literally and figuratively frames "the croaking of frogs" and the "Thin shadow of tule reed" (719). It is precisely such complexities and contradictions that Nelson's editorial license, however unorthodox, preserves. Finally, Nelson's inclusion of the concentration camp poetry in the *Anthology of Modern Poetry* enables us to trace the haiku movement in the United States to its Japanese American beginnings, sounding both its "literary significance" and also its ongoing historical value.

Notes

I am grateful to the American Council of Learned Societies for a yearlong fellowship during 2006 that enabled me to work full time on a project about race and form in American poetry from which this essay derives; to Shari Huhndorf for her comments on an early draft; to Ce Rosenow for sharing her vast knowledge of American haiku and offering valuable suggestions; and to Donald Laird for research help.

1. "*Hokku*" is a term formerly synonymous with "haiku." It refers to the initial 5-7-5 verse in a linked *haikai-renga* sequence, which alternated 5-7-5 and 7-7 verses. Since the *hokku* had to meet several requirements of an introductory verse, it drew notice and became valued in its own right. Early commentators like Pound referred to what we now know as haiku variously as "*hokku*," "*haikai*," or "*haiku*," but "haiku" has long been the preferred term, in Japan and in the West, for separate 5-7-5 poems. For a thorough history of the evolution of haiku, see Kawamoto.

2. Praise for the assumed impersonality of the Japanese character as a quality needed in the West does not preclude racist denigration of the Japanese themselves. Commenting on the infrequency of grammatical subjects in Japanese, Percival Lowell is quick to assure readers that this is not the result of "philosophic profundity. It springs from the most superficial of childish conceptions. For the Japanese mind is quite the reverse of abstract. Its consideration of things is concrete to a primitive degree" (106).

3. The notion that "classical haiku" avoids history and suppresses the self reflects a particular understanding of the Japanese poetic tradition articulated by writers in the United States. These US poets' understanding of their literary past and their shifting responses to it are the subjects of my analysis—rather than a disinterested history of Japanese haiku. Haiku expert Ce Rosenow rightly points out that both Japanese American Kaiko poets and Anglo-American cultural critics and poets respond to a "Buddhist-inflected" haiku trend and do not address the myriad ways haiku poets have traditionally engaged with history, expressed subjective experience, and constructed their poetic personae through haiku. I am grateful for Rosenow's insistence on the significant discrepancies between the "haiku tradition" and the development of haiku in the United States and also for her reminder that Percival Lowell, however much he promoted an Asian stereotype,

should be credited with writing about the East "before many Westerners thought Japanese literature worthy of discussion" (Rosenow).

4. For Nelson, biography *is* history for socialist poets: biography "is almost never primarily a personal story. Writers on the Left live their lives in a conscious struggle with historical conditions and historical ambitions. [. . .] It is the explicit fusion of biography and history in Left poetry that makes the personal lives of these poets relevant" (4–5).

5. There are numerous other instances of de Cristoforo's emphasis on the poets' individuality; see *May Sky* 68, 74, 95, 205, 283–86.

6. The bilingual volume prints the English text from front cover to center and the Japanese text from back cover to center, as is conventional for each language. The page numbers in each section are preceded by an "E" for English and a "J" for Japanese. Not only does this formatting produce a visual English-Japanese "reflection," extending the connotations of "poetic reflections," it also gives a visceral sense of the English and Japanese versions meeting at the center of the book. The poems and commentaries suggest that this is a collision of cultures rather than a cross-cultural truce, and segregating the languages has a powerful estranging effect. In contrast, the *May Sky* anthology combines Japanese and English translations of each poem on the same page, which may signal the later volume's greater spirit of conciliation and optimism as awareness of the wartime crimes against Japanese Americans increased.

7. "The past, in haiku, is nearly always the individual, not the historical past" (Blyth 60). Explaining how haiku emerged from the courtly *waka* tradition, Kawamoto observes that both forms excluded "all 'vulgar' matters such as political and economic, social and historical issues—to say nothing of ordinary things like eating and drinking, personal arguments, or even laughter" (59).

8. De Cristoforo's brother was falsely accused of inciting a riot, incarcerated (and repeatedly beaten) in the isolation pen, and eventually moved to a camp for enemy aliens in New Mexico; her mother-in-law, suffering from cancer, was first denied medical treatment and then sent to Oregon for radiation therapy, accompanied by an armed escort and subjected to repeated humiliations. She died in the camp shortly after her return.

9. De Cristoforo describes the texts of Komuro's two introductions as "summaries" of his original introductions.

10. Internees were first rounded up in local assembly centers, often fairgrounds or racetracks, and then eventually transported to more permanent inland relocation centers, though were they often moved from one relocation center to another.

11. As some readers are aware, Japanese can be written using the Chinese *kanji*, Japanese *hiragana*, and/or the Roman alphabet, *romaji*. The pun on "naturally" occurs in all versions of the poem.

12. Rosenow would avoid the Western word "personification" in reference to "pale faced man," preferring to read "Winter night" and "pale faced man" as an instance of haiku's distinct practice of "internal comparison."

13. "Paleface" and "pale-face" were in usage in the United States from at least 1823, according to the *Oxford English Dictionary*. The term was "chiefly

derogatory" and used "Chiefly in representations of Native American Indian speech and in African-American usage."

14. The haiku paired with these reflections reads, "*Memorized Shape of the Mountain Walk in the Same Direction on Winter Days,*" and like the commentaries it suggests de Cristoforo's paradoxical sense of doom and solidarity with the Modocs.

15. Another de Cristoforo poem about the mountain that does not appear in *Poetic Reflections* or *May Sky* reads, "Foolishly—simply existing / summer days / Caste Rock is there" ("There Is Always Tomorrow" 103).

16. A single photograph appears among the haiku in both the English and Japanese sections of the book, a picture of Castle Rock Mountain. The caption reads starkly, "This is Castle Rock."

17. For instance, editors Gioia, Mason, and Schoerke note "a genuine need for a book inclusive enough to represent the many different, even irreconcilable impulses that enliven modern American poetry" (xli); one of Ramazani's editorial priorities is "to present various modern and contemporary poets who have only recently emerged into prominence" (xxix); McMichael and Leonard gesture to inclusiveness as a fact rather than a principle—"we have added the following authors new to the concise edition"—but their list of mostly women and ethnic writers nevertheless conforms to the general trend toward diversity and inclusiveness (xxx).

18. *Norton* xxvii, *Concise* xxix, *Twentieth-Century* xliv.

Works Cited

Blyth, R. H. *Haiku.* Vol. 1 *Eastern Culture.* 1949. Tokyo: Hokuseido, 1981.

de Cristoforo, Violet Kazue, ed and trans. *May Sky: There Is Always Tomorrow: Concentration Camp Kaiko Haiku.* Los Angeles: Sun, 1997.

de Cristoforo, Violet Kazue Matsuda. "There Is Always Tomorrow: An Anthology of Wartime *Haiku.*" *Amerasia Journal* 19.1 (1993): 93–115.

de Cristoforo, Violet Matsuda. *Poetic Reflections of the Tule Lake Internment Camp 1944.* Santa Clara: Communicart, 1987.

Fletcher, John Gould. *Japanese Prints.* Boston: Four Seas, 1918.

Gioia, Dana, David Mason, and Meg Schoerke, eds. *Twentieth-Century American Poetry.* Boston: McGraw, 2004.

Kawamoto, Kōji. *The Poetics of Japanese Verse: Imagery, Structure, Meter.* 1991. Trans. Stephen Collington, Kevin Collins, and Gustav Heldt. Tokyo: U of Tokyo P, 2000.

Lauter, Paul, et al., eds. *The Heath Anthology of American Literature.* 4th ed. 2 vols. Boston: Houghton, 2002.

Lowell, Percival. *The Soul of the Far East.* 1888. New York: Macmillan, 1911.

McMichael, George, and James S. Leonard, eds. *Concise Anthology of American Literature.* 6th ed. Upper Saddle River: Pearson/Prentice, 2006.

Nelson, Cary, ed. *Anthology of Modern American Poetry.* Oxford: Oxford UP, 2000.

———. *Revolutionary Memory: Recovering the Poetry of the American Left.* New York: Routledge, 2001.

Oxford English Dictionary Online. Nov. 2007. Oxford English Dictionary. 14 Nov. 2007 <http://www.oed.com.>.

Pound, Ezra. "Vorticism." *Ezra Pound: Early Writings, Poems and Prose.* New York: Penguin, 2005. 278–91.

Ramazani, Jahan, Richard Ellmann, and Robert O'Clair, eds. *The Norton Anthology of Modern and Contemporary Poetry.* 3rd ed. 2 vols. New York: Norton, 2003.

Rosenow, Ce. Note to the author. 9 Feb. 2007.

Wilde, Oscar. "The English Renaissance of Art." *The Works of Oscar Wilde: Essays and Lectures.* New York: Putnam's, 1894. 109–55.

◡ 6 ◡

Contexts, Choruses, and Katabases (Canonical and Non-)

Some Methodological Implications of Cary Nelson's Recovery Work

Michael Thurston

A great deal of attention has been paid, justifiably, to Cary Nelson's recovery of numerous poems, poets, and poetic communities repressed by what he has called "the interlocking structures of canon formation and literary historiography" (*Repression* 53). Some of this attention has been negative; early reviews of Nelson's landmark *Repression and Recovery* (1989) often focused on the "bad" poetry quoted, examined, and advocated in the volume. Much more attention, though, has been not only positive but also enacted, as critics influenced by Nelson have taken him up on his invitation to contribute to a wide range of recovery projects. Moreover, some of this recovery work has been institutionalized in such forms as the Oxford *Anthology of Modern American Poetry* that Nelson edited and the University of Illinois Press's American Poetry Recovery series (which Nelson oversaw and some volumes of which he also edited). Thanks to these projects, the work of poets like Edwin Rolfe, Don Gordon, Aaron Kramer, Joseph Kalar, and many others is available both to provide new generations of students with a more complex and capacious sense of what "modern American poetry" might signify and to contribute to our political and poetic imaginaries.

Over the last twenty years, then, Nelson has done an enormous amount to change *what* we read when we read modern American poetry. In this essay, I focus on how Nelson's work also advocates and models changes in *how* we read modern American poetry, for the scholarship that we might see as the "recovery" phase of Nelson's career—including not only *Repression and Recovery* and *Revolutionary Memory* but also Nelson's editions of

poem collections by Rolfe, Kalar, Kramer, and others, and his editorial
work on the Oxford *Anthology* and its accompanying Web site—establishes
a clear set of methodological challenges as well as that very large array of
texts we did not know we had forgotten. In what follows, I describe what
I see as a couple of crucial methodological imperatives arising from Nelson's work, and I illustrate their usefulness both in recovery projects and in
projects not explicitly aimed at recovering the work of neglected poets and
poetic communities.

Reading Contexts and Paratexts

While it might be true that we cannot read books by their covers, it is at
least as true that we *must* read their covers, and not only their covers but
also their endpapers and printers' colophons and paper quality and illustrations (or, perhaps just as significant, their lack of any of these). Appropriately, this message is right on the cover of *Repression and Recovery*, with
its four illustrations between title and subtitle at once representing four
types of literary culture recovered in the book's pages and suggesting that
part of the repressed to be recovered is the visual culture that accompanied modern American poetry. What is advertised on the cover is indeed
enacted in the book's pages, which include eight color plates and more
than fifty halftone illustrations of book and magazine covers and pages.
These illustrations are not only included, of course; they are also read,
and by reading them the way he does, Nelson makes clear that if one is to
recover poems as specific textual acts, however partially (in both senses),
then one must recover them as acts occurring in specific textual sites and
amidst specific sets of other signifying practices. His reading of Langston
Hughes's 1931 poem "Christ in Alabama" is exemplary. Nelson describes
the other texts and the illustration that accompanied the poem when it
appeared on the front page of *Contempo* on December 1, 1931, and concludes, "The poem can aim for a condensed but multiple indictment
[. . .] that the essays cannot achieve," and "The essays in turn root the
poem in an unyielding, pressing set of historical facts that cannot be tran-
scended" (200; the magazine's front page is reproduced on 202–203).
More than this, though, Nelson goes on to argue that "to read the new
black poetry [of the 1920s and 1930s] in journals [. . .] is to see the poetry
as part of a whole critical and transformative social project" (200).

Nelson's tour-de-force reading of Edwin Markham's "The Man with
the Hoe" in the "richly contradictory fin-de-siècle presentation" granted
the poem by the San Francisco *Examiner*'s illustrated Sunday supplement
reprint shows the importance of taking into analytical account not
only such contemporary paratexts as illustrations and surrounding copy
but also the broader institutional matrices (the range of political commitments entangling a newspaper and its parent corporation, for exam-

ple) in and through which the poem performs its cultural work (Nelson, *Revolutionary Memory* 17). Nelson reads Markham's poem in a diachronic context as well, setting it against the horizons of "the great American labor struggles of the preceding decades" and the "hundred years of American labor protest poetry and song" with which Markham would have been familiar from such sources as John Greenleaf Whittier's *Songs of Labor and Other Poems* (1850) (16). This rich contextualization of the poem at once reactivates political energies latent in the poem as it has typically been taught and remembered and foregrounds the disciplinary investments in "literariness" that have rendered those energies dormant. Nelson recovers not only the poem, then, but also the contested strands of political poetics in which it is inevitably enmeshed.

I have not chosen these two examples accidentally, of course; they are influential moments in Nelson's work (the former certainly inspired and influenced my own contextual reading of "Christ in Alabama" [Thurston 98–101]), and each also has affected the Oxford *Anthology*, which includes the illustrated "Christ in Alabama" and the illustrated "Man with a Hoe" in a special section at the back of the book. But Nelson also has carefully attended to (and advocated careful attention to) what he calls "illustrations and design elements that helped shape the cultural work" performed by canonical poets' poems, elements "almost always eliminated from collected volumes" of even the best-known poets' work (*Repression* 193). He analyzes, for example, Gladys Hynes's illustrated capitals for Cantos XVIII and XXII in Ezra Pound's 1928 *A Draft of the Cantos XVII–XXVII*, arguing that Hynes's illustrations "focus the reading the *Cantos* offer of their own historical moment and make that reading accessible to Pound's audience" (194). Of course, Nelson is not the only critic to argue for the importance of illustrations and other bibliographic elements in the small-press editions in which Pound published the first two installments of *The Cantos*; indeed, Jerome McGann's discussions of Pound's "bibliographic text" in *Towards a Literature of Knowledge* and *The Textual Condition* appeared around the same time as *Repression and Recovery*, 1989 and 1991, respectively. I would argue, though, that the model of contextual reading that arises from *Repression and Recovery* and *Revolutionary Memory* together—the practice of reading that combines synchronic analysis of a poem in its publication context (and amidst those surrounding elements Gérard Genette calls paratexts [Genette]) with analysis of the poem's participation in diachronic contexts—enables a richer understanding of the cultural work of both unknown and well-known poems.

An example will make this point more clearly than summary can. Three years before he published *A Draft of the Cantos XVII–XXVII* with Nancy Cunard's Paris-based Hours Press, Pound published *A Draft of XVI Cantos* with William Bird's Three Mountains Press (also in Paris). This volume was a deluxe affair, an oversize book with woven boards, a limited edition with each canto's initial capital printed in red and illuminated by

artist Henry Strater. The book concludes with two cantos set in Hell (XIV
and XV) and a final one in which the poet emerges onto the plains of Pur-
gatory. These "Hell Cantos" have not received much attention from
Pound specialists; they interest me, though, as moments of explicit cultural critique in the poem. Pound performs that critique by mobilizing
the familiar cultural machinery of Dante's system of sins and punishments. The punishments Pound describes here are, as Ronald Bush has
written, satirically scatological and downright "disgusting" (251). Politicians are posed with their wrists bound to their ankles, "Faces" (and, by
implication, feces) "smeared on their rumps," and forced to address the
multitudes assembled in the "ooze" "through their arse-holes." Profiteers
are set to drink "blood sweetened with shit." It is, though, the "betrayers"
and "perverters of language" whose torments are described at greatest
length. As Wendy Stallard Flory has pointed out, while mothers selling
their daughters off to old men are simply equated to "sows eating their
litters," Pound spends nine lines detailing the filth ("foetor," "dung,"
"last cesspool of the universe") the falsifiers are forced to publish on their
bestially "clattering" presses (34). In letters from the early and mid-1920s,
he writes again and again that Cantos XIV and XV were intended as cultural critique. To Wyndham Lewis, for example, he wrote that his "'hell'
is a portrait of contemporary England," and to John Drummond that "the
hell cantos are specifically LONDON, the state of English mind in 1919
and 1920" (Pound, *The Selected Letters* 191, 239). In 1925, Pound wrote to
his father that he "intended to give an accurate picture of the spiritual
state of England in the years 1919 and following" (Terrell 65). That London is the target of Pound's critique is clear within the poem as well;
describing the "utter decrepitude" above the "hell-rot" so evocatively
sketched, Pound compares "the great arse-hole, / broken with piles" to
the "sky over Westminster," and he emphasizes that this hell is populated
by "many English." His critique, indicated by the crimes and punishments
Pound names, is specifically focused on, first, the elements of English and
European society of the 1910s that he blames for the Great War (profi-
teering, monopolistic hoarding) and, even more vehemently, the forces
that produced cultural stultification after the war: censorship (especially
of artistically adventurous discourse), literary envy, Christian conformity,
conservative scholarship, debased politics, the whole "bog of stupidities, /
malevolent stupidities, and stupidities" (Pound, *Cantos* 63). These, Pound
shows, render the potentially productive soil of culture corrupt. His
strong implication is that corrupt culture will yield a disastrous historical
crop. (He makes this more explicit in Canto XVI's purgatorial rehearsal
of the run-up to the First World War.)

Like the illustrations that accompany Markham's poem in its special
supplement publication, Strater's illuminated capital for Canto XIV "un-
derlines the poem's high cultural ambitions" and "underwrites its commit-

ment to eternal values rather than immediate [. . .] historical contexts" (Nelson, *Revolutionary Memory* 21). Centered over the text and surmounted by the red Roman numeral XIV, a monstrous maw gapes to reveal sharp teeth and a number of finned and winged creatures afloat on a suggested fluid current. These creatures might be the tormented shades of the Underworld. Among the humanoid shapes, one's head is shaped so as to suggest a bishop's miter, its face bears a startled or an anguished expression, and it carries a book under one bony arm. The figures are just as easily read, though, as tormenting demons; few are humanoid, and the reptilian and insect-like ones are characterized by sharp fins, fangs, and claws. Taken together, the swimming or swarming creatures and the mouth in which they appear suggest a general sort of mythic Hell. The "I" of the canto's first word (Dante's "Io") lolls like a tongue from the left-hand corner of the demonic mouth and extends alongside the edge of the text's first dozen lines. Where those lines focus not only on specific types of sinners—politicians, prudes, and profiteers—but also on specific individuals, their names rendered as ellipses and last letters but still in many cases identifiable (David Lloyd George and Woodrow Wilson in line three, for example), the illustration and the capital gesture not at the specific historical moment held up for critique in Pound's poem but at the broadly medieval culture of Dante and illuminated manuscripts. McGann writes that *A Draft of XVI Cantos*, along with the 1928 *Draft of the Cantos XVII–XXVII*, marks the culmination of Pound's "appropriation of his Pre-Raphaelite inheritance" (*Textual Condition* 131). But we also might read the illustration as blunting the Hell Cantos' cultural critique. Like other elements of the bibliographic text of *A Draft of XVI Cantos*, Strater's illumination marks the book as a monument aiming for timeless significance; it renders the poem's quite specific sense of social evils both general and cartoonish.

We can further enrich our sense of the poem's cultural work if we add to this paratextual reading the sort of diachronic contextual reading Nelson performs on Markham's poem. Pound's Hell cantos are clearly in the tradition of the *katabasis*, an episode in which a protagonist descends into the Underworld, driven by the need to find or reclaim something (his purpose, his way) or, often, someone (his friend or beloved, a prophetic figure who will reveal some needed knowledge). The canonical origin of the katabasis in European literature is Aeneas's descent to the Underworld in Book VI of the *Aeneid*; Aeneas needs to consult his father, Anchises, in order to determine his mission and fate. Katabasis, then, is there at the roots of the Western literary tradition, and of course it has been commonly deployed and replayed by poets of all kinds since Virgil put down his pen and died and went to Limbo, from which he was called by Beatrice to lead Dante on his katabatic descent into the Inferno. Moreover, as David Pike and others have pointed out, right there at the beginning of what we might call the katabatic canon is the use of the topos for cultural critique (14).

Ronald Macdonald provides an example from *Aeneid* 6: Charon, the boatman who ferries the shades across the River Styx, sees Aeneas coming, armor flashing and sword drawn, and starts ranting about heroes marching down to disturb the natural order. The heroes he means, of course, are those Greeks—Herakles, Theseus, Orpheus—who violate the boundary between the living and the dead. Charon's complaint is Virgil's means of criticizing Greek culture's hubris and sense of privilege; against that horizon, he sets Aeneas, who sheathes his sword and just wants a word with his father, as a paragon of Roman *pietas* (44–48).

One horizon against which we must read Pound's Hell Cantos, then, is the katabatic tradition from Virgil through Dante (and after; it is a key influence, for example, on Blake's *Marriage of Heaven and Hell*), and many critics have undertaken such readings. Indeed, Pound all but demands such a reading in the opening line of Canto XIV—"Io venni in luogo d'ogni luce muto"—a quotation of the fifth canto of Dante's *Inferno* ("I came to a place mute of all light"). To read Pound in this way, though, with an eye on the classical or medieval katabatic horizon, is more closely akin to what Jerome McGann calls "radial reading" than to what Nelson does with Markham's "The Man with a Hoe." Radial reading, for McGann, "involves decoding one or more of the contexts that interpenetrate the scripted and physical text" (*The Textual Condition* 119). The emblem of this kind of reading is "the person who temporarily stops 'reading' to look up the meaning of a word" (119). Confronted with Dante's medieval Tuscan dialect in the first line of Canto XIV, I leave the page to look up the reference and translation, perhaps to note Dante's own acknowledged debt to Virgil, and I bring that information back to the page with me. Nelson's attention to the specific interpretive horizon of labor-related protest poetry in his reading of Markham's poem suggests an additional operation necessary for capturing more of what Pound is up to in Canto XIV. We need to read the poem against the backdrop not only of classical but also of more recent and explicitly political deployments of the katabatic topos. There are, sure enough, just such subterranean streams of the katabatic tradition, including one poem that Pound might well have come across during his long sojourns in the reading room of the British Museum and that would have offered an immediately imitable model for katabatic cultural critique.

James Bronterre O'Brien's "A Vision of Hell, or, Peep into the Realms Below, Alias Lord Overgrown's Dream" is not a poem of which most contemporary readers will have heard. Published in London in the early 1850s, O'Brien's sixteen-page satirical pamphlet circulated narrowly and then disappeared from view. The British Library's copy is bound with a number of other poetic pamphlets from the 1840s and 1850s, all of which sank promptly after making their small splash with even smaller audiences. O'Brien's mission, though, is quite similar to Pound's. "The object of this light Poem," he writes in a note to the reader, "is to turn the tables on those preachers" who use "hell as a sort of artillery on the side of established power." O'Brien turns the tables by endeavoring "to show from what sources Hell must be presumed to recruit its population," arguing that "if God have ordained eternal punishment for any, it can only be for those enormous sinners" who have committed such crimes as "robbing a people of their land—of their free will—of their self-government—of all means of mental and moral culture [. . .] so as to perpetuate their degradation, corruption, and enslavement [. . .]" (2). Chief among such sinners, from the perspective of O'Brien's Irish Catholicism and nationalism, is the recently deceased Sir Robert Peel, who died in 1850 after serving as prime minister of England from 1841 to 1846. Peel is named in O'Brien's long subtitle, which begins "DESCRIBING HIS LORDSHIP's FANCIED REUNION WITH THE LATE SIR ROBERT PEEL IN THE REGIONS BELOW," and his readers' note, which offers Peel as the best representative of the class of "land-usurpers and money-changers" who plunge nations into "poverty, slavery, vice, corruption, sin, and crime."

In this poem, Pound would have found not only a fellow adapter of Dante (O'Brien writes "Oh! for a Dante's muse to sketch / What Peel and Lloyd [Lord Overgrown] that moment felt" [14]) but also a kindred spirit in the condemnation of specific elements of English culture. On first glance, the poems seem dissimilar in this regard. Not only is O'Brien's poem in rhyming doggerel stanzas, it also is clearly provoked largely by the colonial subjugation of Ireland. Pound's unrhymed and unmetered Modernist lines touch only very briefly on this topic, locating "in the ooze" the "murderers of Pearse and Macdonagh," two leaders of the Easter Rising of 1916, and British Captain J. Bowen-Colthurst, notorious for killing Irish political prisoners in his custody (Terrell 66). A crucial set of resemblances, though, is to be found in the poems' castigation of the economic forces seen as dominating English society. O'Brien mentions the British Bank-Charter Acts of 1819 and 1844 in his readers' note and, in the body of the poem, provides a catalogue of those who suffer eternal torment that is worth quoting at length for its similarity with Pound's villains:

> Loan-mongers, landlords, millionaires,
> Contractors, usurers, speculators,
> Stock-jobbers, brokers, bulls, and bears,
> Blacklegs, monopolists, regraters,
> Dealers in spiritual wares. (9)

"Usurers" stands out to the modern reader, of course, since usury and its personification as Usura are central to Pound's project, not only in these cantos ("usurers" are among those condemned in Canto XIV, and Usura appears in Canto XV) but also throughout *The Cantos*, the demonic figure of Usura dominates the famous Canto XLV, for example, and the concept motivates many of Pound's angriest lines. O'Brien's "licensed spoliators," who appear a few lines after those just quoted, prefigure Pound's "profiteers," and his "hired reviewers, / And fabricators of false news" resemble Pound's perverters of language. Especially striking, though, is the "monopolists," another crucial word for Pound that appears in O'Brien's catalogue. Canto XIV concludes with those sinners who most raise Pound's ire:

> monopolists, obstructors of knowledge
> obstructors of distribution. (*Cantos* 63)

Central to Pound's social credit economics and to the politics that follow from it is the notion that the world naturally provides sufficient abundance to prevent the scarcity that leads to war. Scarcity results, then, only when abundance is hoarded (when the naturally equitable distribution of goods is obstructed). Since monopoly, the exclusive control of a commodity, enables the manipulation of a commodity's price through artificial controls on its availability, it is by definition the sort of hoarding Pound condemns. The last lines of Canto XIV set "obstructors of knowledge" between the apposite "monopolists" and "obstructors of distribution," because those who artificially control the circulation of information (as language) enable the malign control of the circulation of goods. O'Brien's poem links these as well; the stanza that condemns merchants and bankers moves to "fabricators," just a few lines later.

What the diachronic context exemplified by O'Brien's "Vision of Hell" helps us see more clearly is Pound's resistance to politics as a means of effecting social change. Where O'Brien frames his poetic pamphlet as part of an effort to bring about social change through the infernal depiction of specific political opponents, Pound vilifies all politicians equally and locates the solution to social ills not in political thought or action (which is just part of the infernal landscape) but in a specific model of philosophical and poetic synthesis for which he, himself, is the exemplar. In Canto XV, Pound names contemporary political parties and movements and consigns to his Hell those who work within the political system to effect change:

> and the fabians crying for the petrification of putrefaction,
> for a new dung-flow cut in lozenges,
> the conservatives chatting,
> distinguished by gaiters of slum-flesh. (64)

Pound includes both ends of the mainstream political spectrum by naming bourgeois socialists and their Tory counterparts. The only difference between the two is that while the Fabians want a nicely decorated, newly designed conduit to move the excrement in which they stand (their specification of the decorative shape of lozenges attests to their misplaced priorities), the Conservatives seem content to stand in the "sh-t" as long as they wear the hides of the poor their policies have skinned. Canto XV suggests, then, the intractable character of the Hell London has become. The various agents of obstruction—profiteers, the press, censors, and clergymen—might be defeated, but the embodied abstraction Usura, the monstrous principle behind their actions, seems immortal, and political action is not only shown to be inefficacious but is itself a sin meriting punishment.

The second half of Canto XV shows the way out of this Underworld. Pound begins by introducing a first-person narrator accompanied by a tutelary figure from the philosophical past. The guide turns out to be Plotinus, and he is armed not only with such wisdom as "Close the pores of your feet!" but also with the shield of Perseus, whose continual reflection of the slain Medusa's head solidifies the muck so that the two can walk on it and make their way toward the light. Pound's Dantean narrator is accompanied by a Neoplatonic philosopher dedicated to the proposition that embodied being is an inferior reflection of a universal and ideal Mind. Plotinus's philosophical wisdom alone, though, does not suffice to rescue the narrator. Instead, it is when the "mirror," a metonym for Plotinus's thought, takes the form of Perseus's mythological shield that it is able to harden "the track" and hammer "the souse into hardness." The shield is a doubly significant metonym. On one level, it figures the legacy of story that Pound inherits from classical culture (via Ovid); on another, it figures the ideal of the artwork as a transformative reflection of the world. Its strong suggestion is that the hell of "LONDON in 1919 and 1920" is to be escaped only by the poet (Pound) who can reflect on that place, that state, through the literary and philosophical traditions as synthesized by his own heroic intelligence and creative will.

Conducting the Poetry Chorus

By now, eighteen years after the publication of *Repression and Recovery*, we might with some confidence say that the recovery and reading of poems' contexts have seeped into the groundwater; while this necessity is not always assumed and cannot yet be taken for granted, it has taken hold as a key methodological means for assessing a poem's cultural work. Another imperative arising out of Nelson's work remains more controversial even among critics and teachers working to recover poems, poetic careers, and poetic communities. In *Revolutionary Memory*, Nelson devotes two chapters to reconstructing what he calls "Revolution's collective voice," the choral character of political poetry in 1930s' America. In each of these chapters,

Nelson presents a "poetry chorus" comprising lines drawn from a number of poets and poems (166–73; 229–31). These choruses serve several purposes. They illustrate and enact the communal and collective understanding of poetry writing (and poetry reading) as modes of political participation in the 1930s, the way in which poems on key political events "offered readers politically committed speaking voices with which they could identify" and so were "in a sense a gift to prospective readers, a text whose authorship was inherently transferable" (145). The poetry choruses offer, in compressed and compelling form, a sense of the collectively authored literary landscape of the American and international Left, a landscape Nelson graphically sketches in his inclusion of numerous magazine covers in both *Revolutionary Memory* and *Repression and Recovery* as well as his suggestive (and still not exhaustive) listing of Left literature anthologies, magazines and newspapers and their widespread locations and various languages (*Revolutionary Memory* 147–50). The choruses embody an alternative epistemology Nelson locates in the Left of the 1920s and 1930s, one devoted not to "expressive subjectivity" but, rather, to "the necessity of disavowing certain forms of subjectivity" (157). What the poetry choruses ultimately demonstrate is that, during the 1930s, around the subjects of revolution and the Spanish Civil War,

> poetry became a form of social conversation and a way of participating in collaborative political action. Poetry was thus in the immediate materiality of its signs dialogic—engaged in a continuing dialogue both with other poetry and with the other discourses and institutions of its day. (157)

Adducing Bakhtin's concept of dialogism, Nelson argues that we can "see the play of difference in a poetic discourse we have long taken to be unproblematically monologic" (157).

For Nelson, the key gain of the poetry chorus is its provocation for a "political aesthetic of the poetic fragment" (159), but his reading and restaging of poems' intertextual modes of participation in a differential discursive field is instructive for the recovery of poetic dialogism in general as well. While the poetry choruses in *Revolutionary Memory* focus on such topoi as the city, the ghetto and the lynching tree, the farm, capital, revolution, and the execution of Federico García Lorca, the method those choruses enact enables us to recapture the dialogic performance of other topoi common in modern poetry. Pound, for example, is not the only poet to cast his cultural critique in the form of the katabasis. Hart Crane detours through the subway-as-Underworld in "The Tunnel," the penultimate section of *The Bridge* (1929), which, as Edward Brunner reminds us, was first published as a stand-alone poem in T. S. Eliot's *Criterion* magazine (Brunner 100–102). Eliot himself deploys the descent narrative in "Burnt Norton" (1936). In each case, the Underworld descent embodies a critical stance toward contemporary culture. Crane quotes snatches of overheard conversation, unfinished ideas, and disconnected phrases that emphasize desire and objectification. His urban Underworld is the dissolution of community, the degradation of history, the replacement of vibrant humanity with signs of wear, exposure, and exhaustion: "verdigris" and "hair / Beyond extinction." The poem captures the dehumanized character of these subterranean urban voices when the "monotone of sound" in the subway becomes "phonographs of hades." The hellish aspects of Crane's journey underground climax in a horrifying vision that condenses urban anonymity, violence, and fragmentation:

> Whose head is swinging from the swollen strap?
> Whose body smokes along the bitten rails,
> Bursts from a smoldering bundle far behind. [. . .] (99)

In "Burnt Norton," Eliot deploys the subway as a similar figure for the fallen world dependent for its redemption on something beyond our power to conceive. The second half of the poem's second movement is set in "a place of disaffection," a place where past and future coexist in artificial light. Under flickering lights, the "time-strained, time-ridden faces" of commuters are "Distracted from distraction by distraction," the constant motion and omnipresent advertisements filling them with "fancies." Like the lovers in Dante's *Inferno*, these commuters are blown by a wind, but for Eliot it is an "Eructation of unhealthy souls" that has been at its belching since before time. The Underworld results from and persists in the pursuit of desire and satisfaction. The tracks of the subway are the emblem of this motion: "the world moves / In appetency, on its metalled ways / Of time past and time future" (Eliot 18).

For Crane and Eliot, as for Pound, the cure for the cultural ills enumerated in their poems lies not in politics but in literary or philosophical change. The speaker in "The Tunnel" begins, "like Lazarus, to feel the slope" and rise from the city's Underworld, but there is no suggestion that the speaker has acted to ascend. Rather, the poem strongly suggests that it is Whitman who brings about this resurrection. The nature and identity of the saving "Word that will not die" is given not in "The Tunnel" itself but in this section's concluding structural and verbal echoes of the closing moments of the earlier "Ave Maria" and "Cape Hatteras" sections. All three end with lines stair-stepped across the page:

Te Deum laudamus
          O Thou Hand of Fire ("Ave Maria" [Crane 50])
My hand
    in yours,
        Walt Whitman—
               so—("Cape Hatteras" [84])
Kiss of our agony Thou gatherest,
        O Hand of Fire
                gatherest—("The Tunnel" [101])

The repeated image of the hand links the saving Word to Walt Whitman, a figure throughout *The Bridge* for the Brooklyn Bridge and its symbolism of connection, so that the deity praised and present in the flames is the poet who sings and celebrates himself and, in himself, all those gathered in his song. Where Crane reaches for the flaming hand of Whitman to pull him from the hellish space of the urban subway, Eliot in "Burnt Norton" offers radical askesis as "the one way" out of the Underground-as-Underworld. The "still point of the turning world," he writes, is "Not here [. . .] in this twittering world," but must instead be sought by a deeper descent: "Descend lower, descend only / Into the world of perpetual solitude"(Eliot 18). In the series of nominalized verbs that follows this imperative, Eliot at once specifies the sacrifice required and enacts the being-out-of-time the sacrifice might enable: "deprivation," "destitution," "Desiccation," "Evacuation," "Inoperancy" (18). The way out of all that the subway represents is a way down into self-denial and self-abnegation, a way of loss and absence and, finally, stillness—"abstention from movement"—that stands in opposition to the world's movement in "appetency."

Virgil famously has the Cumaean Sybil say in *Aeneid* 6 that the way down to the Underworld is easy but that getting back up, reentering history after the sojourn into myth, is tougher. The way up that is chorally indicated by Pound, Crane, and Eliot—the way of Art, Poetry, the Tradition, the Word—might suggest that while the infernalizing of a culture can sharpen a critique, it blunts the edge of any tool that might be brought to bear in efforts to effect social change. In the chorus of katabatic poems of the early twentieth century, though, some voices sing another motif; some poets alloy their katabatic cultural critiques with political diagnoses for contemporary cultural ills and, among these, a few go so far as to imagine political cures.

Perhaps the most entertaining and powerful political diagnosis is the one Sterling Brown offers in the katabatic descent of "Slim in Hell." Sent to Hell as a spy for St. Peter, Slim the trickster encounters Dixie analogues for infernal allusions—a bloodhound for Cerberus, a sign saying "'Dis is it'" condensing Dante and dialect (Brown 89). At first the place seems like a trickster's paradise, but what Slim quickly realizes is that the pleasure dome he sees is decreed by a white Southern sheriff and fueled by the literal consumption of black bodies: "White devils wid pitchforks" throw "black devils on" the fire in Hell's furnace. When he sees how things really are in Hell, Slim says, "'Dis makes / Me think of home." He continues, "Vicksburg, Little Rock, Jackson, / Waco, and Rome" (91), the Southern metonyms here referring to sites of lynchings and/or "race riots" (a euphemism for white-led massacres of African Americans) from the 1890s to the 1920s. Waco, for example, was infamous after the 1916 lynching there of seventeen-year-old Jesse Hall, a mentally retarded African American man who was tortured, hanged, and burned on the town square in front of 10,000 to 15,000 cheering white citizens (Bernstein 4–6). Hell, as St. Peter says at the end of the poem, is Dixie: "Where'n hell dja think Hell *was*?" While this might seem a simple truism, Brown's katabatic poem puts some muscle on the claim by showing this Hell/Dixie to be a racist, exploitative economic system kept in place with deadly violence. In this regard, the poem is part of an array of discourses aiming to make the same point, an array that includes, say, the supplement on "The Waco Horror" published in the July 1916 issue of *The Crisis* to debates over the Wagner Anti-Lynching Act in the 1930s.

Louis Zukofsky's 1934 poems "'Mantis'" and "'Mantis,' an Interpretation" deploy a familiar analogy between the subway and the mythological Underworld (one we can see not only in "The Tunnel" and "Burnt Norton" but also in Pound's "In a Station of the Metro" and in Edna St. Vincent Millay's 1917 sonnet "If I should learn in some quite casual way") and offer a political rather than literary or philosophical vision as the mode and means of salvation. The sestina ("'Mantis'") narrates and meditates upon the speaker's surprise discovery of the title insect in the urban and subterranean space of the New York subway. The mantis draws the speaker's attention to the poor in the station and on the train, but the insect does not symbolize the poor. Rather, the two are linked by the poet's experience of "repulsion." The poet sees both as untouchable, similar in (and, as a consequence, repulsive for) their "helplessness," "separateness," and "ungainliness" (Zukofsky 73). The repulsion, though, is a starting point rather than a conclusion; Zukofsky's reaction to the mantis and the poor provokes "self-disgust" and the shock into seeing that the sestina dramatizes. The content of the vision thus provoked is the machinery of capitalism that at once exploits the labor of the poor and maintains them in the isolation that prevents their realization of this. As Michael Davidson argues, the sestina on its own might run the risk of aestheticizing (and thereby occluding) social tensions but "'Mantis,' an Interpretation" challenges "the totalizing gesture implied by the [sestina's] form and manifested in its utopian apostrophe" (Davidson 122). The interpretation lays bare the devices of the sestina, denaturalizing the form and revealing the labor involved in the production of the poem-as-artifact. Together, sestina and interpretation elaborate a way of seeing that is necessary for the building of a "new world" antithetical to the "oppression of the poor" that is, Zukofsky writes, "the situation most pertinent to us" in the underworld of the present (Zukofsky 77). The defamiliarizing sight of the mantis out of its expected place provokes a shareable realization that, like the mantis, the poor have been driven by forces beyond their comprehension into unnatural (though ideologically naturalized) spaces and processes. The defamiliarizing sight of Marxist analysis in a sestina might perform a similar function.

In "Power," the mid-sequence katabasis of her 1938 "Book of the Dead," Muriel Rukeyser also finds a political version of the conventional prophetic wisdom sought in the Underworld. Accompanied by a tutelary figure analogous to Dante's Virgil—the engineer who designed the power plant—Rukeyser's speaker tours the New Kanawha Power Company's dam and power plant, one result of the labor of the workers whose silicosis deaths inspired the poet's attempt to "extend the document." The two descend a spiral staircase, pause at "the second circle," a "world of inner shade" whose diction punningly invokes the Underworld tradition, and then "Go down" another spiral staircase, "and still go down" insistently descending until even "the last light in shaft" disappears and they are in utter darkness (Rukeyser 50–51). At this nadir of her descent, the speaker encounters this poem's Tiresias or Anchises, a welder in whom Rukeyser condenses the poem's dialectical way of seeing. The welder is dehumanized in and by his labor; "masked for work," he is unrecognizable, his hands covered and his face imprisoned in "a cage of steel" (52). At the same time, though, he is endowed with creative capacities. The welding torch is figured as a tool for writing that is capable at once of "brightening" the welder and "marrying steel." It enables illumination and vision, then, and brings about strong, elemental unions. The dialectical vision she experiences here is central to Rukeyser's transformation of elegiac memory into—if I may borrow Nelson's phrase—revolutionary memory. It is through the dialectical understanding of labor discovered in the katabatic descent that Rukeyser imagines the transformation of dead workers' bodies into "seeds of unending love" (72).

The chorus of political katabases establishes a counterpoint to the chorus of katabatic poems whose cultural critiques are not attached to political programs for social change. Brown, Zukofsky, and Rukeyser clearly write with an awareness of Pound, for example (Zukofsky is explicit about this). It is in Britain that a contrapuntal voice answers the Eliotic katabasis of "Burnt Norton." A contemporary and friend of W. H. Auden and a poet edited by Eliot for Faber and Faber, Louis MacNeice was living in London during the fall of 1938. In his 1939 volume *Autumn Journal*, he writes a poetic account of that fraught season and, at a climactic point, stages an Underworld descent whose political vision answers Eliot's religious imperatives. The chief drama of MacNeice's poem is the inexorable intrusion of the public, political, and historical into the private spaces, thoughts, and activities of the poet. Nowhere is this more pressing than in the sections dealing with the Munich Accord. In his apartment across the street from Regents Park, MacNeice listens as "Hitler yells on the wireless" and as trees are cut down on nearby Primrose Hill ("they want the crest of this hill for anti-aircraft"), and he wonders whether to bother choosing fabric for curtains or to "stop the cracks for gas or dig a trench" (MacNeice 22–23). When Neville Chamberlain signs the Munich agreement, thereby averting war for the moment, the poet's relief is palpable—"once again / The crisis is put off and things look better" (28)—but so is his guilt over this relief. It is this guilt that drives MacNeice to travel to Oxford for the parliamentary by-election, which had become something of a referendum on the Munich agreement, the journey that he casts in katabatic terms.

MacNeice's trip is cast as an Underworld descent, at first subtly, through the insistent repetition of circular imagery, and then more openly (the countryside is "damp and dark and evil"), and finally explicitly: "I take the steep / Plunge to Henley or Hades" (45). At the end of the day, the katabatic resonances come once more to the foreground:

> So Thursday came and Oxford went to the polls
> And made its coward vote and the streets resounded
> To the triumphant cheers of the lost souls—
> The profiteers, the dunderheads, the smarties. (47)

Supporting the Chamberlain government and Munich, the majority of Oxford voters have at least momentarily turned their city into what is, from MacNeice's point of view, a Hell of souls lost in their own self-interest, ignorance, or calculation. Ashamed of his earlier fear for his own skin, MacNeice castigates those in whom he sees that aspect of himself as well as those who do not realize what he has come to realize—that at this historical moment, even the skeptics like himself, even "the nicest people in England," who are predisposed against "solidarity and alignment," must come together "against the beast / That prowls at every door." (47)

Where Pound depends on Plotinus bearing Perseus's shield, MacNeice, within and through the same topos, advocates direct political action. More specifically, he advocates political action around the battlefields of the Spanish Civil War. Often held up—by himself as well as many critics—as an embodiment of political skepticism, MacNeice in *Autumn Journal* narrates his own coming to political commitment. Read alongside one another as constituents of a chorus performing modern riffs on the katabatic topos, Pound and MacNeice go beyond simply illustrating the ways in which poets with varying aesthetic and political commitments deploy the same narrative, allusions, and conventional associations (in this case, even the same word—both Pound's and MacNeice's hells contain "profiteers"). Reading them as voices in the chorus, we recover a wider and richer sense of the ways in which some specific poetic strategy—like the katabasis—can be put to work in the service of not only divergent but even competing cultural agendas. As Nelson reminds us in *Repression and Recovery*, though, "Literary history is never an innocent process of recovery. We recover what we are culturally and psychologically prepared to recover and what we 'recover' we necessarily rewrite" (11). Writing during a moment in which poets debate, in their works (e.g., Seamus Heaney's *Station Island* and Derek Walcott's *Omeros*) and in the pages of literary journals (e.g., Stephen Burt, Daisy Fried, Major Jackson, and Emily Warn debating the question "Does poetry have a social function?" in the January 2007 issue of *Poetry*), the potentials and (almost always) perils of political poetry, I am driven to see in the katabatic chorus of the early twentieth century a broader continuum of possible relationships between poetry and political commitment than is admitted by Heaney's or Walcott's agonized avatars or by the young poets of *Poetry*. Rereading Pound and Eliot and Crane, recovering the broader katabatic chorus of which their works were only a few voices, we can see how, in the hands of Brown or Rukeyser, the apparently conservative or reactionary political poetics of Pound and Eliot can be rearticulated to programs of social change, and how, in the hands of a poet like MacNeice, the katabasis can help a poet work his way out of the shadows of Pound and Eliot and into what MacNeice's friend Auden, in his own poem on Spain, called "to-day the struggle." We can see, as Nelson has urged us to see, "varied cultural roles for literariness," and we can discover ways to take up, as Nelson urges to take up, "different, even contradictory, subject positions from which literariness can be valued" (41). Among his many contributions to our contemporary understanding of poetic possibility, this one seems to me one of Nelson's most important.

Works Cited

Bernstein, Patricia. *The First Waco Horror: The Lynching of Jesse Washington and the Rise of the NAACP*. College Station: Texas A & M UP, 2005.

Brown, Sterling A. *The Collected Poems of Sterling A. Brown*. New York: Harper, 1983.

Brunner, Edward. *Splendid Failure: Hart Crane and the Making of "The Bridge."* Urbana: U of Illinois P, 1985.

Burt, Stephen, Daisy Fried, Major Jackson, and Emily Warn. "Exchange: Does Poetry Have a Social Function?" *Poetry* 189.4 (January 2007): 297–309.

Bush, Ronald. *The Genesis of Ezra Pound's Cantos.* Princeton: Princeton UP, 1976.

Crane, Hart. *Poems of Hart Crane.* Ed. Marc Simon. New York: Liveright, 1987.

Davidson, Michael. *Ghostlier Demarcations: Modern Poetry and the Material Word.* Berkeley: U of California P, 1997.

Eliot, T. S. *Four Quartets.* 1943. New York: Harcourt, 1971.

Flory, Wendy Stallard. *Ezra Pound and the Cantos: A Record of Struggle.* New Haven: Yale UP, 1980.

Genette, Gérard. *Paratexts: Thresholds of Interpretation.* Trans. Jane E. Lewin. Cambridge: Cambridge UP, 1997.

Macdonald, Ronald. *The Burial-Places of Memory: Epic Underworlds in Vergil, Dante, and Milton.* Amherst: U of Massachusetts P, 1987.

MacNeice, Louis. *Autumn Journal.* London: Faber, 1939.

McGann, Jerome. *The Textual Condition.* Princeton: Princeton UP, 1991.

——. *Towards a Literature of Knowledge.* Oxford: Oxford UP, 1989.

Nelson, Cary. *Repression and Recovery: Modern American Poetry and the Politics of Cultural Memory, 1910–1945.* Madison: U of Wisconsin P, 1989.

——. *Revolutionary Memory: Recovering the Poetry of the American Left.* New York: Routledge, 2001.

O'Brien, James Bronterre. *A Vision of Hell, or, Peep into the Realms Below, Alias Lord Overgrown's Dream.* London: Holyoake, undated (early 1850s). British Library shelf mark 11651a.69.

Pike, David L. *Passage through Hell: Modernist Descents, Medieval Underworlds.* Ithaca: Cornell UP, 1997.

Pound, Ezra. *A Draft of XVI Cantos of Ezra Pound for the Beginning of a Poem of Some Length.* Paris: Three Mountains, 1925.

——. *The Cantos.* New York: New Directions, 1973.

——. *The Selected Letters of Ezra Pound, 1907–1941.* Ed. D. D. Paige. London: Faber, 1971.

Rukeyser, Muriel. *U.S. 1.* New York: Covici, 1938.

Terrell, Caroll. *A Companion to the Cantos of Ezra Pound.* Orono: National Poetry Foundation, U of Maine, 1984.

Thurston, Michael. *Making Something Happen: American Political Poetry between the World Wars.* Chapel Hill: U of North Carolina P, 2001.

Zukofsky, Louis. *All the Collected Short Poems, 1923–1964.* New York: Norton, 1965.

PART 2

CORPORATIZATION AND THE POLITICS OF THE ACADEMY

◡ 7 ◡

Worlds to Win

Toward a Cultural Studies
of the University Itself

Marc Bousquet

Who among us hasn't longed to be in charge for just one day? Oh, the things we would change! Virtual U gives you that chance—the chance to be a university president and run the show.

—William Massy, "Virtual U Strategy Guide"

There are many ways of understanding what we mean when we speak of the "corporatization" of the university. One valuable approach focuses on the ways campuses actually relate to business and industry in quest of revenue enhancement or "cost containment": apparel sales; sports marketing; corporate-financed research, curriculum, endowment, and building; job training; direct financial investment via portfolios, pensions, and cooperative venture; the production and enclosure of intellectual property; the selection of vendors for books, information technology, soda pop, and construction; the purchase and provision of nonstandard labor, and so forth (e.g., Barrow, Bok, Kirp, Newfield, Noble, Sperber, Washburn, White). Through these activities, most individual campuses and all of the various "independent" or "self-governing" institutions of the profession are "commercialized," inextricably implicated in profoundly capitalist objectives, however "nonprofit" their missions.

Included in this line of analysis are diverse bedfellows. Its unabashed right-wing comprises those celebrating commercialization, especially the $17 billion a year for-profit education industry itself, including, in addition to Trump and Sperling, celebrity junk-bond felon Michael Milken. The left wing of this approach is led by such contributions as *Campus, Inc.* and *University, Inc.*, respectively, Geoffrey White's scathing collection of exposes of "corporate power in the ivory tower," and Jennifer Washburn's monograph on the "corporate corruption of higher education." There is also a "center" to this discourse. The center comprises such widely read recent efforts by prominent university administrators as Harvard University President Derek Bok (*Universities in the Marketplace*) and the acting dean of Berkeley's Goldman School of Public Policy, David Kirp (*Shakespeare, Einstein, and the Bottom Line*). The common theme of centrist efforts is that they claim no alternative to "partnership" with business and "making peace with the marketplace." Distressingly, more than a few unions of the tenure-stream faculty have adopted a position similar to those of Bok and Kirp, accepting the necessity of "partnership" with corporate enterprise and adopting the protection of tenure-stream faculty "rights to intellectual property" as a higher priority than, for instance, addressing casualization and the installation of a radically multitiered workforce.

An important second line of analysis focuses not on commercialization but on organizational culture. Among the best-known examples of this approach include Bill Readings's study of the ideology of "excellence," in connection to the active effort by university administrations to transform institutional culture, and Slaughter, Rhoades, and Leslie's examinations of "academic capitalism," the phenomenon through which university management both encourages and commands faculty to engage in market behaviors (competition, entrepreneurship, profit-motivated curiosity, etc.). In both cases, the particular merit of the projects is the sense of agency: each discusses changes in the academic workplace that have come about in consequence of clearly understood and clearly intended managerial, corporate, and political initiatives. There is no mystery in these accounts. Management has the explicit intention of inducing the faculty to relinquish certain values and practices and adopt a new organizational culture carefully crafted by management.

The "organizational culture" approach avoids the "victim of history" narrative popularized by Bok and Kirp, in which there is "no alternative" to commercialization. It also sees "the university" as a complex and contradictory place, in contrast to the vestal virgin or ivory tower tropes dominating such accounts (see Newfield). At least since the early 1970s, when labor economist Clark Kerr theorized the "multiversity" and Reisman chronicled the rise of "student power" over "faculty dominance," it has been extremely useful to view the academy as a complex organization hosting multiple, generally competing, institutional groups, each with its own evolving culture, and, further, to see cultural change as related to the struggle between the groups (i.e., to see the vigor of 1960s student culture, for instance, as closely connected to the rise of "student power" relative to the powers of administration).

Cary Nelson is one of very few scholars to have effectively united both strands. On the one hand, with the salvo of books he fired off between 1994 and 1997 (*Higher Education Under Fire, Manifesto of a Tenured Radical, and Will Teach for Food*), he emerged as the single most important spokesman in the humanities regarding the commercialization of higher education. At the same time, he simultaneously developed what remains the single most influential cultural studies approach to the university's competing subcultures, derived in substantial part from his own career of providing leadership to US proponents of the Birmingham school. Nelson's 1999 collaboration with Steve Watt, *Academic Keywords*, successfully positions Nelson as the Raymond Williams of US higher education; his most recent (2004) collaboration with Watt, *Office Hours: Activism and Change in the Academy*, provides an enduring ethnography of academic radicalism worthy of Birmingham school luminaries Hoggart, Hebdige, and Hall. While Nelson's reputation in cultural studies is founded on his own research in the Spanish Civil War, working-class poetry, and his authoritative collections, he is most like Raymond Williams for me in his reflexive consideration of the academy itself. It is not saying too much to suggest that the vast interlocking corpus of Nelson's work on the structural transformation of higher education amounts to, à la E. P. Thompson, *The Making of the Academic Working Class*. As he told me in a 2002 interview,

> being a college professor is going to be a genuine lower class life. It's going to be the kind of life where you cannot afford to send your own children to college. It will offer minimal job security, extremely low income, and increasingly less intellectual freedom. It's going to shift from being Aronowitz's "last good job in America" to one other lousy job in America. And it seems, from the vantage point of someone who has had a pretty good ride in higher education, a huge loss.

To my mind, the utterly indispensable contribution that Nelson makes is his Birmingham-inspired sense of the distinctness of academic subcultures. In the same interview, he analyzed the permatemping of higher education as the production of "separate worlds," so that "a tenured faculty member could teach in the English Department for years and never meet any of the large numbers of part timers on the staff, never learn their names, never recognize their faces."

Most studies follow the lead of 1970s scholarship in considering the rise, through the 1960s, of at least three increasingly distinct cultures—faculty, student, and administration. The lion's share of the attention during that period was on student and faculty cultures. However, the circumstances supporting the flourishing of those cultures have long since eroded. With the increasing economic segmentation of higher education, and the long period of political reaction beginning circa 1980, the sense of a vital "student" culture is generally absent from US mass culture and scholarly literature alike (with the exception of the graduate employee labor movement, of which Nelson, again, has been the leading chronicler). Because the traditional figure of the tenure-track professor is now a small minority of the instructional force in US higher education, the sense of a "faculty culture" also has been undermined. As a result, as Nelson has taught us, investigating "faculty culture" means investigating the multiple subcultures of the persons doing the work formerly done by the tenurable faculty: part-time pieceworkers, graduate student employees, undergraduate tutors, and full-time, nontenurable instructors. For Nelson, this is a form of apartheid, "a structured blindness" created by activist administrations:

> The mechanisms by which those worlds are kept separate are vigorously and intricately applied by the departments. You don't give part timers offices in the building. You don't post their names, and you don't bring them into faculty meetings, and they teach in spaces that are separate from where regular faculty members teach. A lot was done to just make them invisible on campuses where they exist in significant numbers.

Nelson's sense of administration as an intentional agent in faculty culture is a critical advance for a reflexive cultural studies of the university.

Even as the 1970s sense of strong faculty and student cultures has dissipated, management culture has moved in the other direction entirely—becoming ever more internally consistent and cohesive. The culture of university management has the power and, crucially, the intention to remake competing campus cultures in its own image. In fact, the extent to which we increasingly see campus administrations as dominant over other campus groups has much to do with what we see as the success of administrative culture, for its capacity to transmit its values and norms to other groups. As I relate in my own book pervasively influenced by Nelson, *How the University Works*, since the 1960s faculty have certainly organized—with greater and lesser success, depending on immense variables—but campus administrations have in the same period enjoyed a massively increasing sense of solidarity. The managerial caste has grown by leaps and bounds, and it is tightly knit. Through a complex and vigorous culture of administrative solidarity, university management sees itself as a culture apart from faculty. More than just "apart," management is often aligned *against* the faculty (say, when the faculty seek to bargain collectively or to make "shared" governance meaningful). Even when it is not aimed at defeating a particular faculty initiative, management culture is pitched toward a continuous struggle with faculty culture. Informed by the rhetoric of "change," an administrative solidarity continuously shores itself up in opposition to the attitudes, behaviors, and norms felt to describe traditional faculty culture. Faculty values and practices targeted for "change" generally include those associated with relative autonomy over the direction of research and conduct of teaching.

In large part, the self-recognition by management of an emerging culture of its own flowed from the extent to which university administration through the 1970s increasingly took traditional faculty beliefs and practices as an object of study. Informed by trends in corporate management, the "educational leadership" discourse increasingly zeroed in on what Chaffee and Tierney dub "the cultural drama of organizational life" (*Collegiate Culture*). Management theory turned away from the human resources model of developing individual potential. Turning to a more social-psychological frame, managerial discourse began to describe "the underlying cultural norms that frame daily life at the college" (37) as the root of most managerial problems (i.e., as an obstacle to "organizational change"). This phase of management theory—the "leadership" discourse—also saw organizational culture as the wellspring of all possibilities. As the new crop of "institutional leaders," "change agents," and "decision makers" saw it, transforming institutional culture could accelerate change, reduce opposition, and sweepingly create in individuals the desire to change themselves to greater conformity with institutional "mission."

If this sounds Orwellian, or a bit like Foucault goes to business school, it should. In adopting a management theory founded on the dissemination of a carefully designed organizational culture, campus administrations were like most US corporate management in putting to practical use the lessons in cultural materialism they had learned in humanities classes. It is no exaggeration to say that through management theory the ranks of corporate executives and upper-campus administrators are wholeheartedly cultural materialists to a greater extent than the faculty of most humanities departments.

Rather than the dedicated cultivator of "human resources," they now envisioned themselves as an intellectual vanguard—as the institution's meta-culture, the "change agents" whose change agency was expressed through cultural invention, whose "leadership strategies" were aimed primarily at "the social construction of collegiate reality" (Neumann). Plainly put, higher education administration pervasively and self-consciously seeks control of the institution by seeking to retool the values, practices, and sense of institutional reality that comprise faculty and student culture. And it has succeeded wildly. To a certain extent, the left wing of the cultural approach to the corporatization of the university (the critical study of "academic capitalism") simply provides an assessment of the extent to which the right wing has accomplished its overt agenda. A significant fraction of tenure-stream faculty readily engage directly in the commercialization of research, the enclosure of intellectual property, market behavior such as competition for scraps of "merit pay" rather than a collective demand to keep up with the cost of living, an increasingly managerial role over other campus workers in connection to the continual downsizing and deskilling of traditional faculty work, and so forth. And as they do, we are seeing them embrace exactly the "culture of quality" and "pursuit of excellence" that the administration has intentionally designed for them. When I asked Nelson what he thought of the media fantasy of a university teeming with "tenured radicals" like himself, he exploded with laughter. Eventually gaining his breath, he sputtered, "Oh, heavens no. Heavens no. At best a very weak liberalism characterizes the university faculty as a whole—certainly not real political radicalism." Indeed, he observed that most faculty welcome management's designer culture. They especially welcome the "structured blindness" toward the working conditions of everyone else on campus: "It's a blindness that's available to tenured faculty who choose not to see," he explained. "They could choose to investigate. They could choose to find out about the other people who work on campus, but by and large they choose not to."

Management's Dashboard: William Massy's "Virtual U"

The culture of university management is aggressive, pervasive, and self-sustaining, as Nelson and others have observed. It has its own language, journals, traditional gathering places—and now, games. William Massy's "Virtual U" is a "computer simulation of university management in game form" (Sawyer 28). Designed by a former Stanford vice president with a $1 million grant from the Sloan Foundation, the game models the range of powers, attitudes, and commitments of university administration. In short, it provides a window into one of the more widespread versions of administrative consciousness and worldview—the ideal administrator in the world of "resource allocation theory," "cybernetic leadership," and "revenue center management." The use of such simulations, models, and games is widespread in bureaucratic, professional, service, and manufacturing training environments. The "serious gaming" trend has seen the emergence of games designed to promote environmental awareness, armed forces recruitment, white supremacy, religious tolerance, better eating habits, approaches to living with chronic diseases, and so on. Wherever there is real-world rhetorical and practical purpose, institutions and activist organizations have commissioned games to propagandize, train, inform, and recruit. Both the US armed forces and Hezbollah recruit through downloadable PC-based games. Even public budgeting has resulted in an at least two gaming simulations designed to influence voters by shaping attitudes toward spending, in New York City and the Massachusetts state legislature.

Massy's game is a budgeting simulation. It draws upon two prominent strains of thought in contemporary university management, the "cybernetic systems" model of university leadership developed by Robert Birnbaum and resource allocation theory, specifically the principles of revenue center management (RCM), of which Massy is a leading proponent. It also is signally influenced by the Hong Kong design team selected by Massy and the Sloan Foundation, Hong Kong's Trevor Chan. Massy and the Sloan Foundation specifically selected Chan for his prior success with the PC game *Capitalism* ("The Ultimate Strategy Game of Money, Power, and Wealth," reviewed by *PC Gamer* as "good enough to make a convert out of Karl Marx himself"). Massy and Sloane felt Chan's game represented a "good match" with their "similar" vision of management strategy, and the code underlying Chan's *Capitalism 2* serves as the base for many of the modules in Massy's game.

There is only one viewpoint possible in Massy's "Virtual U." Players can choose to be the president of several different kinds of institutions, but presidency is the only possible relationship to the campus. One cannot choose to play Massy's budget game as a student, faculty member, taxpayer, employer, parent, alumnus, or nonacademic staff. The reasons for this design decision are abundantly clear and profoundly ideological. To the audience Massy addresses, only administrators are "decision makers." Only the presidency offers a viewpoint from which to "view the whole institution." As a result, every other standpoint in the game has reality only insofar as it represents a "challenge" to presidential leadership.

Faculty, students, staff, and all other constituents are treated in the game as "inputs" to the managerial perspective. The players have the power to "adjust the mix" of tenure-track and nontenurable faculty, as part of their overall powers to "allocate resources as they see fit." The ease with which nontenurable faculty can be dismissed is accurately modeled. Storing hundreds of faculty "performance profiles," the simulation permits university presidents to troll through the records—including photographs—of faculty in all ranks in every department. As in real life, presidents may terminate the employment of the nontenurable with a keystroke—advancing a great variety of their presidential policy goals with relative ease. What is actually being taught here? Players have to fire adjunct faculty while looking at their photographs. One thing that is being taught is the exercise of power in the face of sentiment: players quickly learn that one cannot have an omelette without breaking eggs.

In contrast, the tenured faculty are represented as a much more difficult "leadership challenge." They cannot be easily dismissed—so many
leadership priorities could be swiftly reached if only all of the funds tied
up in tenurable faculty were released! But the tenured have to be offered
expensive retirement packages to free money for other "strategic purposes." And as in so many other ways, the faculty tend to act irrationally
in response to retirement incentives.

While the tenured faculty may represent a headache for the player-
president, they do not represent any real opposition in the world of the
game. There are no unions. In fact, as bored game players frequently reported, the game is almost impossible for the player-president to "lose,"
because no one else has any meaningful power. This is particularly significant because it successfully models the virtually unchallengeable
legal-political-financial-cultural supremacy underwriting contemporary
management domination. The only question is, how much victory can
one administrator stomach over ten years?

Admittedly, Massy's ambition is to train a leadership cadre in the
habits of benevolence. Underlying the game's approach to the relationship of administrators to faculty is Robert Birnbaum's "cybernetic systems" model, which synthesizes much of the new organization and
management theory of the 1980s into a moderately more faculty-friendly
form. Birnbaum amounts to a "left wing" of the university management
discourse. The extent to which this is a "left" wing is highly relative. On
the one hand, Birnbaum genuinely feels that education required a different kind of organizational management than business corporations.
Within limits he defends the sometimes anarchic and unpredictable nature of "loosely coupled" academic organizations, through which administrative subunits retain conflicting missions and identities at least
partially independent of organizational mission. Birnbaum correctly
notes that the corporate wing of the leadership discourse decries his
moderately more faculty-friendly posture "as a slick way to describe waste,
inefficiency, or indecisive leadership and as a convenient rationale for
the crawling pace of organizational change" (39). Recalling the current
popular trope for faculty managers of "herding cats," he sums up his own
view of "effective leadership" by quoting Clark Kerr's ambition to keep
the institution's "lawlessness within reasonable bounds" (196). The book
with which he launched his retirement was an effort to debunk three
decades of "management fads" in higher education, including total quality management (TQM) and Massy's own RCM.

On the other hand, Birnbaum, together with many in his discipline,
is the author of an approving portrait of management's strategic deployment of faculty committees and faculty institutions as the "garbage cans"

of governance. Drawing on a trope circulated by Cohen and March and enthusiastically adopted by the leadership discourse a decade earlier, Birnbaum notes the utility to "leadership" of establishing "permanent structural garbage cans such as the academic senate." He observes that task forces, committees, and other receptacles of faculty garbage are "highly visible, they confer status on those participating, and they are instrumentally unimportant to the institution" (171). Their real function is to "act like buffers or 'energy sinks' that absorb problems, solutions, and participants like a sponge and prevent them from sloshing around and disturbing arenas in which people wish to act" (165). As in Massy's model, for Birnbaum the word "people" ultimately means administrative "decision makers." "People" should keep the faculty garbage "*away* from decision arenas" (165, emphasis in original). Serving as coeditor of the ASHE reader on organization and governance in higher education throughout the 1990s, Birnbaum's views on the "cybernetics of academic organization" were widely influential, at least among those who were committed to models of university governance as leadership by strong management qua benevolent indulgence of one's "followers."

Essentially the cybernetic model is about managing feedback loops in an awareness of systematic interconnectedness. Viewing management as a "social exchange," Birnbaum emphasizes the extent to which management enters a preexisting environment "in which there are many 'givens' that restrict to a great extent what can be done," and that while it is possible for a president to transform a "Neil Simon comedy [. . .] into Shakespeare," it requires incrementalism and the willingness to provide others with at least the sense of agency, so that, as Birnbaum cynically notes, "In future years, they can reminisce about how *they* transformed themselves" (228, emphasis in original). He concludes that leaders have to listen to the organizational environment—or, more accurately, *monitor it*—and cannot simply command. "Leaders are as dependent on followers as followers are on leaders," and "Presidents should encourage dissensus" (23, 216).

This promotion of dissent is not to encourage organizational democracy, but to provide more accurate information to "decision arenas" and reduce "leader error" in the larger service of more effectively inducing changes in the behavior and value of organization members.

At its core, the cybernetic management model is not about enabling *speech* per se on the part of nonleadership constituencies, it is about harvesting information. While faculty or student speech can be a source of information, speech is not the only or even the primary mode through which presidential "data are collected" (218), hence the "assessment movement" sweeping administrations across the country. In contrast, Birnbaum often models the administrator as a speaker, often a very creative one, the author, director, or impresario of organizational saga and myth, with the power to "interpret organizational meaning." Rather than "inducing the alienation that may arise from giving orders," presidents should "try to get people to pay attention to matters of interest to the administrator" (207). This is not about faculty democracy, it is about the usefulness to administrations wishing to create "organizational change" of a *sense* of democracy. Where propaganda, and the creation of organizational myth or mission, fails, leadership can always induce "organizational learning" with funding. Over time, units that fulfill their institutional mission receive funding increases; units that do not lose funding: "the subunit 'learns' through trial and error in a process akin to natural selection" (191).

Both Massy and the Sloan Foundation are explicit in their intention to promote a managerial model of systems theory in "Virtual U." As in Birnbaum's vision, the arc of the game is fundamentally incremental. Player-presidents get results slowly over time by tinkering with the environment in which other constituencies act, rewarding certain behaviors and punishing others, primarily with funding: "Many of the decisions don't produce explicit reactions, but instead initiate trends and behaviors that evolve toward a desired result by the manager." If Birnbaum might be called an "organizational Darwinist," then Massy is a managerial Malthus. In his essay "Lessons From Health Care," Massy praises the system of managed care for insurers' capacity to intervene in the doctor-patient relationship. Because an insurer's "denial of payment triggers organizational learning," hospitals, clinics, and practices "will be less likely to perform the procedure again in similar circumstances" (197).

The same principle, of feeding those who collaborate with management's vision of "institutional mission" and starving out the opposition, governs every dimension of Massy's management training game. The game's organizing concept is the representation over a ten-year period of the consequences of presidential adjustments in annual budgeting. As Massy's collaborator at the Sloan Foundation has it, "money" is the "yarn" that knits this vision together: "Every decision translates, directly or indirectly, into revenue or expense. In considering how to convey the university as a system, we concluded that there was no better way than the annual budgeting process. The way the player, or the president, finally sees the whole institution synoptically is through financial flows" (Ausubel 4). Primarily employed in education schools (Columbia University, New York University, University of Kansas, etc.) as a teaching aid in graduate classes in educational leadership, the game's scenarios are generally introduced with a version of the driving fiscal imperative: "Your task [. . .] is to maintain steady revenue, at minimum, and preferably grow revenue and spend it in ways that advance the institution."

The game is meant to bring forth a particular administrative subjectivity. One dimension of the administrative personality it success-fully evokes is information overload. The managerial desktop is full of data, with each datum representing a competing claim on resources. These resources can be translated into livelihoods and potential good deeds, or, as Massy has it, "the diversity of values that abounds within any higher education institution" (5). The overall effect is of fatigue, includ-ing moral fatigue: "Each group argues for its view in terms of high prin-ciples, often reinforced by the fact that success also furthers self-interest." The reduction of reality to revenue flows becomes a solution for the chief feelings of the administrative standpoint, information overload, and something that might be called "value fatigue." As one University of Southern California administrator quipped to David Kirp, "If you don't have a vision, RCM becomes your vision." The game teaches a very spe-cific set of feelings and values to potential future administrators. It teaches the utility of maintaining a large disposable faculty both for meeting financial targets and for quick restructuring to meet new presi-dential priorities. It teaches what I call a "management theory of agency" in which managerial decisions appear to drive history.

It even teaches what can be called a "management theory of value," in which the labor of "decision makers" (à la George W. Bush, "I'm the decider!"), and not the strenuous efforts of a vast workforce, appears to be responsible for the accumulation of private and public good in the university labor process. As one community college president using the game puts it to his students at Columbia University: "Senior administra-tors are the engines that push an institution forward—and like a big train, the larger the institution the more engines must be strung to-gether to drive the institution forward" (Hankin). In the down-is-up world of education administration, it becomes possible for a group of New York University students playing Massy's game to conclude that the game's "Improve Teaching" scenario would be best served by a massive acceleration in the hiring of adjunct lecturers. Ultimately, the game teaches these future administrators the pedagogy that Paul Lauter sees is already immanent in the institutions that it models:

> Universities teach by what they are. When a great university with an $11 billion endowment helps impoverish an already indigent city by using outsourcing to push down dining hall wages, it teaches who counts, and who decides in today's urban world. When a great university stiffs its retirees at $7,450 a year while setting up its CEO for a $42,000 a month pension, it teaches who is important and who is not. When the American city in which a great university

carries out its medical research has a higher infant mortality rate than Costa Rica, lessons about priorities are being delivered. When 60–70% of the teaching hours at a great university—and at many not at all great universities—are carried out by a transient faculty, many of them paid below the poverty line and provided with no benefits, offices, or job security, a redefinition of teaching as a "service industry" is being implemented. (54)

Really two distinct worlds of faculty experience are being modeled in "Virtual U." The world of tenured faculty must be more ponderously influenced, involving a fairly strenuous effort by administrators. Relatively speaking, it takes a lot of administrator sweat and frustration to surmount the obstacles represented by the tenured—who ultimately must be provided their retirement incentives to get out of the way, requiring the constant creation of new forums/garbage receptacles for their opinions. Subject to the Malthusian financial discipline and organizational mythmaking of the leadership cadre, as extensively theorized by Birnbaum, Massy, and others, the first world of the tenure stream is certainly no picnic for most faculty occupying it.

The second world the game models for the "other" faculty, the nontenurable majority, is rather different. These folks can be dismissed quickly and cleanly. Despite representing the majority of the faculty, they require a minimal fraction of management time and attention. The extensive use of them permits game players to advance most dimensions of the institutional mission with greater speed. And in this dimension of the game play, the premium on management's capacity to swiftly "adjust the mix" of labor to its own changing sense of "mission" is where we find Massy and the Sloan Foundation's vision of the future.

At a University of Pennsylvania meeting full of administrators, game engineers, and potential users of the game, Sloan Foundation Project Director Jesse Ausubel described his own background in modeling systems used for real-time command and control of complex energy-industry operations (such as an oil refinery). Somewhat wistfully he observed that the current release of "Virtual U" is for "teaching and learning, not real-time operational control." However, he continued, "It would not surprise if some of the people in this meeting help *advance the state of the art in university simulation, so that in 10 years, we have models that serve for control, for decisive management.* For the present, and it is a huge step forward, we have a game" (3, emphasis added). In the future, the Sloan Foundation promises us, all labor will act informationally, in the interests of real-time control by a yet more decisive management. There will be no more noodling around with even the trappings of faculty democracy.

Cultural Studies of the University, From Above and Below

One tantalizing question begged by management's wildly successful social engineering of faculty culture is this: Under current conditions, to what extent do tenure-stream faculty represent the possibility of an opposition, a counterculture? With the spread of acceptance among the tenure-stream faculty of academic-capitalist values and behaviors, and acquiescence to an increasingly managerial role with respect to the contingent, there is little evidence of anything that resembles an "oppositional culture." Indeed, it has become increasingly difficult to speak of anything resembling "faculty culture" apart from the competitive, marketized, "high-performance" habitus designed for them by management. One study of this question regarding community college faculties in the United States and Canada concluded that despite evidence of antagonism between the faculty and administrations on individual issues, and a degree of concrete opposition located in faculty unions, tenure-stream faculty were generally subject to a profound "corporatization of the self" that produced a pervasive "environment of employee compliance with institutional purposes" founded in management's success at fostering a primary identification with the employing institution "over and above" an alternative affiliation with, for instance, one's discipline, any sense of a separate faculty culture, or even the union (Levin 80–81). Of course there are exceptions, and self-consciously militant faculties have made their mark in California, New York, Vermont, and elsewhere, including the South. But even most collective bargaining faculties have not addressed such core issues of administrative control of the workplace as the massive creation, over the past twenty years, of a majority contingent workforce. Instead, Nelson observes, most faculty, including humanities faculty, have adopted the ethos of the "capitalist entrepreneur—self-interest rules. What's happened in the discipline is that uncompromised self-interest can be seen as heroic. [This comes about] when faculty members are encouraged and eventually required to abandon all else but their own careers."

As Nelson's work makes clear, however, there is nonetheless an emergent, vigorous culture of faculty opposition—just not in the tenurable minority. Instead, the rising faculty culture belongs to the unionization movements of contingent faculty and graduate employees, who together comprise what AAUP accurately calls the "new majority faculty." On the face of it, it would seem even more difficult to speak of a "culture" of the contingent workforce. This is a group whose precarious position is overwhelmingly designed to disable solidarity, face-to-face encounters, and the emergence of a sense of common culture and communal interest. Additionally, graduate employees and adjunct faculty face not only the

employer as a challenge when organizing but also other workers, including tenure-stream faculty and their unions who, Keith Hoeller points out,
have in many cases bargained the multitier system of academic labor into
existence. It is a group whose purchase on the word "faculty" itself is precarious, as Joe Berry has underlined: "Every time a [tenure-track faculty
member] or administrator uses the word 'faculty' to refer only to the full
time tenure track faculty, one more piece of grit is ground into the eye of
any contingent within earshot" (87).

Despite the precarious hold that the contingent have on their very
identity as faculty, they have succeeded in forging an emergent culture of
opposition, a culture that sustains and promotes a movement to transform policy, standards, knowledge, appropriations, and the law itself.
Nelson has singled out the California Faculty Association, representing
the Cal State system has for developing an activist culture that has gar-
nered serious results for continent faculty and in negotiating increases in
tenure track hires system-wide:

> I admire the leaders of the California Faculty Association. I have
> spent some time with them. Their meetings are very spirited. They
> understand the economics of higher education. There are no
> blinders on them. They are smart. They're articulate. They have
> been shifting increasingly toward direct action and community ac-
> tivism. Just within the last year, they forced a series of petitions with
> twenty thousand signatures on the board of trustees for the Cali-
> fornia State University system. They clamored their way into the
> meeting and got their petitions handed over, and marched in the
> street outside with a very large puppet of the chancellor of the Cali-
> fornia system in effigy.
>
> When the chancellor went off to New York they called friends
> there and arranged for them to arrive with picket signs where the
> chancellor was. They began to make the chancellor of the whole
> system yield. He was safe from their clamorous protest nowhere
> that he went. His life was just going to be interrupted all the time
> by part timers and full timers who believed that the part time fac-
> ulty deserved a better deal. [They] joined the part timers and full
> timers in cheerful and creative activism.
>
> When they finally signed the contract, the first thing the chan-
> cellor said in California was, "Does this mean that the puppets will
> finally be gone?" (laughs)
>
> The puppets had gotten under his skin. It's not like you'd think
> that was a tactic that could be politically successful, but it had an
> emotional impact on the chancellor, enough that he was ready to
> move on. He was ready to see an end to the protest. The solidarity

that the California Faculty Association has promoted—not perfectly, not without difficulties, not without a long learning curve—makes for a better workplace and a better academic community.

Nelson's admiration for the creative culture struggle and commitment to direct action of what he calls the "academic proletariat" is a reflection of his own commitments. After writing in admiration of student protesters who occupied a "supposedly takeover-proof" administration building on his own campus, leading the university at last to enter contract talks—and urging that contingent faculty follow their lead, Nelson himself, while serving as AAUP president elect, got himself arrested on the barricades surrounding the union-busting New York University administration.

As a long-term officer and subsequently president of the AAUP, Nelson has done a great deal to move that organization onto the terrain of contingent faculty issues. In doing so he freely acknowledges that he sees himself as part of a global and twenty-first-century struggle for greater equality: "The potential for overlapping and intensified workplace justice campaigns is one of the few things about which I'm genuinely hopeful. We need to being thinking of ourselves as a community [and] to wrest control of institutional mission and priorities from the small groups of businessmen who seem to be controlling it increasingly. It can be done. If people are organized and work together, they can regain collective control over the mission of the institution." Seeing the linkages between student and faculty movements is just the beginning for Nelson, who sees in individual issue campaigns "the conceptual underpinning" for regional, metropolitan, and global movements. Those linkages often are democratic practices of hegemony, securing the consent of the dominant to the more just rule of the dominated. In a way, Nelson himself has been seduced, even hegemonized, by the militant, oppositional culture of the contingent, in the same way he has been fascinated throughout his career by the Industrial Workers of the World (IWW), the Abraham Lincoln Brigade, and the radical imagination wherever he finds it. We may not (yet) have returned to the proletarian militance of the 1930s and its prospects for a radical expansion of democracy; nonetheless, as AAUP president, Nelson leads us and is himself led by the rising culture of the contingent. There is hope.

Works Cited

Ausubel, Jesse. "Virtual U: Origins and New Release; Remarks to the First Adopters Workshop." U of Pennsylvania, 1 Feb. 2002. 1 June 2007 <http://www.virtual-u.org/documentation/ausubelremarks.asp>.

Barrow, Clyde W. *Universities and the Capitalist State: Corporate Liberalism and the Reconstruction of American Higher Education, 1894–1928.* Madison: U of Wisconsin P, 1990.

Berry, Joseph. *Contingent Faculty in Higher Education: An Organizing Strategy and Chicago Area Proposal.* Diss. Chicago: Union Institute, 2002. 1 Feb. 2006 <http://www.chicagococal.org>.

Birnbaum, Robert. *How Colleges Work: The Cybernetics of Academic Organization and Leadership.* San Francisco: Jossey, 1988.

Bok, Derek. *Universities in the Marketplace : The Commercialization of Higher Education.* Princeton: Princeton UP, 2004.

Bousquet, Marc. *How the University Works: Higher Education and the Low-Wage Nation.* New York: New York UP, 2008.

———. "An Intellectual of the Movement: Interview with Cary Nelson." *Workplace* 5.1 (Oct. 2002). 2 June 2007 <http://www.workplace-gsc.com>.

Chaffee, Ellen, and William Tierney. *Collegiate Culture and Leadership Strategies.* New York: American Council on Education, 1988.

Hankin, Joseph. "TD4010: College and University Organization and Administration: Spring 2002." Syllabus, Columbia University. Available at www. virtualupdate.org/Features/Previous%20Issues/V/N2featuresA.html>.

Hoeller, Keith. "Equal Pay Means Equal Raises, Too." *Chronicle of Higher Education* (Aug 16, 2005). 1 June 2007 <http://www.chronicle.com>.

———. "Treat College Part-Time Faculty Fairly." *Tacoma News-Tribune,* 7 Oct. 2006. 1 June 2007 <http://www.coastcca.com>.

Kerr, Clark. *The Uses of the University.* 5th ed. Cambridge: Harvard UP, 2001.

Kirp, David. *Shakespeare, Einstein, and the Bottom Line: The Marketing of Higher Education.* Cambridge: Harvard UP, 2004.

Lauter, Paul. "Content, Culture, Character." *Works and Days* 41/42, 21.1–2, (2003): 51–56.

Levin, John S. "Faculty Work: Tensions between Educational and Economic Values." *Journal of Higher Education* 77.1 (Jan./Feb. 2006): 62–88.

Massy, William. "Reengineering Resource Allocation Systems" and "Lessons From Health Care." *Resource Allocation in Higher Education.* Ed. William Massy. Ann Arbor: U Michigan P, 1996. 15–48, 193–222.

———, et al. "Virtual U Strategy Guide." 1 June 2007 <http://www.virtual-u.org/downloads>.

Nelson, Cary. *Manifesto of a Tenured Radical.* New York: New York UP, 1997.

———, ed. *Will Teach for Food: Academic Labor in Crisis.* Minneapolis: U of Minnesota P, 1997.

———, and Michael Bérubé, eds. *Higher Education Under Fire: Politics, Economics, and the Crisis of the Humanities.* New York: Routledge, 1994.

———, and Stephen Watt. *Academic Keywords: A Devil's Dictionary for Higher Education.* New York: Routledge, 1999.

———, and Stephen Watt. *Office Hours: Activism and Change in the Academy.* New York: Routledge, 2004.

Neumann, Anna. "The Social Construction of Resource Stress." *Organization and Governance in Higher Education.* ASHE Reader Series. Ed. Christopher M. Brown. 5th ed. Boston: Pearson, 2000.

Newfield, Christopher. *Ivy and Industry: Business and the Making of the American University: 1880–1890.* Durham: Duke UP, 2003.

Noble, David. *Digital Diploma Mills: The Automation of Higher Education.* New York: Monthly Review Press, 2002.

Readings, Bill. *The University in Ruins.* Cambridge: Harvard UP, 1996.

Reisman, David. *On Higher Education.* San Francisco: Jossey, 1981.

Rhoades, Gary, and Sheila Slaughter. *Academic Capitalism and the New Economy.* Baltimore: Johns Hopkins UP, 2004.

Sawyer, Ben. "Serious Games: Improving Public Policy through Game-based Learning and Simulations." Washington, DC: Woodrow Wilson Center, 2001.

Slaughter, Sheila, and Larry L. Leslie. *Academic Capitalism: Politics, Policies, and the Entrepreneurial University.* Baltimore: Johns Hopkins UP, 1997.

Sperber, Murray. *Beer and Circus: How Big-Time College Sports Is Crippling Undergraduate Education.* New York: Owl, 2000.

Washburn, Jennifer. *University, Inc.: The Corporate Corruption of American Higher Education.* New York: Basic, 2005.

White, Geoffry, ed. *Campus, Inc.: Corporate Power in the Ivory Tower.* Buffalo: Prometheus, 2000.

∽ 8 ∽

THE ORGANIZATION MAN

Michael Bérubé

When I was hired by the University of Illinois at Urbana-Champaign in 1989, I had a moment of wondering just what I had gotten myself into. That moment had everything to do with Cary Nelson, and I will spend the first few pages of this essay explaining why. It was clear to me—and, apparently, to some of the Illinois faculty members I met on my campus visit—that Cary saw my work as potentially conversant with his own. To my astonishment, he had asked, during my MLA interview, whether I thought that "general" literary history could still be written now that I had completed a "case study" kind of reception history that focused on the careers of individual writers. I learned later that Cary had just finished writing *Repression and Recovery*—a book that, it is fair to say, wound up being a decisive turning point not only in Cary's own career as a critic and theorist but also in the academic study of American literature, of modern poetry, and of the writing of the American Left. At the time, had I been told that anyone would consider my unwieldy, idiosyncratic dissertation on the careers and institutional reception histories of Melvin Tolson and Thomas Pynchon in the same mental breath with Cary's sweeping and definitive study, I would have considered the idea preposterous. And yet I found myself in a hotel room in New Orleans at the 1988 Modern Language Association (MLA) convention, where Cary was asking me if, based on what I had learned about the minutiae of reception aesthetics in late-twentieth-century American letters, sweeping and definitive studies like his were still viable at all.

"Um, yeah," I replied, "I guess so—I mean, I'd write a more sweeping study myself if I could, but these two guys wound up taking all of my time." From that point on, I saw my work on Tolson and Cary's on modern poets we have wanted to forget as complementary. I tried to write a kind of microhistory of neglect, focusing on one African American poet whose work fits neither in the Harlem Renaissance nor in the Black Aesthetic; indeed, it does not seem to fit under any heading except that of "Tolsonesque poetry of the postwar era." Cary, in contrast, threw down a gauntlet and presented us with the work of dozens of disparate writers in the modern period, daring us to acknowledge our ignorance of American literary history and our despair over the impossibility—and yet the indispensability—of literary history.

In the introduction to *Marginal Forces/Cultural Centers*, which was written just after I had read *Repression and Recovery*, I framed this complementarity like so:

> Nelson argues that we have swept dozens of writers from the map of modern poetry, and I agree, for Tolson is prominent among them. [. . .] But by the same token, Nelson's invocation of "repression" foregrounds a key problem for critics attempting to theorize the noncanonical. To put a complex question simply, can we account for the noncanonical more satisfactorily in latitudinal literary histories or in individual reception histories? On one hand, I cannot agree that each of the writers Nelson discusses was neglected—or repressed—in the same way. On the other hand, I cannot coherently counterargue that neglect operates only at the level of individual writers, whether these be Tolson, Blake, and Donne or (among Nelson's many examples), Amy Lowell, Edwin Rolfe, and H. H. Lewis. For if we persist in the belief that repression and neglect always come, so to speak, in individually wrapped slices, directed at individually "neglected" writers, then we also hypothesize "neglecters" for each of these writers, eventually conflating neglect and repression. Neglect is never benign, but though it is always motivated, it may not always be conscious. We cannot, in other words, indict all but a handful of the world's five billion citizens with the charge of neglecting Tolson. (13)

Almost two decades later, this passage strikes me as unfortunate—for two reasons. One, I frame my book's complementarity with Cary's in such a way as to make a virtue out of dire necessity—after all, one of the reasons I focused my study of neglect on one poet, Tolson, was that I did not have the intellectual and historical breadth to attempt anything else; I had done a great deal of archival work on one figure, but nothing like the kind of archival work Cary had done for *Repression and Recovery*. Two, I confused two distinct and difficult questions—I was trying to distinguish between an active process of repression and a passive process of neglect, even while acknowledging that *Repression and Recovery* "plays productively with the political and psychoanalytic sense of 'repression,' elaborating, as no reception theory has yet been able to do, on how the process of canon formation entails also procedures of exclusion that are both motivated and unconscious, active and passive, repressive and neglectful" (12). But I also was trying to acknowledge that neither "repression" nor "neglect" is purely active or passive. We can repress knowledge precisely to prevent ourselves from knowing that we know it, or ought to know it, just as we can only be said to "neglect" things of which we have some plausible reason to be aware. (That is why I admitted that we cannot blame people in general for "neglecting" Tolson's work.) Much later in *Marginal Forces*, I admit that it is all but impossible to think of neglect as passive:

> What do we mean by "neglect"? Is there a pure form of neglect? What would it look like? An unsolicited manuscript that was never published or, worse, "neglected" in the strict Latin sense of "not read" at all? Possibly, but here the Latin sense seems to contradict the commonsense notion that a "neglected" object must be somehow available for attention or neglect, hovering someplace on the edge of consciousness—where it remains, being systemically "overlooked." We can thus usually be said to be "neglecting" some of our duties, or our appearance, or our friends and relatives; but we are not normally accused of "neglecting" things of which we are completely unaware. (133)

I wrote some of this material before reading *Repression and Recovery*, and some of it after, but in retrospect it looks like an extended dialogue with Cary's work from start to finish. Accordingly, I was stunned and somewhat embarrassed a few years later, in 1995, to read Alan Wald's account of my relation to Cary. In a bracing review of *Marginal Forces*, Wald wrote, "My own understanding of *Repression and Recovery* is that it is intended as a prolegomenon, a general call aimed precisely at eliciting individualized studies of the repression mechanisms, which Nelson subsequently himself inaugurated with his biographical work on the Marxist poet Edwin Rolfe. Simply put, Bérubé unnecessarily magnifies his differences with Nelson, and perhaps others, in some of the areas on which he chooses to focus" (297). Perhaps I did magnify my differences with Cary unnecessarily; perhaps I thought I was competing for shelf space. If so, then I have to conclude that my conception of my work as complementary to Cary's involved a bit of delusional thinking, for *Repression and Recovery* has been far more influential than *Marginal Forces*, and deservedly so. The book launched (as Wald suggested) an entire series of new studies and reevaluations of the Modernist period—and of the relation of poetry to political conviction and political organization. Some of these studies, of course, were undertaken by Cary himself (as Wald suggested), as he delved further into the work of Edwin Rolfe, of the poetry and iconography of the Spanish Civil War, and of the revolutionary memory so many of us have apparently wanted to forget. The best that can be said of my first book in that vein is that it set a standard for comparative studies of Tolson and Pynchon that has yet to be surpassed.

But that is not the reason, upon my arrival at Illinois, I had a moment of wondering what I had gotten into. I knew by then—right from the start—that Cary and I shared a critical sensibility and a love for finding out about fascinating writers most people had not heard of. I also knew—and this was just as important—that we shared a similar sense of humor. In fact, this was the first thing I learned about Cary, and to appreciate it fully you need to recall how nerve-wracking and uncomfortable some MLA interviews can be, particularly the ones that start off with some variation on, "Begin, ephebe!" At Virginia, we had been counseled by our graduate placement director to never accept an offer of coffee or tea during an interview, on the grounds that it could be one more thing for a nervous candidate to worry about— milk, sugar, hot liquids, and shaky hands. Cary, upon welcoming me into the room, asked me if I would like a cup of coffee, and I gratefully accepted, because I needed a cup of coffee, whereupon Cary turned to Zohreh and said, with his famous precipitously arched eyebrow, "*He took the coffee.*" (You could hear the italics.) It was a deft and charming way of signifying the parameters of the interview setting, and it made me like Cary immediately. It also made me wonder—as I wondered aloud, at the time—just how long the coffee had been sitting on the breakfast tray.

I saw in Cary not only a potentially sympatico colleague but, in some ways, a kindred spirit. What was there to worry about? Why would I have had even a moment of concern about coming to Illinois as a young assistant professor? Well, it had something to do with Cary's gift for tact and diplomacy. He often spoke, in those days, as if he were the department pariah—a Ginsbergian bearded wild man who disrupted department meetings every so often by bursting in and bellowing, "Repent! The end is near!" and then reciting the work of W. S. Merwin. (He had, but a few years earlier, published an essay in the *ADE Bulletin*, "Against English: Theory and the Limits of the Discipline," and apparently at least one of his colleagues *did* take his suggestion that African American literature be required of all English majors as the ravings of a wild man.) After Cary had told me a few (actually, a great many) choice stories about his favorite colleagues and their foibles, I began to get the impression that Amanda Anderson (who came to Illinois the same year) and I had been hired as a kind of fluke, and that the entire department would turn on us once they realized what their Ginsbergian wild man had brought back to Urbana from New Orleans. "Well, I'll say this much," Cary replied when I tentatively gave voice to this moment of concern. "More often than not, if I want to get something done in the department, I get up and argue against it."

Great, I thought. I had better start making friends.

The supreme irony of all this—and the reason I burden this essay with memories of texts and encounters from the distant past—is that over my next twelve years at Illinois, I came to realize that Cary Nelson is in fact one of the best organization men in the business, and there is no reason for me to speak only of those twelve years—even though I am no longer Cary's colleague, I have served with him on executive committees in the MLA and the AAUP since 2002. Now I know that organization men tend to get a bad rap. By calling Cary Nelson a good organization man, I do not mean simply that he knows how to raise money for the AAUP, or that he knows how to raise its national profile. He has done both, but that is not the point. I mean, instead, that few people in our profession have demonstrated such a commitment to the greater good of academe as a whole. Beginning in the early 1990s, when the sudden re-contraction of the job market after two or three years of "false recovery" led to the permanent job system crisis we now know, the nature of which is at once revealed and disguised by the fact that universities hire three new part-time teachers for every tenure-track assistant professor, Cary has been at the forefront of struggles for graduate student unionization, for the rights of adjuncts, and for professional working conditions for all faculty and graduate students. This is not news, of course. But I want to stress the familiar and sometimes highly amusing contrast: the Cary Nelson who can be so witheringly contemptuous or flamboyantly exasperated with the more self-indulgent or malevolent or simply addlepated members of the professoriate is the same Cary Nelson whose contempt or sense of exasperation is triggered most readily by members of the professoriate who have no conception whatsoever of the common good.

This is, I think, the key to Cary's lively sense of moral outrage. I recall vividly his horror over one of the MLA committees to which he had been elected in the mid 1990s. He returned from Astor Place appalled that the film specialists seemed to believe that it was their job to represent film specialists; and early modern scholars seemed to believe that they should seek to advance the interests of early modern scholars; and linguists or medievalists seemed to believe that someone needed to speak of linguists or medievalists. It looked, Cary said, like sub-subdisciplinary identity politics gone mad—and no one knew or cared to hear that there were English and modern languages professors working one-year contracts for $900 to $1,500 per course.

Recently I had two encounters that shed an eerie light on Cary's sense of outrage. In the fall of 2006, I spoke to a faculty member who objected to a passage in *Higher Education Under Fire*, which claims that "for decades American universities have fostered a kind of *idiot savant* academic culture" (25). "In all honesty, that was Cary's line," I replied, "but I'll defend it anyway." I explained that Cary and I were thinking of professors who know a great deal about incredibly difficult and recondite matters but who have no clue about how their university actually works—and I admitted that in the years since 1993 (when we wrote that introduction) or 1995 (when it was published), times had changed somewhat, and younger faculty hired in the past decade or so seemed to be generally more informed about the engine rooms of their institutions and the economics of the business. Marc Bousquet's work is, by any measure, the best example of the new generation's attention to the working conditions of academe, and certainly no one would accuse him or the writers for *Workplace* of being "idiot savants" about the academic job system (see Bousquet, *How the University Works*). And yet not a week after I had that conversation, I ran into a young faculty member at Penn State who informed me that senior members of his department had warned him not to get involved with the AAUP because it could be held against him in his tenure evaluations. "That," I said, "is precisely why you need to join AAUP now—to protect yourself against unscrupulous colleagues who engage in illegal behavior." Sometimes, I think, Cary's line about idiot savant faculty culture—and it was, after all, his line—is only too kind to some of the miscreants and fools who populate our campuses. But even when one is not dealing with unscrupulous colleagues, miscreants, and fools, there is still so much in academic culture that prevents us from thinking about what we share in common as professionals and as teachers, regardless of our disciplinary commitments and our institutional affiliations, so much that encourages us to think only in terms of individual reward and sub-subdisciplinary identity politics. Cary Nelson is outraged by all of it, and rightly so.

I want to briefly touch upon some of Cary's work in the MLA and the AAUP. In the late 1990s, Cary—with the help of Bousquet and the other leaders of the Graduate Student Caucus—passed a remarkable slate of initiatives and resolutions that changed the character of the MLA as an organization and helped redirect its attention to the working conditions of its members. Prior to the Nelson-Bousquet era—and I am sorry to say, *after* the Nelson-Bousquet era, when I served on the MLA Executive Council and Delegate Assembly Organizing Committee—the Delegate Assembly devoted most of its time passing resolutions for a single, common form for fellowship applications or demanding that the United States withdraw from North America. Nothing in between—nothing in the middle distance where MLA resolutions actually could have an impact on MLA policies and practices. Thanks to the Nelson-Bousquet era, however, the MLA now strongly supports the unionization of graduate students and adjuncts; it has conducted a comprehensive wage survey in the profession and announced wage floors for teachers of English and the modern languages; and it will not meet in hotels that are undergoing labor disputes, for to do so is to weigh in on the side of management. The MLA is not an ideal scholarly organization by any means, but it is vastly different than it was twenty years ago, and some of its changes for the better can be attributed to the work of Cary Nelson. About the AAUP I will say less, because Cary's work there is still ongoing. All I will say is that I am more impressed with Cary's AAUP work to date than with anything I have ever seen in any academic organization.

The funny thing is that in some ways Cary and I are still working out these questions of neglect and repression. If, as I suggested many years ago when I was trying to do my little Wittgensteinian number on "neglect," we can be said to be "neglecting" some of our duties but not those things of which we are completely unaware, then perhaps Cary's academic activism can be seen as an attempt to remind his fellow professors of the professional duties many of them are neglecting, and of the way the profession continues to perpetuate the exploitation and abuse of its most vulnerable members. (I will not say that adjuncts are "repressed," because I do not want to evoke the inevitable comparison to the famous scene between King Arthur and Dennis the Peasant in *Monty Python and the Holy Grail*, but I will certainly say that they are exploited and abused.) I know, of course, that some adjuncts and graduate students have not been altogether happy with the ways Cary and I have tried to take up their cause, and I know even more acutely that no one likes a scold. Nevertheless, the simple fact remains that through the 1970s and 1980s, few senior scholars in the humanities—*remarkably* few senior scholars, really—turned their attention to the working conditions of their less fortunate colleagues, and the likely working conditions of most of their graduate students. Perhaps one might say that in pursuing a leadership role in the national AAUP, Cary Nelson has been devoting his time and energy to uncovering and redressing academic realities we have wanted to forget.

Of course, a few professors remain dedicated to neglecting the working conditions of academe; a few even find Cary's efforts somehow risible. For example, Emory University professor of English Mark Bauerlein, writing in 2005, adduced Cary's work as evidence of the decline of theory and the self-indulgence of leading theorists:

> As theorists became endowed chairs, department heads, series editors, and MLA presidents, as they were profiled in the *New York Times Magazine* and invited to lecture around the world, the

institutional effects of Theory displaced its intellectual nature. It didn't have to happen, but that's the way the new crop of graduate students experienced it. Not only were too many Theory articles and books published and too many Theory papers delivered, but too many high-profile incursions of the humanities into public discourse had a Theory provenance. The academic gossip in *Lingua Franca* highlighted Theory much more than traditional scholarship, David Lodge's popular novels portrayed the spread of theory as a human comedy, and *People* magazine hired a prominent academic feminist as its TV critic. One theorist became known for finding her "inner life," another for a skirt made of men's neckties, another for unionizing TAs. It was fun and heady, especially when conservatives struck back with profiles of Theorists in action such as Roger Kimball's *Tenured Radicals*, sallies which enraged many academics and soundly defeated them in public settings, but pleased the more canny ones who understood that being denounced was better than not being talked about at all (especially if you had tenure).

The passage starts off plausibly enough. There was a decade when theory became the Lingua Franca of the discipline, and there was a decade in which *Lingua Franca* covered the foibles of theory—and not always, it should be said, to "highlight" the phenomenon in a flattering way. But the second half of this passage goes dramatically off the rails—first by likening the unionization of teaching assistants (TAs) to finding one's "inner life" or wearing a necktie skirt, and then by trying to claim (1) that Roger Kimball's *Tenured Radicals*, published in 1990, somehow "struck back" against things that happened five to ten years after its publication, and (2) that Kimball "soundly defeated" his theory antagonists "in public settings." The last claim is especially strange, since Kimball's book was dismantled in most "public settings" where its readers knew anything at all about the history of the academic study of literature (Louis Menand's review in *The New Republic* was utterly devastating, and neither Menand nor *TNR* were particularly enamored of theory at the time), or, indeed, anything about anything at all. But for my present purposes, what is really remarkable about Bauerlein's essay is its sneering suggestion that the task of unionizing teaching assistants is "fun and heady," sort of like wearing a racy skirt. At least Bauerlein cannot be said to be "neglecting" the subject of TA unionization.

But why should I be so perverse as to value "organization" at all? Is not "organization" a synonym for "institution," and why should anyone on the academic Left be so invested in institutions so hierarchical and traditional as universities? In *Marginalized in the Middle*, Boston University sociologist and public intellectual Alan Wolfe criticizes Cary and me for defending academe from the Right's various onslaughts. Contrasting us with the late 1960s radicals who occupied university buildings, Wolfe writes that we sound "remarkably like the very people the left once criticized" (20). Because Cary and I think the professoriate has been badly misrepresented, and sometimes slandered, by the likes of Dinesh D'souza, Lynne Cheney, and David Horowitz, Wolfe paints us as gray-flannel organization men: "One could hardly imagine a more conservative language, even if those speaking it think of themselves as leftists of one sort or another" (20). Apparently one cannot be "on the Left" and defend universities at the same time. Is Wolfe serious, or is he just scoring some cheap debating points? It is hard to say, because in a later essay, his *New Republic* piece of 2003, "Anti-American Studies" (also available in Wolfe's *An Intellectual in Public*), he describes Cary and me as "advocates of class struggle within the university" simply because of our support for graduate student and adjunct unionization. Unions are agents of class struggle, oh my! Just wait until Wolfe finds out what his teaching load will be after Cary and I establish the dictatorship of the academic proletariat. But apparently, people like Cary Nelson can be "conservatives" and "advocates of class struggle" at the same time, depending on the ever-changing rhetorical needs of people like Wolfe. All I can say about Wolfe's marginalization in the middle, on this front, is that it must be hard out there for a "centrist." For the rest of us, I would hope that the idea of organizing for the common good—because, you know, there is power in a union—would not be quite so strange or radical as Wolfe tries to make it sound.

Over the past two decades I have learned this above all about Nelson— he is a salient exception to the rule—a paid-up member of the academic Left who thinks organizationally, and acts organizationally, for the greater good of college teachers throughout the country, and even for the greater good of the next generation of college teachers. It has been one of the most pleasant surprises of my career. The Ginsbergian wild man who told me that he gets things done in his department by standing up and arguing against them has turned out to be such an extraordinary—and extraordinarily effective—organization man.

Works Cited

Bauerlein, Mark. "Theory's Empire." *Butterflies and Wheels.* 6 July 2005 <http:// www.butterfliesandwheels.com/articleprint.php?num=134>.

Bérubé, Michael. *Marginal Forces/Cultural Centers: Tolson, Pynchon, and the Politics of the Canon.* Ithaca: Cornell UP, 1992.

———, and Cary Nelson. *Higher Education Under Fire: Politics, Economics, and the Crisis of the Humanities.* New York: Routledge, 1995.

Bousquet, Marc. *How the University Works: Higher Education and the Low-Wage Nation.* New York: New York UP, 2008.

Kimball, Roger. *Tenured Radicals: How Politics Has Corrupted Our Higher Education.* New York: Harper, 1990.

Menand, Louis. "Lost Faculties." *New Republic* 9.16 (July 1990): 36–40.

Nelson, Cary. "Against English: Theory and the Limits of the Discipline." *ADE Bulletin* (Winter 1986): 1–6.

———. *Repression and Recovery: Modern American Poetry and the Politics of Cultural Memory, 1910–1945.* Madison: U of Wisconsin P, 1989.

Wald, Alan. "Contradictions of the Canon." *The Minnesota Review* 41–42 (1995): 292–97.

Wolfe, Alan. "Anti-American Studies." *New Republic* 10 Feb. 2003. 14 Oct. 2006 <http://www.tnr.com/doc.mhtml?i=20030210&s=wolfe021003>.

———. *Marginalized in the Middle.* Chicago: U of Chicago P, 1996.

∽ 9 ∽

THE HUMANITIES, THE UNIVERSITY, AND THE ENEMY WITHIN

Stephen Watt

Perhaps Yale should change the motto on its university seal to read "America's foremost robber baron university."

—Cary Nelson, *Will Teach for Food*

We had a [deadwood colleague] like that on campus some years ago, since retired. [. . .] Before then he had enough free time to work at a men's clothing store in the local mall. It wasn't then (nor is it now) permissible for a full-time faculty member to take extra work like that without permission. Now, he'd have to lie on his annual "Conflict of Interest" form. [. . .] But twenty years ago gentlemanly honor prevailed. He just didn't possess it in sufficient quantity.

—Cary Nelson, "Moonlighting," in *Academic Keywords*

Nearly fifteen years ago, in the spring of 1993, the Unit for Criticism and Interpretive Theory at the University of Illinois at Urbana-Champaign hosted a conference convened by Cary Nelson and Michael Bérubé that led eventually to the publication of their fine anthology *Higher Education Under Fire* (1995). One context for the volume, and for Nelson's later *Manifesto of a Tenured Radical* (1997), was the torrent of criticism levied against the contemporary university and its faculty by such pundits as Roger Kimball, Dinesh D'Souza, and Charles Sykes.[1] Allegations like D'Souza's of a widespread "illiberal education" and Sykes's of a rampant "profscam," much like old generals in the aphorism, never seem to die; they rise phoenix-like whenever a neoconservative has an ideological ax to grind on the neck of the professoriate. Recently in my local newspaper, for example, a letter writer inveighed against the unspecified excesses of Indiana University's "insanely liberal" faculty, evoking, as Kimball does, images of Berkeley in the 1960s and the tenured radicals it helped cultivate. Today, for the most part, such musty diatribes have been displaced by other concerns and different, more formidable, challenges. In their introduction to *Higher Education Under Fire* Nelson and Bérubé anticipate one of these by urging us not merely to "defend the university unilaterally from unprincipled attackers comfortably housed in right-wing think tanks" but also to undertake the "more hazardous enterprise [of] criticizing specific university policies and practices from within" (9). The latter project is the principal aim of the pages that follow and, as we shall see, the hazards in doing so are several, precisely because such a critique must inevitably confront some of the very issues distorted by the Right throughout the 1980s and 1990s.

I want first to identify several potentially dangerous policies and practices at the current research university, then offer suggestions for resisting them and the institutional motivations they represent. It also must be said, and here is where my argument veers perilously close to those of Kimball and Sykes, that the behaviors of some faculty have exacerbated the dilemmas the humanities face at present and, in some cases, rendered humanists less effective in ameliorating them. Such an observation, however, should not be dismissed as inherently D'Souzean or Syksean but rather entirely Nelsonian, for as ferocious as he has been in responding to reactionaries outside the academy, Nelson has never hesitated to turn his keen wit against a corporate university like Yale all too willing to impoverish its workers, or against faculty who have abdicated from the responsible discharge of their duties. Would that these colleagues had succumbed only to the relatively innocuous temptation of working at a men's clothing store while pretending to be a teacher-scholar like the feckless Americanist Nelson lampooned in our book *Academic Keywords: A Devil's Dictionary for Higher Education* (1999). Regrettably, some colleagues do far more damage to the departments in which they work and the disciplines they purport to value. Those who know Nelson's work—and our collaborations—are familiar with his tenacity in exposing the elitism of the MLA and securing places for graduate students on its executive council, in documenting the misdeeds of academic superstars, and in revealing some writers' brazen demands that editors fork over exorbitant permission fees when compiling textbooks like his Oxford *Anthology of Modern American Poetry*.[2] Provoking such a discussion, however, taking up the challenge of internal critique posed by Bérubé and Nelson in *Higher Education Under Fire*, prompts the following questions: What distinguishes such an analysis from the muckraking of external critics of the university like Kimball and Sykes? How can we identify damaging behaviors in the academy without replicating the crass charges of those who would reject nearly everything Nelson has stood for in nearly four decades of principled activism? What, more generally, are humanists to do? These questions occupy the conclusion of what follows.

Stated in another way, this essay will advance a kind of double understanding of the last phrase of its title, the "enemy within," an allusion to Brian Friel's early play of the same title and its staging of a dual conflict all too familiar to today's humanists. As *The Enemy Within* begins, Friel's protagonist Columba, a sixth-century priest and founder of monasteries, resides in relative seclusion with his fellow monks on the island of Iona, pursuing a life of contemplation and spiritual engagement far removed from the turbulence of Irish politics. Not unlike contemporary scholars, some of Columba's colleagues occupy themselves with biblical exegesis, translation, and transcription. Early in Act One, a scribe reads verses from the gospel of Saint Matthew, chapter 10, in which Jesus explains one connotation of "enemies within" by predicting an inevitable conflict between love of God and love of family:

> Do not think that I come to send peace upon the earth; I come not to send peace but the word. For I come to set a man at variance against his father. [. . .] And a man's enemies shall they be of his own household. He that loveth father or mother more than Me is not worthy of Me. (20)

As the scene progresses, Columba, given to memories of an idyllic Ireland that may no longer exist, reveals a second resonance of "enemy" through his struggles to suppress his longing to return home. He is successful at doing so until a messenger arrives with news that his cousin is surrounded by a rival's army and needs Columba's help. Initially steadfast in his devotion to the contemplative life, Columba wavers and finally relents, reconfirming the double meaning of "enemy within." This latter enemy, the enemy within humanists themselves, like the masochist's fetish, often is metaphorized by enticing images frozen in time to "exorcise the dangerous consequences" of movement and change (Deleuze 31). Faculties in the humanities, like masochists, are prone to adapt such fetishes, clinging desperately to a past when their disciplines were more central to the mission of the university. In short, they coexist with the enemy within their universities, and they do battle with another within themselves.

I can offer as a defense for these allegations only my experiences as the former chair of a large English department who, after five years in the trenches, stepped away from administration to assess what he had learned. In this regard, three topics come immediately to mind: first, that the humanities face more powerful adversaries within the university than those ideologues who sought to sway public opinion in the 1990s; second, that while describing the university as harboring enemies of the humanities might appear alarmist or melodramatic, it is nonetheless obvious that the number of faculty and administrators who espouse values radically inimical to ours is growing; and, third, again, that too often we are our own worst enemies at a time when, like the Hollywood producer Robert Duvall visits in *The Godfather*, we can ill afford to "look ridiculous." At the risk of arrogance or immodesty, I must add that unless they have negotiated with deans and trustees, balanced impossibly tight budgets, attempted to hire prima donnas with gargantuan senses of entitlement, and labored to broker peace treaties among hopelessly deluded, in some cases certifiable, colleagues, most faculty have little idea of how things work at the university. As a dejected Columba laments in Friel's play, "You must pray for me [. . .] because I am ringed with enemies" (20–21). Prayer, sadly, might not provide sufficient prophylaxis from the forces at work in the corporate university of the new millennium—and from the ill-conceived directions in which many institutions of higher education are headed.

I begin by nominalizing one emergent link in this chain of enmity, something that might be called the "scientification" of university values. This process-cum-ideology evolved rapidly during my tenure as a department chair and manifested itself in a myriad of ways: from the annual "conflict of interest forms" that monitor faculty activity and income generation to "refinements" in the processes of tenure and promotion; from the appointment of deans to the formation of boards of trustees and other governing bodies who manage, often ineptly, the postmodern university. As Bérubé and Nelson predicted fifteen years ago, the life sciences in particular have ascended to a position of dominance on campuses like mine,[3] and, not surprisingly, procedures common to scientific disciplines have now been implemented in important campuswide assessments, often to the disadvantage of humanities faculty. At present, for example, my university has embarked upon a vigorous advertising campaign trumpeting the abilities of a recent life sciences initiative both to save lives and promote economic growth; moreover, the initiative represents a successful partnership between the university and larger corporations that might help sustain it during a time of inadequate legislative support. What reasonable person could oppose the goals of curing cancer and employing a greater percentage of the workforce in this burgeoning area?

Of course, I do not, but several phenomena have devolved from the launching of such initiatives that might give one pause. As Nelson and I reported recently in an article about the multiple insanities (or inanities?) of tenure and promotion reviews,[4] several scientists at Indiana were amazed when, in leading a discussion of tenure procedures to some forty department chairs, I alluded to the practice of offering honoraria to outside reviewers. In an almost visceral reaction, one chair from the sciences leapt to his feet to express his disapproval, demurring that the writing of such letters was a "professional obligation." His objection was easily parried by the reminder that, in the humanities, a tenure and promotion review often requires reading books as well as articles, a burden scientists seldom undertake, then providing a detailed review of these very substantial materials. Just how much of the summer is one obligated to sacrifice, I asked, for institutions so inconsiderate in some instances as to send smudged copies of books rather than the books themselves? Then, in the fall of 2006, at a seminar for new department chairs on the assembly of tenure dossiers, a university administrator broached the topic of "bibliometrics." This practice, common to many scientific disciplines, requires a candidate for tenure to demonstrate her or his influence on a field by painstakingly listing citations to her or his work in peer articles, an often inaccurate, not to mention time-consuming, activity. At this meeting, chairs of disciplines such as English who have not embraced such measures were advised to explain in tenure files why bibliometrics was *not* part of their tenure deliberation, and the direction of the conversation then became clear: this is now—or will soon be—the default position of the university. Departments in the humanities will be required to defend their recalcitrance in choosing to remain so hopelessly unscientific.

Yet as many scientists acknowledge, citation indexes are notoriously unreliable, in part because one of their proveniences is the unethical behavior of journal editors. That is, one colleague in geology confided to me that he knew several editors who demanded that contributors to their journals add citations in their bibliographies to these same journals to enhance their perceived prestige. Yet even if it is not the product of academic puffery, can a mere list of citations clarify the use to which a colleague's work has been put or the esteem with which it is held in a professional community? Can it reveal the relationship between an author and the author of a source he or she cites? Can it effectively gauge the importance of the referenced research, its centrality to an argument or wider critical discourse? Of course not, but the practice—like that of increasingly wide criminal background checks for new faculty members and more intrusive conflict-of-interest forms—has been encouraged by trustees seemingly obsessed with the detailed assessment of faculty (while, of course, the actions of these same trustees remain largely free of or impervious to such oversight).[5] The result is a *faux* objectivity passing itself off as unimpeachable scientific data, and such practices are occurring across the country, inflecting standards in tenure, salary, and broader budgetary reviews.

Further, during tenure and promotion deliberations, department chairs in the humanities are at times required to mount lengthy rebuttals of negative commentary in tenure dossiers in ways influential scientists can avoid if they choose, as I learned when one of our finest candidates in recent years was abused by a college committee because one of the eight letters solicited from external referees was negative. The departmental vote was 35 to 0 in favor of tenure, and the candidate's record was enviable in all areas: outstanding teaching and service, a published book from a major press, two coedited anthologies, numerous articles, and so on. So when the negative referee admitted that she or he was working on a closely related project and might therefore be too biased to make a balanced assessment of the published book, I made the mistake in my chair's report of too readily agreeing. In fact, the referee's analysis *was* stilted and, in parts, deliberately misleading, but my saying as much was construed as either a knee-jerk reaction or a blithe dismissal that, in turn, angered some members of the college tenure committee. The dean scheduled a meeting with me, administered a perfunctory scolding, and asked me both to write a more sustained rebuttal of the negative letter and to solicit more internal memoranda of support—the departmental vote of 35 to 0 supporting the candidate being, apparently, too ambiguous to decipher. I complied, with the result that the case was approved.

At about the same time, as an administrator confessed to me, the chair of a powerful Science Department found himself in a dilemma similar to mine and also was asked to provide further documentation to support his department's positive recommendation. He flatly refused and admonished members of the college committee, suggesting that they did not know enough even to have an opinion on the matter. They should shut up, vote yes, and move on, which is exactly what they did.

Of course, there is much more evidence of the scientification of the university than these examples provide, and many of them are more material than ideological or procedural. There was a time when the university attempted to retain a balance in the disciplinary expertise of its deans and higher administrators, appointing one cadre from the sciences and social sciences, another from the arts and humanities. At least where I live, this sense of balance has been obliterated. Then there is the more material matter of the university's physical plant, its buildings and the condition of its classrooms and offices. Two years ago at Indiana, a new humanities building designed to provide badly needed classrooms, lecture halls, and office space was ranked at the top of the capital priority list. The dean of the College of Arts and Sciences, highly supportive of the building and confident that it would be built, convened a blue-ribbon panel to study the architectural, technological, and other requirements of such a construction, and the committee worked diligently for the better part of a year. But a few months later, after a multidisciplinary science building was already under construction, two new science buildings and a computer technology building were announced as next in line (as was, needless to say, a $55 million expansion of the athletic facilities). The humanities building, once perched at the top, had vanished from the priority list.

Deeply concerned, chairs from Humanities Departments met and were joined in their efforts by several colleagues in the sciences, one of whom offered immediate help by calling trustees to meet with us. Within a few *hours*, amazingly enough, the meeting was scheduled and when the president of the board arrived, he greeted all of the science chairs by their first names; he knew all of them well and had worked with them previously. He had to be introduced to the four humanities chairs in the room, as he had no idea who any of us were, which is hardly surprising when one looks at the composition of boards of trustees or regents at many universities. At Indiana, three of the nine are lawyers (one of whom works in medical technologies), two are doctors, one is a law student, and two are or have been corporate executives. Five are over sixty-five years old, eight of the nine are men, and more than half are political appointments made by our Republican governor (and former director in the George W. Bush administration). The alumni association conducts elections for two of the positions, and the official position of the university has been in the past that no seat should be reserved for faculty. As the trustees also approve the formation of faculty-corporate relationships, they are literally the business partners of many of our colleagues in the sciences. In 2004, for example, Indiana University received a $53 million grant from the Lilly Endowment to fund genomic and proteomic research through its Metabolomics and Cytomics Initiative. The initiative is modeled in a corporate fashion with scientists and administrators serving as executives, and shortly after its inception the University Media Service announced, "Some of the nation's top venture capitalists are being introduced today [September 7, 2005] to top life science researchers and entrepreneurs at the Indiana Future Fund Entrepreneurial Forum."[6] Thus it follows that in 2007, as the university sought an additional $80 million from the legislature to broaden this project, it would adapt the motto "Turning Breakthroughs into Business."

It comes as no surprise, then, that while most humanists are more or less strangers to the trustees, they are on a first-name basis with powerful scientists. Yet these same scientists, for the most part, are not the "enemy within"; rather, the ethos of corporate science, and the idea of the university as first and foremost a hub of new business, is. In fact, many scientists on my campus have proved to be staunch allies of the humanities, and we need to strengthen our relationships with them. One distinguished chemist even donated recently a quarter of a million dollars to the English Department to support its fellowship funds, though—like the entrepreneur-scientist he is—he both wanted my commitment to increase the growth of the funds and a kind of warrant to review our development plans, because he feared we would do nothing with the gift other than spend it.

I view this gift and its context as a kind of parable, for even scientists who want to support the humanities view us with a certain suspicion. We are like talented children admitted to expensive private universities: a treasure to cherish, on the one hand, a kid to pay heavy tuition for, on the other. Or, to put it differently, before meeting with the trustees, the chemistry and psychology chairs coached several of us about how to conduct ourselves after the trustees arrived: you know, things like, "Don't talk to them about office space for graduate student teachers because they don't like the idea that students teach"; and "Imagine you're in an elevator with the trustees going up ten stories. You have to tell them what you want them to remember in that amount of time." You get the idea: it is the movie *Wall Street,* and humanists are nervous Charlie Sheens waiting all day to wrest just one minute of time from Gordon Gecko's hectic schedule. Influential scientists on campus are already inside Gecko's office acting as fully empowered partners in the running of the university, while humanists languish in the waiting room wondering if the university will actually create the space necessary to accommodate the students they are expected to teach.

An extreme example of this issue emerged at the beginning of 2007 at the University of Alabama in Tuscaloosa with the hiring of football coach Lou Saban at the unprecedented salary of $4 million a year over an eight-year contract. To be sure, the inflated salaries of college coaches and the effects of intercollegiate athletics on the university are hardly news, as Murray Sperber has so tirelessly documented in such studies as *College Sports, Inc.: The Athletic Department vs. the University* (1990). But this case is especially egregious. In 2004, a decrepit and highly scheduled classroom building on the Tuscaloosa campus was so infested with bats that classes were suspended as some faculty feared for the well-being both of undergraduates and the instructors who taught them, many of whom were graduate student employees not covered by health insurance in their contracts. The following semester, the university retained the ICES Corporation, a facilities analysis firm from Stone Mountain, Georgia, to review buildings on campus and file a report. The report was eye-opening in recommending the gutting or substantial renovation of many buildings, even those not mired in guano. In one sense, as Stephanie Dawkins reported in *The Crimson White* (February 16, 2005), the thrust of the ICES study was not surprising: because of long deferred maintenance and the fact that "most UA buildings were built in the 1960s, the second most in the 1920s," nearly $50 million needed to be invested to restore many of the buildings into full and safe use. Add this serious problem to the fact that the state of Alabama "funds education at one of the lowest per-pupil rates of any state in the country," as a legislator observed in opposing the appointment of Saban as the highest paid football coach in

America (Johnson, *Tuscaloosa News*, January 5, 2007), and the picture of misplaced priorities becomes clear.

As might be expected, a champion of the hiring rationalized that the coach's salary does not come from the "academic side of the university"; and the president of the university in the same January 5, 2007, article in the *Tuscaloosa News* applauded the choice as well, arguing that the landing of such a high-profile coach would benefit "student recruitment and donor giving." Perhaps some "students" *do* choose schools on the basis of such a criterion, but in many instances the claim is disingenuous in the extreme. Indeed, virtually all full-time students on campuses such as Indiana and the University of Louisiana-Lafayette, as I learned on a recent trip there, pay a thirty-dollar per semester "athletics fee" that goes directly into the coffers of the Athletic Department, and they do not like it. Like some aspects of the scientification of the university, such a huge university investment in athletics places other priorities well before the quality of the education that students receive. Classroom buildings may be falling down, they may be befouled by animal excrement, and they may not exist in sufficient number in the first place—but sports are more important, and economic development across the state is more important.

And so is the accumulation of capital. As Lynne Munson, an adjunct fellow at the Center for College Affordability and Productivity reported in the fall of 2007, many American colleges and universities are among the nation's "wealthiest institutions." She reports that, as of 2007, some sixty-two schools can boast of endowments exceeding $1 billion. So while a school like the University of Michigan plans to spend $61.9 million for student financial aid for the 2007 academic year, Munson points out that this seemingly huge amount actually represents less than 1% of its endowment. Even a small liberal arts college like Grinnell holds approximately $1 million in its fund for *each* of its 1,500 students (Munson 15A). There is little question that a college's or university's investments accrue far more than 1% a year, even in years in which the stock market performs below expectations. When I managed my department's foundation accounts, the expectation was that each one would generate 5% a year, and we planned our expenditures from these accounts accordingly. Last year's bullish market on Wall Street meant that college and university endowments, on average, rose 17.7%, leading one to wonder just why tuitions also needed to rise at rates that outpaced inflation. The answer typically proffered is that university foundation accounts are constituted largely of dedicated funds that can be used only in the narrow manner stipulated by donors and the gift agreements they have brokered, but Munson argues that this is largely a cop-out, as nearly half of such agreements are in fact totally unrestricted. Meanwhile, undergraduate students borrow more to attend school, and graduate student employees are driven deeper into debt as they join the ranks of the working poor in the communities in which they live.[7]

This is the public university of the twenty-first century, but in addition to decrying such maladjusted priorities, humanists have to change as well, adapting to this environment and doing things differently. Cardinal Newman's idea of the university as a haven for noninstrumentalized learning, as a place simply to think while pursuing a generous education of "useful uselessness," has been supplanted by a vision of the university as a center for commerce and a catalyst for scientific and technological development.[8] So while humanists must do all they can to create intellectual community and to promote the life of the mind that attracted them to the profession of humane letters in the first place, they also must understand the extent to which, returning to the line spewed by Francis Ford Coppola's film producer in *The Godfather*, people in our position cannot be made to "look ridiculous." Sadly, in this changing environment, we embarrass ourselves on almost a weekly basis, or at the very least suggest to those managing the university that we may be more trouble than we are worth. In an article in the MLA's *Profession 2004*, for example, Reed Way Dasenbrock, dean at the University of New Mexico, and English professor, put it this way:

> When arts and sciences deans get together, like any group with something in common they share horror stories or war stories. [. . .] The department in first place in these stories is nearly always the foreign language department. [. . .] If there is a clear candidate for second place, it is the English department. (63)

Dasenbrock's anecdote hardly surprises me, as nearly every administrator I have ever met, after learning that I chaired an English Department, either shook her or his head in sympathy or cracked a joke about combat pay, loony bins, or dangerously elevated blood pressure. Assuming that the monsters in Dasenbrock's horror story are accurately identified, why do administrators feel this way? And how should humanities faculty respond to their depiction as institutional monsters or pariahs, bogeymen and women who haunt administrators' dreams and daily lives?

In my experiences, several factors account for the transmission of such narratives.[9] One, of course, is ideological gridlock and meltdown in Humanities Departments over what administrators typically regard as largely practical decisions. When a department invites several candidates to campus to interview for senior positions, for example, it must be able to reach consensus and, on occasion, defend its enthusiasm for the candidate who is, from a cursory reading of the *curriculum vitae*, the *least* productive scholar. That is, departments that plead the urgency of hiring

authorizations *must* be able to recruit successfully and not allow inter-
necine skirmishing to grind the process into dust. A chair must be able to
control her or his most self-important colleagues from unilaterally firing
missives—or is it missiles?—to deans (and, it should go without saying,
thoughtful deans should refuse to receive such uninvited tomes without
vetting them with the chair). And, most important, in an era of unprecedented movement for younger scholars, an era in which senior faculty
are retiring in large numbers, and younger scholars replacing them are
commanding comparatively lavish recruitment or retention packages,
departments must not neglect the faculty who remain and have remained loyal to the institution. Some, like the professor who was moonlighting at the men's clothing store, are merely going through the
motions of a now enervated career and suffer from a *réssentiment* no gesture can appease. But others are not so adrift and must be recognized for
their achievements. In my five years as a chair, the most disaffected colleagues came from the full professor rank irrespective of the facts that
many earned the department's best salaries and were beyond the anxieties produced by those annual hazing rituals known as the tenure and
promotion processes.

Yet another liability emerges in our unexamined presumption that
we still matter to the contemporary university. In his book *Shakespeare,
Einstein, and the Bottom Line* (2003), Berkeley professor of public policy
David Kirp points to both faculty apathy *and* a decisive turn away from
Newman's idea of the university as one origin of our devalued status
on campus:

> Much like Swiss watchmakers, liberal arts professors offer what is
> widely regarded as a luxury item to a shrinking clientele. Because
> these academics treat the value of their subject as self-evident, not
> something that needs to be explained anew, in recent years they
> have lost much of their audience.[10] (258–59)

Kirp affects a subtle rhetorical shift here, as blame for the sorry state of
affairs of the humanities is shifted from career-obsessed undergraduates
and their parents to faculty too arrogant to explain why Chaucer's Can-
terbury, or Swift's Dublin, or Proust's Paris are important for today's students. What he seems to advocate might be called "presentism," and
although there is no rationalizing of everything we teach in careerist or
instrumental terms, presentism is not always already dubious, nor is the
notion of defending anew the importance of what we teach. Why should
we not demonstrate the relevance of what we teach to an enhanced purchase of contemporary life and thought, as Linda Charnes does in her recent book *Hamlet's Heirs: Shakespeare and the Politics of a New Millennium*

(2006)? Or, to state the question another way, why should we automatically presume that American students in the twenty-first century will value literatures and cultures of the fourteenth, sixteenth, or eighteenth centuries? How can we defend the value of such curricula in a climate defined by scientification and commerce?

Then there is the matter often distorted by those external critics of the university from Lynne Cheney to D'Souza, Sykes, and others. For the lack of a more precise expression, let us call it "political correctness." In his essay "Affirmative Action" in *Academic Keywords*, Nelson quite compellingly argues for the centrality of women and writers of color in the canon of American literature; indeed, throughout his career, when one considers the groundbreaking work he has undertaken in introducing the poetry of the American Left to new generations of students, Nelson has made good on his claim that we should collectively respect projects that recover "the rich part of our literary heritage that has been repressed or forgotten" (44). In contrast, as Nelson discusses, internal critics of these developments, such as John M. Ellis in *Literature Lost: Social Agendas and the Corruption of the Humanities* (1997), assume that the results of so-called political correctness are "always destructive" (31). Nelson's rejoinder to Ellis's claim that "race-gender-class perspectives" necessarily rob literatures of "historical context" and instead channel the energies of scholars "into resentment" (*Literature Lost* 226) argues that just the opposite is usually the case. It is on this point, I think, that we might distinguish Ellis and D'Souza from Nelson. The former critics regard curricula as zero-sum games in which objects of study added to any subfield necessarily activate a commensurate subtraction of time-tested objects of value; thus, innovation, politically correct or not, is inherently and always "destructive." Nelson's and similar positions embrace a more catholic, radically opposite calculus by maintaining that the traditional object of study may actually be enhanced by a more capacious sense of canons and writers. Moreover, subjecting such orthodoxies to the principled critique enacted by canon study is a long-respected tradition within the humanities.

It is within this tradition of internal critique that the following also must be said: what might be called a brittle political correctness has calcified into a new orthodoxy in many departments, impairing their ability to thrive in the contemporary university. This is, quite obviously, a difficult observation to unpack, but the damage caused by this new orthodoxy can be real and resides within many disputes that department chairs are asked to adjudicate on a monthly, if not weekly, basis. Many of these, needless to say, are no more than minor provocations. Largely ideological disputes on PhD examinations—progressive colleagues disparaging the staid intellectual project of a student trained by archly conservative ones, or vice versa—or in salary reviews are now so common as to be unexceptional. Similarly insignificant, in most cases, are the growing number of interventions of a new generation of "hovering parents" connected by a wireless umbilical to their children through e-mails, fax machines, and cell phones. In those halcyon 1960s, students called home once a week on Sunday when the rates were less expensive; today, students arrive at chair's offices expecting to insert a parent into formal appeals about attendance requirements that demand that students actually appear in class, stringent paper grading, and more.

But these dilemmas, some of them inherently political, are most often easily negotiated. Chairs are not likely to agree, for example, that *Time* magazine is a radical Zionist periodical unfit for use in the composition classroom, as a Christian fundamentalist parent simultaneously complained to me and the president of the university; chairs, one hopes, will not agree that missing half of the meetings of a class, even if the absences are related to physical disability, should be excused when a syllabus clearly demands attendance. We are not yet a completely virtual university. And most chairs will not immediately capitulate to a parent who complains to a dean about an assignment in a composition class to decode a semiotically rich advertisement for condoms, whatever its political intent (although such an assignment might be reconsidered after assessing its ramifications—surely other ads might work as well). Such conflicts are inevitable disruptions of a chair's daily schedule. So too are those more serious occasions when instructors decide to sleep with their students and are reported pursuing the tryst in such exotic venues as a dormitory room in full view of a freshman roommate—or two. (In truth, this indiscretion *did* have the potential to cause serious damage to our reputation, as several administrators hastened to remind me.)

But an uncritical political correctness can cause more damage to departments at the highest levels of the university than even this last example would; after all, even wealthy and well-connected Science Departments have their share of sexual predators or just plain idiots. Two examples might suffice. Eager to hire a more diverse faculty, a laudable, increasingly important goal for all institutions, my colleagues in creative writing passed on to me the resumés of three finalists for a junior position. After reviewing them, I called the committee chair and asked about the educational background of one of the candidates. After assuring my colleague that, in fact, the issue was not clarified on the *curriculum vitae*— that it, in fact, listed no undergraduate degree and only a one-year MFA—I should have prepared myself for the response: "Does it matter?" Suffice it to say that the relative absence of much formal education *does* matter when hiring university faculty, and fortunately I was able to retrieve the materials before all but one administrator could review them and ask me later, "What the hell is going on over there?" A prolific senior writer with a long list of publications and little postsecondary education might be one thing, a notable exception, but precisely why should scientists with distinguished PhDs, prestigious postdoctoral fellowships, and other credentials respect a junior professor of English who has *never* attended a residential college or university? Why *should* the university take a department or program seriously that lobbies to hire such a candidate?

Not long after this, the phone in my office rang—another complaining parent. Nothing unusual about this, but the question she asked was: "Can you explain to me how coming to class in drag, or attending a drag queen pageant, improves student writing?" I registered my surprise, professed ignorance of the matter, and then confessed that the question required further reflection and investigation. The next day, the instructor who made the assignment came into the office and expressed her dismay over the inquiry: other instructors had made similar assignments—no big deal—and what about academic freedom, a topic about which Nelson has written so passionately and intelligently? Perhaps, the course coordinator replied, but one question remains: "How does this assignment relate to the announced goals of the class, the most important of which is to improve students' expository writing?" There was no answer. Throughout my five years as chair, several instructors and tenured faculty alike similarly constructed syllabi that scarcely reflected the catalogue description of a course or other sections of a large lecture but rather ones that suited their own, largely political, interests. In doing so, solipsistic or unthinking faculty in effect dare an administrator to challenge them and force a confrontation over the issue; absent such an exchange, students expecting a course in, say, American fiction or basic writing are instead held captive in a course on an entirely different body of literature and expected to agree with every political position an ideologue utters. And when the complaints filter out beyond the department, it begins to appear to the university that we have lost our sense of a discipline, that we are floundering in a wave of personal excess that should not be countenanced—or supported.

So what might we do? In conclusion, I suggest the following steps that might improve our chances of survival at the contemporary university:

1. We must stop destroying ourselves from within. I reviewed an English Department recently in which one disgruntled professor announced to the campus newspaper that the departmental IQ was lowered when it began to hire faculty in business and technical writing. What is gained by making such an aspersion? In this case, department meltdown was the inevitable result, which in turn prompted higher administrators to view the department as a problem that required immediate intervention and, perhaps, a leaner budget. For better or worse, the English departments at

most Research One schools include specialists in writing, and this will be the case for a very long time. Most important, literary and cultural critics need to recognize that the expertise of such colleagues can aid in forming relationships with other units on campus and also might be cultivated to forge relationships with entities external to the university that can help support all of our graduate students.

2. Humanities departments need to inaugurate development projects and cooperate fully with development officers at the college and foundation. When reviewing the aforementioned same department, one that just a decade ago was highly regarded as a top-twenty English Department, I was surprised to learn that it claimed only *one* active foundation account that funded a single doctoral student out of well over 100 candidates. In contrast, my department benefits from the funds in nearly thirty accounts, two of which are worth over $3 million that can be leveraged to broker fellowships, internships, teaching reductions for graduate students, and so on. Most humanists do not understand that departments cannot initiate budgetary negotiations with deans by stretching out an abject hand in a plea of poverty; instead, academic units must possess funds at their disposal and new ideas to broker. Most humanities departments lack the wherewithal and the will to cultivate their own independent revenue flows, thinking that alumni associations and colleges will do everything for them. They will not.

3. In the new ethos of scientification, the pursuit of external funding can only grow more aggressive. And at many research universities, internal funding allocations are predicated on an applicant's documented efforts to obtain an external grant or award. Yet in many humanities departments, far less than half of the faculty ever takes the time to identify and apply for relevant external funds, as our colleagues in the sciences do as a matter of course. We can no longer afford such complacence, as pleas of poverty ring hollowly absent the effort to seek funding on our own. To be sure, too many faculty on research leaves means a scheduling nightmare for chairs, and some deans will exploit these successes by authorizing only the hiring of adjuncts as temporary replacements, thus often recouping funds from the teaching budget for their own coffers. This growing managerial problem, like the need at the departmental level for attentive fund management, is a direct consequence of the ascendance of the sciences and corporatism at the new research university.

4. Last, and most important, faculty must monitor the activities of boards of trustees or regents and act decisively when they make mistakes—which they do with shocking regularity. Near the conclusion of the 2005–06 academic year, nearly 700 faculty on the IU-Bloomington campus sent a vote forward to the trustees demanding a review of the president they had inexplicably appointed three years earlier. The event that served as the

catalyst for the protest was the president's scuttling of a year-long committee's work to select a new chancellor for the Bloomington campus. As it
turned out, none of the three candidates recommended by the committee
was suitable to the president, one of whom was a superb dean in the College
of Arts and Sciences supported by almost all of the chairs in the college.
Needlessly humiliated by the process, this capable dean secured employment elsewhere, as did several other superior administrators and colleagues
who had strongly supported him. A similar impasse galvanized factions at
the University of Iowa in 2006, when the board of regents rejected all four
candidates for university president unanimously recommended by a hard-
working search committee (chaired, in fact, by a regent!). By November,
faculty, student leaders, and staff had taken steps toward the writing of a resolution of no confidence in the board, and the governor was poised to intervene in the dispute. In December 2006, an entirely new search was
announced, and it was uncertain if the consulting firm that had produced
only *one* candidate for the previous search would be retained. Perhaps the
$195,277 charged by the firm to identify this lone candidate could be spent
more wisely.[11]

So yes—sadly, the humanities at the contemporary university are
imperiled to say the least, and in the years since *Higher Education under
Fire* and *Manifesto of a Tenured Radical* were published, things have mu-
tated in dangerous directions for which much of our history and our
comforting fetishes have ill prepared us. We either adapt to these changing conditions—while advocating the more ecumenical goals of a generous education—or we suffer from increased marginalization and poverty.
For all of these reasons, Nelson's work on the profession and academic
politics will continue to be crucially important, as will all of our responses
to enemies within the university of the new millennium.

Notes

1. See particularly the chapter "Canon Fodder: An Evening with William
Bennett, Lynne Cheney, and Dinesh D'Souza" (*Manifesto* 97–114). Here Nelson
relates an anecdote about being accused in a campus newspaper article of despis-
ing any poetry written before 1950 and after 1972, a charge connected to the efforts of the "loony Left" to ban writers such as Shakespeare from college curricula.

2. For a discussion of Nelson's efforts to reform the MLA, see *Office Hours*
(97–116); for a discussion of the economics of textbook reform, also see *Office
Hours* (165–80). His most sustained critique of academic superstars can be found
in *Academic Keywords* (260–80).

3. In their introduction, Bérubé and Nelson note, "Our colleagues in the
sciences, drawing on a long and illustrious tradition of research with tangible
consequences, find it relatively easy to defend their teaching loads and their
costly research centers" (10).

4. See "Tenure and Promotion Goes Crazy."

5. My evidence for this claim will have to remain anecdotal. I was informed by a high-ranking university administrator that the board of trustees urged the implementation of such practices, and when I protested to the dean of faculties about a vaguely timed and poorly executed criminal background check for a new faculty member, I was referred to a trustee whose response to my inquiry was both dismissive and condescending.

6. See "BioCrossroads' Life Sciences Forum Arrives at a Time of Fast Growth in Bloomington," <http://www.Newsinfo.iu.edu/news/page/normal/2403.html>.

7. In *Office Hours*, published in 2003, Nelson and I reported that graduate student debt at Indiana had tripled in the decade of the 1990s. It has now more than quadrupled.

8. See Simon (46–56), who borrows the phrase "useful uselessness" from Young (48).

9. See my "Collegial Propositions," esp. 26–28.

10. I am indebted to my former dean, Kumble Subbaswamy, for introducing me to Kirp's book and this particular argument.

11. For information about this widely covered debacle, see Morelli, Hiatt, and Valentine. Stories about the search have run consistently in the *Iowa-City Press Citizen* and *The Daily Iowan*.

Works Cited

Bérubé, Michael, and Cary Nelson, eds. *Higher Education under Fire: Politics, Economics, and the Crisis of the Humanities.* New York: Routledge, 1995.

"BioCrossroads' life sciences forum arrives at a time of fast growth in Bloomington." Indiana University Media Relations. 22 Feb. 2008 <http://newsinfo.in.edu/news/page/normal/2403.html>.

Charnes, Linda. *Hamlet's Heirs: Shakespeare and the Politics of a New Millennium.* New York: Routledge, 2006.

Dasenbrock, Reed Way. "Toward a Common Market: Areas of Cooperation in Literary Study." *Profession 2004.* New York: MLA, 2004. 63–73.

Dawkins, Stephanie. "Maintenance to Cost UA Millions." *The Crimson White.* 16 Feb. 2005 <http://www.cw.ua.edu/news/display>.

Deleuze, Gilles. "Coldness and Cruelty." *Masochism.* Trans. Jean McNeil. New York: Zone, 1989. 9–138.

Ellis, John M. *Literature Lost: Social Agendas and the Corruption of the Humanities.* New Haven: Yale UP, 1997.

Friel, Brian. *The Enemy Within.* Dublin: Gallery, 1979.

Hiatt, Kurt. "UI's Search Firm Found Only One Finalist." *The Daily Iowan.* 30 Nov, 2006 <http://www.dailyiowan.com/home/index>.

Johnson, Bob. "Salary Raises Concern about Priorities." *Tuscaloosa News.* 5 Jan. 2007 <http://www.tuscaloosanews.com/apps/pbcs.dll>.

Kirp, David L. *Shakespeare, Einstein, and the Bottom Line.* Cambridge: Harvard UP, 2003.

Morelli, Brian. "Fallout Continues from Regents' Decision." *Iowa City Press-Citizen.* 21 Nov. 2006 <http://www.press-citizen.com/apps/pbcs.dll>.

Munson, Lynne. "College Tuitions Rise While Endowments Simply Swell." *USA Today* 18 Oct. 2007: 15A.

Nelson, Cary. *Manifesto of a Tenured Radical.* New York: New York UP, 1997.

———, ed. *Will Teach for Food: Academic Labor in Crisis.* Minneapolis: U of Minnesota P, 1997.

Nelson, Cary, and Stephen Watt. *Academic Keywords: A Devil's Dictionary for Higher Education.* New York: Routledge, 1999.

———. *Office Hours: Activism and Change in the Academy.* New York: Routledge, 2003.

———. "Tenure and Promotion Goes Crazy." *Inside Higher Education.* 11 May 2005 <http://www.insidehighereducation.com/views/2005/05/11/nelson>.

Simon, Roger I. "The University: A Place to Think?" *Beyond the Corporate University: Culture and Pedagogy in the New Millennium.* Ed. Henry A. Giroux and Kostas Myrsiades. Lanham: Rowman, 2001. 45–56.

Sperber, Murray A. *College Sports, Inc.: The Athletic Department vs. the University.* New York: Henry Holt, 1990.

Valentine, Danny. "Regents to Start Search All Over Again." *The Daily Iowan.* 8 Dec. 2006 <http://www.dailyiowan.com/home/index>.

Watt, Stephen. "Collegial Propositions." *Symploke* 13.1 (2005): 18–29.

Young, Robert. "The Idea of a Chrestomathic University." *Logomachia: The Conflict of the Faculties.* Ed. Richard Rand. Lincoln: U of Nebraska P, 1992.

☙ 10 ☙

EVERYDAY LIFE AT THE
CORPORATE UNIVERSITY

Jane Juffer

I was recently asked by the dean of the College of Liberal Arts to meet with a vice president in outreach at Penn State to see if I could help him with a proposal related to "Hispanic culture." I went, reluctantly, cognizant that this was one of those funding opportunities I could not, as director of Latina/o studies, afford to pass up. The vice president, a Latino, did his sales pitch for a six-hour seminar for Anglo managers of Hispanic employees in businesses throughout Pennsylvania. As more Hispanics move into areas of the state where little is known about Hispanic culture, companies want to hire Hispanics yet find that cultural conflicts arise—hence, the marketing appeal of the seminar. Then came the Web presentation: a series of colorful images and flashy titles advising managers that they can learn to do the following: understand and describe Hispanic cultural traits and values; gain greater awareness of their attitudes and behaviors; identify stereotypes; recognize verbal and nonverbal aspects of communication; and learn basic phrases in Spanish.

Should you not be asking the College of Business for this program, I asked? Why liberal arts?

Because it is all about culture, he responded. What non-Hispanics need to learn is culture, for, as the proposal states, culture is behind our behavior on the job, and the mixture of cultures often becomes a source of misunderstanding and conflict in the workplace. I realized I was feeling especially protective of the word "culture" and resenting the way he bandied it about to encompass such things as whether an employee makes eye contact with the boss, or what to do if employees want tortillas in the cafeteria. Yet a little voice reminded me that elsewhere I have argued that Latino cultural studies has to engage with business if it wants to have significant effects in the "real world."

But I could not stop myself. After listening politely and nodding my head for ten minutes, I let loose: "I find it very hard to imagine how one could reduce the complexity of Latino culture to a six-hour seminar. How a Chicano from California will react in the workplace is significantly different from how a recently arrived Guatemalan will. You could end up reinforcing stereotypes and papering over conflicts in the interest of profit. I would want to address the hierarchical structure of the workplace and ask if the company is taking advantage of undocumented labor."

"You mean you don't think it's possible that a program like this could do any good at all?" he asks. And I pause, feeling terribly judgmental. I don't know, I admit. But I don't think I am the person to do it, and I try to explain, less harshly, the different perspective that people in the humanities are likely to have on business. "Oh, yes," he says. We couldn't have you in there, indoctrinating the workers to overthrow the evil capitalists!" I feel like he has instantly put me in my place, a feeling that intensifies when he recounts an anecdote about how, when advising companies in Georgia, he found several that only warned its Spanish-speaking employees about dangerous equipment in English, resulting in some on-site accidents.

I begin with this anecdote because it speaks to central and potentially productive tensions in cultural studies in an age of globalization—a tension that can be found in Cary Nelson's work as well as that of other scholars who have addressed the growing corporatization of the public research university. On the one hand, we may be tempted to respond to the corporate university as we would to any institution that provides little space for alternative voices from the Left—with critique, seeking a position on the outside, or at least on the margins of, the corporation. On the other hand, we may recognize the danger of nostalgia in this notion of culture as opposition. Is there really any outside to power? Addressing this tension, I argue, requires that we recognize the historical moment and the particular space from which we are operating and devise practical, everyday strategies of engagement with the corporate university as well as with other corporations. Unless we do this, there is little hope of putting into practice the cultural studies maxim that we attend to the institutional conditions that shape our work. There is simply no way around corporatization, as Nelson and his coauthor, Stephen Watt, say in *Academic Keywords: A Devil's Dictionary for Higher Education*: "Corporatization is here to stay. It cannot be stopped, but it can be shaped and, where appropriate, resisted" (94).

What does it mean to shape and resist corporatization? In both *Academic Keywords* and *Office Hours*, Nelson and Watt offer many practical suggestions for how to do the former so the latter might be possible; in fact, their work is exemplary in its attention to academic labor conditions and the need for collective action such as unionization and increased faculty participation in university governance. In contrast, many critics of the corporate university coming from the loosely defined field of cultural studies have focused on resistance without inquiring into the mundane questions of what it means to engage in governance—how does one actually help shape the corporate university, not just engage in moral condemnation? These critics imagine themselves, in the terms of Michel de Certeau, to be the tacticians fighting the strategists. Tacticians are the weak, the marginal, the mobile, the insurgent, those who through their unpredictable movements through time and space make brief but ultimately unsuccessful incursions into the spaces of the strategists, who are the powerful, those who control capital and property. "A tactic is determined by the absence of power just as a strategy is organized by the postulation of power," says de Certeau (38).

While many critics of the corporate university lament the loss of power in the humanities that corporatization has entailed, there also is a certain relish in occupying that position of marginality, from which one can speak, seemingly, in purer moral tones. The tactician evades power, because power equals complicity with the corporation. This co-optation takes many forms, but perhaps the most dangerous for the tacticians is the possibility that the study of culture will be put to utilitarian, profit-making purposes. As Stanley Aronowitz warns, "The university is the only way some professors can pursue esoteric knowledge, that is, scholarship that has few or no practical uses. This is especially true for natural scientists and humanists whose focus is on theoretical or historical issues" (12). Unfortunately, Aronowitz says, "for the preponderance of the professoriate, research and scholarship are no longer as they once were, performed as a 'vocation' in the religious sense. In keeping with the desacralization of their profession, academics call what they do a 'job'" (12). Similarly, Masao Miyoshi laments the fact that "Culture—arts and literature—is being driven out of academia, just as in the old days, and has every sign of being reorganized into media, entertainment, and tourism—all consumer activities—that would be assigned a far more legitimate role in the emergent global economy" (18). He adds, "Although some minimal room is still left for serious inquiry and criticism in academia, such space is rapidly shrinking, and the ranks of independent eccentrics are fast thinning" (37).

The eccentric tactician shuns all realms of utility: job training, practicality, and profits. Yet this avoidance reveals the problem with de Certeau's bifurcation of the world into tacticians and strategists: in remaining a tactician in order to enact resistance, one avoids the very sites where resistance is most necessary and in fact likely to occur. Most of the critics of the corporate university have assumed a transcendent position, eager to distance themselves from outreach programs and the like, disingenuously ignoring the fact that the position from which they critique—and their salaries—are produced by those very forces of corporatization. I argue, in contrast, that to engage with everydayness is precisely to think of what we do as a job—a sometimes not very pleasant job—much as the students we are training, both graduate and undergraduate, need to consider their education as job training, sometimes in the most utilitarian sense. Cultural studies must reject the idea that the role of the public intellectual requires a distanced critique and think instead as organizers, even if that means collaboration with the strategists. Writing off the corporate world as always already co-opted means writing off thousands of students who want jobs in that corporate world. Furthermore, many of these students are first-generation college students, some of them students of color, who do not have the luxury of thinking of education is nonutilitarian terms. Who are we as academics, especially those of us with tenure, to deny our students a good salary and job security? We should rather see corporatization as an opportunity for intervention, one that cannot effectively happen from an imagined outsider position.

Collaboration *requires* strategies based on information, and this is what the work of Nelson and Watt provides, in their careful documentation of the structural conditions shaping higher education. However, I also part company with their work insofar as the authors remain partially invested in identifying themselves as tacticians for whom effective response relies on a distance from certain corporate-identified arenas. Most specifically for my purpose here I question how Nelson and Watt, even as they disdain nostalgia, continue to assume that "culture"—which, when all is said and done, really means literature—is the one true arena of dissent, an arena that needs to be saved if corporatization is to truly be resisted. In this view, culture stands in opposition to job training, a practice that should be opposed because it is empty of critique. Speaking as director of a newly forming Latina/o studies "program" at a corporate university, I show how any notion we have of culture must demonstrate its engagement with the corporate world, and that this engagement is not only a necessary part of survival for ethnic studies programs but also a possible route to intervention.

I do not pretend that negotiating the twists and turns of the corporate world is an easy task. As Nelson said after I gave a version of this article at the conference in his honor at the University of Illinois, working with the corporate university puts one on a "slippery slope"; he added that he was "more pessimistic than ever about the corporate university." His comments drew many sympathetic nods from the audience, and my response, again arguing for engagement, prompted no support. Yet I would point out that it is easy to condemn the corporation, ignoring the very site from which one speaks, especially since no one (at least at a cultural studies conference) wants to be seen as colluding with capital. It is much more difficult—and, I would argue, effective—to figure out how to work not as a transcendent intellectual masquerading as a public intellectual but rather as what Foucault called the specific intellectual: the one who has "gotten used to working, not in the modality of the 'universal,' 'exemplary,' the 'just-and-true-for-all,' but within specific sectors, at the precise points where their own conditions of life or work situate them" (126). In fact, I believe that notions of "outside" and "inside" are no longer operative, if they ever were, for there is simply no outside to globalization and corporatization. As Bill Readings argues in his *The University in Ruins*, there is no point to waxing nostalgic about the old, "truly democratic" university where culture provided narratives of legitimation, for "Change comes neither from within nor from without, but from that difficult space—neither inside nor outside—where one is. To say that we cannot redeem or rebuild the University is not to argue for powerlessness; it is to insist that academics must work without alibis, which is what the best of them have tended to do" (171).

Culture as Alibi?

Working from a precise institutional location seems to be what Nelson and Watt urge, especially in their critique of "faculty at prestige institutions" who "continue to dig for fool's gold in their imagination and predict the return of good times" (*Office Hours* 2). They argue that no amount of "cultural persuasion" about the value of humanities-based research will save the day; what is necessary is serious collective action that addresses the political and economic conditions of higher education within a global economy—conditions that are making academia, along with the rest of the world, increasingly vulnerable to exploitative, profit-driven agendas.

So what is the role of culture and cultural studies in this new world? Stepping outside of the safe confines of the imagination requires one to recognize that the long-standing legitimating discourses for the humanities no longer exist. For example, the very structure of an English department, premised as it is on the notion of a national literature, is antiquated in a world run by global corporations. In keeping with the promise not to be nostalgic, Nelson defines the New World order in his chapter "The Humanities and the Perils of Globalization":

> As the old ties that bound literature to nation are undone and high culture's traditional capacity to underwrite empire becomes irrelevant, a desperate struggle ensues to find new ways of attracting investments in literary institutions. These investments are already under way, but their nature and function have undergone sea change. Nations traditionally invested in literature

and the humanities in part because of their symbolic capital; literature could be used at once to mystify and naturalize power relations. But our cultural accounts have crashed overnight. Global commerce does not need our symbolic capital. (*Office Hours* 86)

The loss of cultural capital cannot be recovered, he adds, simply by "internationalizing literary studies and putting national literatures in dynamic dialogue either with traditions they have influenced or texts written in resistance to dominant powers, much as those comparative enterprises are worthy and desirable" (*Office Hours* 92). A world economy does not need "a historical world culture in quite the same way that a nation-state needed a national culture" (92)—a need that generated jobs for literary critics invested in the practice of illuminating how culture both undergirds and resists power.

If the nation-state no longer needs national literature, then critics of the nation-state's racist, sexist, classist, and homophobic practices also are unnecessary. They may sound a dissent in the form of noncanonical poetry, but no one will be listening—not because of hegemonic power but merely because literature no longer has any purchase—literally. As Nelson notes, it has become increasingly difficult to convince university presses to publish critical work on alternative poets and writers: "Our regret is that the rise of World Bank culture means we may not be able to do the interpretive work for the newly recovered work of the Left. Without that work much progressive literature will remain largely empty of meaning, its potential for cultural and political work severely curtailed" (91). Although this chapter does not contain a "solution" for the crisis in academic publishing, Nelson says here and elaborates elsewhere that we must work to restore the "economic and institutional infrastructure" necessary to support humanities work—an infrastructure that globalization, with its emphasis on "instrumental curriculum," has eroded (91).

Note the disjunction in Nelson's argument: On the one hand, high culture no longer matters in a global economy, and there is no going back. On the other hand, humanities funding needs to be restored so scholars can continue to do the work of the Left. It would seem that the point of collective action is to restore a traditional notion of humanities, grounded in the study of literature. But why, if the nation-state is truly dead? What interventions will more poetry anthologies make in a world that no longer cares about poetry? Of what importance is canon revision when no one cares about the canon? If we are truly *not* to use culture as an alibi, then perhaps we need to rethink our notion of what counts as culture, expanding it far beyond literature and decentering its ability to effect social change. Even as he acknowledges that the articulation of culture and nation no longer matters, Nelson seems unable to come up with a new articulation of culture, revealing the nostalgia amidst the cynicism. In urging the discipline of English to reflect on its past, for example, he says, "We need to recover our collective institutional history, department by department, and then we need to find a way to share that history and reflect on it as national disciplines" (25). Yet if these disciplines are no longer politically effective, then how much reflection is necessary, and when does reflection become nostalgia?

Perhaps there is no need for nostalgia, for there is plenty of cultural work to be done in the new global economy. It turns out that global commerce really does need our symbolic capital, as the anecdote with which I began this essay illustrates. The question is how we will respond to that need. Doing so effectively, I argue, requires us not to counterpose culture and utility, as Nelson frequently does, as in this quote: "The international effort to make job training, foreign investment, and revenue generation the primary focus of higher education, while defunding humanities based cultural critique, remains in its early stages and can be stopped" (4). Note the set of binary characteristics here: globalization is aligned with job training and profit, while the humanities are aligned with culture and critique. The critic's job as tactician is ensured. Yet the desire to "stop" the erosion of these binary oppositions may prevent effective critique. We must look rather for the *intersections* of globalization, job training, cultural production, and ethical engagement (a phrase I prefer to "critique," which assumes an outside). I turn to Latina/o studies to examine those possibilities.

Latina/o Studies and Diversity Management

The replacement of the nation-state by the transnational corporation is apparent in Latina/o studies programs across the country. While some cuts in ethnic studies programs are being made, many large universities are now funding some form of Latina/o studies precisely because they recognize the field's potential to assist in training students for the transnational labor force. This potential includes disciplines engaged in cultural studies. Hence, as I have found at Penn State, requests for funding are more likely to be granted if made under the rubric of job training than under the area's integral importance to an understanding of US history, politics, or culture. Indeed, we have reached the age when big business joins forces with universities to defend affirmative action in the interest of developing a diverse and well-trained workforce. In 2000, General Motors filed a brief to *support* the University of Michigan's affirmative action admissions practices, stating that "only a well-educated, highly diverse work force, comprised of people who have learned to work productively and creatively with individuals from a multitude of races and ethnic, religious, and cultural histories, can maintain America's global competitiveness in the increasingly diverse and interconnected world economy" (qtd. in Schmidt A46).

Job training is linked to that problematic corporate buzzword "diversity." For many humanities-based critics of the corporate world, diversity management is a strategy for managing conflict, for erasing the systemic nature of racism, sexism, and homophobia in the interest of a smoothly functioning workplace that happily recognizes "everyone is different." A diverse workforce in which everyone gets along means a more profitable company better able to gauge the desires of a diverse consumer base. Thus for universities seeking to fulfill the corporate world's need for a diverse workforce, students of color become hot commodities, for the value they themselves represent to future employers, and because they are able to "sensitize" Anglo students to cultural diversity. International students and domestic students of color are lumped together as one homogeneous Other that can be recruited to serve as authentic resources for Anglo students, as indicated in this comment from Penn State's "Framework to Foster Diversity":

> Meaningful diversity initiatives MUST encompass BOTH domestic and international groups, and success in one arena does not allow units to forgo aggressive action in the other. [. . .] In fact, one of our deficits is the limited number of international undergraduate students, which restricts opportunities of our domestic students to develop the type of cross-cultural experiences that will make them attractive to future employers.

The broadness—and emptiness—of the word "diversity" means that ethnic studies programs must struggle to contextualize and historicize—to point out, for example, that Latina/o studies is a distinct field from Latin American studies, and that many Latinas/os are not "foreigners" but rather US citizens whose families have resided here for generations.

The emphasis on job training as a discourse of mastering the Other seems especially common in states with historically small Latina/o populations, where Latina/o studies is seen primarily as a way to train non-Latina/o students to work with what the United States now recognizes as "the fastest growing minority group" in the country. Iowa, for example, recently requested that the state be declared an "Immigration Enterprise Zone," largely exempt from federal immigration quotas in order to facilitate Latina/o and other immigration to replace an aging workforce. Between 1990 and 2006, Iowa's Latina/o population grew nearly fourfold, to 114,700; Latinos still comprise only 4% of Iowa's population, but they are the state's largest racial minority. It comes as no surprise, then, that the Latina/o studies program at Iowa State advertises itself largely in terms of job training for an Anglo population. "What do you know about the fastest-growing population group in the United States?" is the opening line. Next to a photo of the program's director, the page trumpets the value of getting a degree in Latina/o studies to prepare for "today's changing job market," for, it advises, "Latinos are now the largest ethnic 'minority' in America, and that means that today's college students need to know how their life will change because of the dramatic growth of this population group." The job opportunities will require "multicultural literacy," which the program defines as "the knowledge needed to be successful in a society whose ethnic composition is rapidly changing," and which is "rapidly becoming the advantage you might need in today's competitive job market." The page enumerates likely career options, including marketing, health care, and law enforcement agencies "who want officers who can relate to Latinos and other ethnic groups."

In this fraught nexus of diversity and excellence, Latina/o students become even better qualified than Anglo students to work for transnational corporations who desire employees with a "special expertise" in Latina/o and Latin American culture. Latina/o students at Penn State say they are regularly sought out by advertising companies, for example, who recognize the market potential of what is now the largest minority in the United States. College counseling services feature career guides that advise Latina/o students to deploy their "heritage" to demonstrate their special knowledge of the Latin American consumer's "lifestyle."

Obviously, it is not just about money. Diversity training has a moral component due to its advertised ability to help people understand differences and thus make "the team" function more smoothly. In this context, humanities courses—which for some students have little relevance to future careers—become useful insofar as they teach "cross-cultural communication," whether through a literary text or learning a "foreign" language such as Spanish. The study of "culture" is posited as a useful tool in understanding "Others." The University of Wisconsin-Madison, for example, advertises the conjunction of economic and culture in its "World Affairs and the Global Economy" program with a quote by former US Secretary of State Lawrence Eagleburger: the university "is doing something very important by bringing together people who know the business world and the university's liberal arts faculty, which know a good bit about the sociology and culture of other countries."

Linking the market value of diversity to the educational imperative of moral training makes diversity initiatives seem like less of an imperative and more of an individual choice. Diversity training encourages the subject to *choose* to take multicultural courses, become more culturally sensitive, and generally welcome diversity in order to become both a better worker and a better person. As the University of Indiana's Department of Human Resources says, "diversity" is "a customer service issue." Diversity management gives the illusion of consent to a process that, in effect, restores selection to individual bodies of governance for whom diversity is most prominently a question of corporate excellence. Students are not really choosing, of course—they are being shaped by a context in which corporate desires for well-trained, culturally sensitive employees are guiding curricular choices. Completing one's diversity requirements indicates that one has completed moral training and is now ready to graduate, entering the workforce as a properly trained, moral subject.

All of this would suggest that students are merely dupes—in fact, that is what the academic critics assume. There is no discussion in either of the books on academic labor by Nelson and Watt, for example, about whether students naively accept this diversity training; the assumption is that any time culture becomes "instrumentalized" (a word that appears frequently in *Office Hours*, always in a pejorative context), it is no longer worthy of being called "culture." Culture offered in the form of diversity training is commodified culture, without a critical edge. We see this view of culture in the work, for example, of Henry Giroux, one of the most alarmist critics of the corporate university, who says, "No longer a space for political struggle, culture in the corporate model becomes an all-encompassing horizon for producing market identities, values, and practices" (9). What is to be gained, I ask, by searching for a noncommodified realm of culture? Where might that exist? Nelson is more savvy than Giroux about the imbrication of culture and economy, given his careful attention to academic labor structures and to the economic conditions of publishing. Yet he is still reluctant to fully embrace the new formations of culture under globalization—formations that require professors to work with students who want corporate jobs and to acknowledge that (high) culture is not the only realm where critique occurs.

The Contradictions of Everyday Life

An on-the-ground engagement with students reveals possibilities obscured in the division between tactician and strategist. Yes, Latino students want to capitalize on these new professional opportunities. Yet that does not mean they blindly accept the drive for profit. In fact, these students have sometimes been more astute than cultural studies scholars about how to transform job opportunities into moments of activism. For example, Penn State students in the Latino fraternity Sigma Lambda Beta and the local chapter of the National Hispanic Business Association several years ago sponsored a forum on sweatshop labor. The forum was advertised under the headline "We Are the Future" and described like this:

An open forum on how we as the future leaders of corporate America can affect the treatment of OUR PEOPLE while still maintaining efficient global trade. *Our goal is not to blame anyone for what has happened,* but to come up with ideas on how to better the current conditions in the 3rd world nations that are now being exploited. If we don't fight for their rights, who will? (emphasis in original)

The students draw on concepts familiar to a tradition of Chicano, Puerto Rican, and African American studies that grew out of the student movements of the 1960s: empowerment, community building, fighting oppression, and a connection to "third world nations." These tenets of activism are articulated to capitalism and corporate efficiency, a domain that in the 1960s would have seemed antithetical to activism. Unlike some professors, however, students are not nostalgic; they have recognized the opportunities of the current moment. They see that universities are not removed from power but rather one site of governance where influence can be exercised precisely because the corporate university is a player in the global economy and yet does not want to be seen as exploitative. In fact, in the last decade, the antisweatshop movement has recognized that the corporate university is characterized not by a lack of morals, as critics would have it, but by a proliferation of calls to be moral, and not purely in the interest of individual autonomy and profit but in the interest of the university community that has moral obligations to the global community.

This call to be moral, like diversity training, will not automatically translate into ethical action, but it does present opportunities for intervention, as Nikolas Rose recognizes in his description of the infusion of morals into political discourse under neoliberalism:

The subject is addressed as a moral individual with bonds of obligation and responsibilities for conduct that are assembled in a new way—the individual in his or her community is both self-responsible and subject to certain emotional bonds of affinity to a circumscribed "network" of other individuals. [. . .] Conduct is retrieved from a social order of determination into a new ethical perception of the individualized and autonomized actor, each of which has unique, localized and specific ties to a particular moral community. (176–77)

Diversity training addresses students as individuals responsible for their own moral conduct—it is not the responsibility of the state or the corporation to police behavior (as in affirmative action) but rather that of the autonomous actor. These actors are expected to conduct themselves in moral fashion, and this conduct is articulated to a "network" of other individuals—this network may be the university as a team (as in the chant at football games, "We are Penn State") or the corporate team. Either way, this sense of moral conduct is assumed to benefit the team in all sorts of ways, including profit—an idea that the business students have accepted but also called into question. Are third-world workers really benefiting from the diversity rhetoric? If universities really support diversity, goes the antisweatshop activist argument, then they would stop working with companies that exploit third-world labor. Because the notion of community is still operative, the space of the university presents an opportunity for social activism, and the corporate university presents students with the opportunity to press administrations to recognize the contradiction of the Nike logo and the idea of education as moral training.

The students thus demonstrate how calls for moral action that all too easily devolve into diversity rhetoric about mastery of the Other can be, with some effort, kept open, out of the recognition that, as Readings puts it, one's obligations to others are never fulfilled. The act of questioning what our responsibilities are to "our people" is an example of what Readings urges as an ethical alternative to moralisms: "There is no emancipation from our bonds to other people, since an exhaustive knowledge of the nature of those bonds is simply not available to us. It is not available because the belief that we could fully know our obligation to the Other, and hence in principle acquit that obligation, would itself be an unjust and unethical refusal to accept our responsibility" (189).

What is missing from Nelson and Watt's work is a recognition of the contradictions and complexities of everyday life and their generative, if not always reconcilable, possibilities. I provide another example in the form of Viviana, a student in my "Introduction to Latina/o Studies" class in the fall of 2006. Born and raised in Puerto Rico and recently arrived in Pennsylvania, Viviana was an articulate critic of US colonization of the island. She was a major in civil engineering and an officer of the local chapter of the Society of Hispanic Professional Engineers. She helped organize a workshop in November called "Diversity within the Corporate World: Managing across Cultures," which brought in management guru William Cruz to teach students how to "develop cross-cultural management and communication skills, recognize differences in values across cultures, distinguish the six patterns of nonverbal communication, and recognize incorrect ways to deal with these differences." According to the flyer "Are You Ready for Corporate America??" that Viviana handed out in class, endorsements such as "I felt as an Anglo male, I was not on trial for my beliefs, only that we need to be aware of differences and try to work for compromise and understanding," were included. The flyer illustrates the criticism of diversity management as a discourse that glosses over conflict in the interest of corporate profit. Viviana did not hesitate to organize this workshop to help Latina/o students get jobs, even as she critiqued the effects of US corporations in Puerto Rico. Similarly, at a recent meeting of leaders of Latina/o student groups on campus (November 2007), the National Hispanic Business Association leader talked about the group's upcoming event, the Dress for Success Fashion Show, in which students model clothes considered appropriate by job interviewers. In the next breath, the group agreed to participate in a spring forum on connections between black Puerto Ricans and African Americans on campus.

We must rearticulate the general notion of critique upon which cultural studies scholars have based their analysis of the corporate university. In their analysis, culture is the realm that will free us from the false consciousness produced by commodification. Thus is affirmed the role of the cultural critic (especially the literary critic) as the one who teaches true (oppositional) culture. Ironically, however, this emphasis on freedom coincides with the diversity management discourse. Under diversity management, the subject is free to enter the global economy as a person who has fulfilled his or her moral obligations by learning about other cultures. For cultural critics, the subject is free when he or she refuses to enter the global economy because doing so indicates the rejection of the corporation's pretense at moral obligations. While the diversity discourse may seem more politically dangerous because it masquerades as a moral position that may be used to elide power, the cultural critique is equally dangerous insofar as it also refuses to engage with power. Ignoring the fact that students must get jobs in the global economy—or even worse, criticizing the desire for jobs as crassly utilitarian—leaves no way to engage with students such as Viviana who want—and need—these jobs. The objective should not be to reject the connections between Latina/o studies and job training but rather to articulate those connections so as to increase the very possibility of better jobs, and, in the meantime, to demonstrate to students (or let them demonstrate to us) that cultural studies is useful for thinking about work conditions.

It is possible, for example, to examine how diversity functions across commodified sites precisely to engage culture at those sites, which are inevitably part of the marketplace, such as bookstores, the music industry, and the telecommunications industry. In so doing, we explore the important question of what it might mean to work at one of those sites. The challenge is to truly think in interdisciplinary terms (another maxim of cultural studies), which requires one to think about the ethical possibilities *in the relationship between* the humanities, business, education, engineering, information sciences, health services, and other fields. Although Nelson calls for "solidarity" among faculty rather than "entrepreneurial individualism" (*Office Hours* 37), it is clear that arts and humanities scholars will be the vanguard: "If the system loses much of its arts and humanities research capacity, the intellectual caliber of the relevant disciplines will rapidly decline. That means their critical purchase on contemporary culture will diminish, a development some will welcome" (2). In contrast, I argue that the current moment offers the arts and humanities the opportunity to investigate how other disciplines outside the humanities are in fact interested in ethics. It behooves us to pursue truly interdisciplinary exchanges—or risk being rendered, again, ineffectual and irrelevant.

Institutional Pragmatism

As director of Latina/o studies, I have been quite brutally confronted by the crisis in funding for the humanities of which Nelson and Watt write in both *Academic Keywords* and *Office Hours*. We have struggled to put together an undergraduate minor with only a handful of faculty, no staff, and no physical space. Our Latina/o studies committee has proposed seven new courses to constitute the minor in the last two years, and although we now have the courses on the books and the student demand, we do not always have the people to teach them. As a stopgap measure, in the spring of 2006 I began searching for money to bring in a qualified professor from the Penn State Altoona campus to University Park for the fall semester to teach our new course "Latina Feminisms." I secured $2,750 from the dean of liberal arts and the same amount from the Rock Ethics Institute, but we were still $2,500 short of the $8,000 needed to compensate Altoona. I wrote to the associate dean of liberal arts, pleading for the money, and received this e-mail response:

> Jane, it looks like budgets are very tight everywhere. Including here. Unless there are other sources, you'll have to ask Altoona to contribute by accepting less money than (usual for course releases), or find the $$$ elsewhere somehow. [. . .] Sorry I can't fix it.

A quick tour of campus made it clear budgets are not actually tight everywhere. Spanning the major street in town is the shiny new multimillion dollar facility of the Information Science and Technology program. A mile away is the seemingly ever-expanding, multimillion-dollar Beaver Stadium—a structure that on any football game day becomes the third largest city in Pennsylvania. I composed a letter to football coach Joe Paterno, thinking he might contribute just $2,500 of his football budget or his Nike endorsement money to Latina/o studies. In the meantime, however, our request for funds to the Office of the Vice Provost for Educational Equity was granted, and the professor was able to offer the course.

The fact that we had to scramble for $8,000 to pay a tenured professor so that we could proceed with the minor illustrates the urgency of what Nelson and Watt identify as the gradual defunding of the humanities. It is indeed tempting to retreat, in condemnation, of these seemingly corporate values. Yet where does that leave us? Certainly with limited appeal to students, perhaps especially Latina/o students, since the majority of them do not major in the humanities. Of the thirty students in my fall 2006 introductory class, only three majored in the liberal arts (none in English), with the others coming from a wide range of areas, including education, communications, international policy, forensics, accounting, hotel management, health and human development, and business. In all of these disciplines, "culture" is a relevant, albeit slippery, term, and they are open (as was the outreach manager with whom I began this piece) to discussion about its uses. To say culture is useful is not to give up on critical thought—in fact, it requires us to be especially "thoughtful" about our practices rather than relying on the isolated and often antiseptic practice of textual criticism. "Institutional pragmatism," as Ien Ang calls it, requires us to "take the notion of 'utility' out of the sphere of marginality and seriously address it as we continue to think through our own politics of knowledge."

How might we apply our research so as not to abdicate a thoughtful, ethical position? I have already begun to answer this question: engage on the ground with students and recognize that they are capable of complex positions that generate unexpected possibilities. Also, pursue the cultural studies mandate to consider culture in its material forms—such as publishing and distribution—which will bring us into the realm of job training. There is nothing inherently special or enlightening about culture, in other words. In studying the immigration debates in Congress, students in my Latina/o studies classes are able to make an argument for the legalization of undocumented immigrants based on the history of US intervention in Latin America—without ever having read a novel, poem, or other "cultural" text. This argument overlaps in some ways—though not in others—with business support for legalization based on corporate needs for labor. How does one convince these business leaders, then, that all workers deserve to be treated fairly and equally?

I thus arrive at my next suggestion. Crossing fields and disciplines, we may identify common areas of struggle, such as the ethical treatment of workers, out of which to carve ethical spaces. Consider another example: a recurrent issue in Latina/o studies is which term to use, Latina/o or Hispanic? Many would argue that the former has more of a grassroots origin, whereas the latter is a category created by the US government to homogenize and facilitate management of diverse populations. Yet in some areas of the country, "Hispanic" is the preferred term and has no negative connotation. And "Latina/o" itself can be a homogenizing term, even with the slash to encompass women and men. It offers cohesiveness and solidarity, but it also erases differences in the country of ancestral origin. Some prefer identifying by Chicana/o, Puerto Rican, Dominican, and so on, yet that carries the risk of dividing Latinas/os and retaining national affiliations that are no longer relevant or desired by some. These issues are not particular to the realms of "noncommodified" culture, however. They are just as important in advertising and marketing, television and film, political campaigns, organizing around health issues, and other areas. The questions raised by academics and activists regarding the limits and advantages of identifying as Latina/o are not that different from those raised by demographers, politicians, and marketing executives. In my "Introduction to Latina/o Studies" class, we approached the question of identity from a variety of disciplinary perspectives without trying to reconcile them or oppose them. We had a lively discussion, for example, about the reality show *Survivor*'s strategy of dividing competitors into teams based on race, with "Latino" being one of the racial groups. Is Latino a race, we asked? Is it a strategy to draw viewers? Could it increase solidarity among Latinos? Does it mean television executives are becoming more cognizant of the power of Latino viewers? Is that all based on spending potential?

Institutional pragmatism does not require the kind of consensus on which easy diversity management relies. Our Latina/o studies initiative recently received a small grant from the Institute for Arts and Humanities at Penn State to hold a symposium on the issue of new Latina/o communities in Pennsylvania. As Latino populations grow and disperse—in Pennsylvania and throughout the country—they are sometimes welcomed as a critical labor force and sometimes encounter racism and xenophobia. The town of Hazleton, Pennsylvania, for example, made national headlines in the summer of 2006 when it passed a draconian anti-immigrant ordinance that fines employers and landlords of undocumented immigrants and requires that all city documents be printed in English only; the ordinance was later ruled unconstitutional, but it "inspired" other towns in Pennsylvania and elsewhere throughout the country to pass similar laws, including Altoona, which is just forty miles down the road from State College.

Ironically, the Latino influx into Hazleton over the last decade has revitalized the town's stagnant economy; that resurgence is now being threatened as Latinas/os, both documented and undocumented, move given loss of business. Our symposium will bring together different players in these developments—Anglo town officials, Latino activists and residents, civil liberties attorneys, academics, students—to discuss these local issues within the broader national and global contexts that shape them. The goal is to bring to non-Latino residents of Pennsylvania a greater understanding of Latina/o history, culture, politics, language, and religion so there is less of a tendency to react sympathetically to inevitable moments of xenophobic backlash. The goal also is to restore jobs and business vitality to the community, and undoubtedly many of those jobs are caught up in the global economy that so many cultural critics disdain. How useful would a symposium be that did not acknowledge that cultural work is effective (not inherently co-opted) when it engages with utilitarian issues such as job training?

This essay is dedicated to all the students in my Latina/o studies classes at Pennsylvania State; thanks for making the struggle worthwhile.

Works Cited

Ang, Ien. "Who Needs Cultural Research?" Working paper. Consortium of Humanities Centers and Institutes. U of Western Sydney, 2001. 22 Feb. 2008 <http://chcinetworking.org/angfv.html>.

Aronowitz, Stanley. *The Knowledge Factory: Dismantling the Corporate University and Creating True Higher Learning.* Boston: Beacon, 2000.

De Certeau, Michel. *The Practice of Everyday Life.* Berkeley: U of California P, 1984.

Foucault, Michel. "Truth and Power." *Power/Knowledge: Selected Interviews and Other Writings, 1972–1977.* Ed. Colin Gordon. New York: New Press, 1980. 109–33.

Giroux, Henry. *Corporate Culture and the Attack on Higher Education and Public Schooling.* Bloomington: Phi Delta Kappa Educational Foundation, 1999.

Miyoshi, Masao. "Ivory Tower in Escrow." *boundary 2* 27.1 (1999): 7–50.

Nelson, Cary, and Stephen Watt. *Academic Keywords: A Devil's Dictionary for Higher Education.* New York and London: Routledge, 1999.

———. *Office Hours: Activism and Change in the Academy.* New York and London: Routledge, 2004.

Readings, Bill. *The University in Ruins.* Cambridge: Harvard UP, 1996.

Rose, Nikolas. *Powers of Freedom: Reframing Political Thought.* Cambridge: Cambridge UP, 1999.

Schmidt, Peter. "General Motors Joins U. of Michigan's Defense of Affirmative Action in Admissions." *The Chronicle of Higher Education,* 28 July 2000: A46.

∽ 11 ∽

WHO'S AFRAID OF CULTURAL STUDIES?

Lisa Duggan

Cary Nelson was not my teacher, nor am I a colleague in his field of political poetry. He influenced me most as a kind of impressario of US cultural studies during the 1980s and 1990s. Along with Paula Treichler, Peter Garrett, and others, Nelson changed my intellectual and political life from 1989 to 1991, in what seemed to me the unlikely place of Urbana, Illinois.

When I arrived at the Unit for Criticism and Interpretive Theory at the University of Illinois at Urbana-Champaign in the summer of 1990, I had no idea what was waiting for me. I vaguely knew that the Unit was a center for something being called "cultural studies," but as an "almost" PhD in social history, I did not have a clear grasp of what that meant. I was thirty-six years old in 1990, having taken my sweet time finally finishing the PhD degree that led me to the postdoctoral fellowship at the Unit. I had only had my head expanded and my life transformed once before; I did not know that was about to happen again.

In 1969, when I was fifteen and a sophomore in high school, I was selected by my public high school principal to participate in a program designed by the Junior League in Richmond, Virginia—a peer counseling program for teenagers with drug problems. My principal and the Junior League ladies saw me as part of the "solution," but they had no real understanding of the "problem." Fortunately for me and unfortunately for them, they brought in a team from the Rubicon drug rehabilitation facility in Richmond to train us, sixteen white, working-class teenagers from Richmond's largely segregated public high schools (the Junior League had excluded the black high schools, where they believed the "problem" was located rather than the "solution").

The Rubicon facilitators, the brothers Barry and Alan Barkan, appeared to me as truly exotic creatures—Jewish Maoists from New York City! They did not teach us much about drug use, but they did not preach their political views either. They used classic community organizing techniques to introduce us to the workings of the city in which we lived—by taking us to court, to the hospitals, the jails, the neighborhoods, and the full range of schools. It was 1969, and we were all radicalized. The Junior League ultimately fired Rubicon's Barkan brothers for "undermining family values." And life went on from there.

But my life was never the same afterward. I had learned how to connect the modes of daily life to the larger political economy of the city, nation and globe, and I had learned that numb depression could be converted to rage, to understanding, and to action in a larger world.

In 1990, when Unit director Peter Garrett brought me in as their postdoc, my world expanded at a dizzying pace yet again. The heyday of cultural studies there was just peaking—the big conference that generated the huge Routledge *Cultural Studies* anthology (1991) had taken place the year before; the impresarios who made it all happen were Nelson, Treichler, and Lawrence Grossberg.

So what was so special about cultural studies? In 2007, it isn't a clear designation for a specifiable body of work, and it is now as often used to denigrate scholarship as to praise it. In the 1980s and 1990s, as the Birmingham School's work had begun to circulate more widely in the United States, the framework for "cultural studies" derived from the British school initially prevailed. As I discovered it at the Unit in Urbana, where for me Nelson and Treichler were central figures, cultural studies had produced a collective life that was politically engaged, interdisciplinary, deeply serious, and yet ridiculously fun. To me, then, it represented life lived whole as a radical intellectual activist—a way of being I had first encountered when I met the Barkan brothers. Nelson provided a particularly riveting example of the kind of intellectual and political vigor—opinionated, obstreperous, direct—that joined scholarship, institutional politics, and everyday activism in ways that make the complacent uncomfortable. Yet Cary was not self-marginalizing; he remained at the center of university life in multiple arenas, despite his refusal to conform to the rules of proper decorum in the university. He, along with Treichler, Garrett, Sonya Michel, Amanda Anderson, Alan Hance, Michael Bérubé, Janet Lyon, Carol Neely, and many others, provided a context at the university that did not merely tolerate my presence as a token queer scholar but immediately placed new queer theories and politics at the center of the work and concerns of the Unit. At that time I did not realize how rare and fragile such contexts can be.

Cultural studies was the central context for my experience in Urbana-Champaign, but feminism was in a state of turmoil and transformation there in 1990 as well. After years of rallying around the bullhorn of Andrea Dworkin and antipornography feminists, many of the local and university feminists were fed up and searching for new directions. By 1990, a critical mass of students, faculty, and local activists began to displace the centrality of "cultural" feminism. When I arrived, Madonna was the posted "Organic Intellectual of the Month." The students in my women's studies class were among the organizers of an intervention into the antiporn politics of the local Take Back the Night march—they joined in as Sluts against Rape. And at the Unit's faculty seminar, the junior women hatched a plan to intervene in the domination of the agenda and discussions by the senior male faculty. We met before seminar time to go over points we wanted to make. We agreed not to make eye contact with the men when they were speaking, and to refer to each other's points by speaker's name whenever we spoke. We did not sit together, and we did not reveal our plot. We were highly successful in disconcerting the men, including Cary (who, nonetheless, stuck with us; some other senior men dropped out), and redirecting discussions. Feminism in Urbana took many forms.

My teaching at the University of Illinois, while a Unit postdoc, and then as visiting women's studies faculty in the fall of 1991, was the high point of my life as a pedagogue to date. I have a framed 8 × 10 studio portrait of my queer theory class on my desk at home, and I am still in touch with most of the people in it. We read all the new work in queer studies then emerging, in a state of voracious excitement. At the end of the semester, they gave me a pair of leather chaps that I am wearing in the class portrait. And after class, faculty and students hung out, brainstormed new Organic Intellectuals for the coming months, took joy rides out to the Imported Swine Research Area, and drank margaritas at the Fiesta Café. Life and learning overlapped. My own intellectual horizons expanded exponentially, and I had more fun than I thought possible in a university context.

But what were the conditions that made this kind of experience possible? Nelson played a central role in bringing Birmingham School cultural studies to Urbana-Champaign, and to the United States in general. This cultural studies project brought Left class politics together with cultural politics, and with what was called "identity politics" in the United States. This moment of intense engagement with questions of race, class, gender, sexuality, and nation produced productive cross-fertilizations from different locations for scholarship. In addition, this cultural studies project addressed multiple audiences, within and outside the university, bringing together scholarship and activism in new formations (as was also happening within ACT UP during those same years). The battle over democracy was engaged in a wide range of publications, public institutions, and spaces, and the lines between "economics" and "culture" and "scholarship" and "activism" blurred significantly, even if they did not entirely dissolve. As Nelson and his coeditors explained in the introduction to *Cultural Studies*,

> [. . .] cultural studies in fact has no distinct methodology, no unique statistical, ethnomethodological or texual analysis to

call its own. Its methodology, ambiguous from the beginning, could best be seen as a bricolage. Its choice of practice, that is, is pragmatic, strategic, and self-reflective. At Birmingham, a central goal was "to enable people to understand what [was] going on, and especially to provide ways of thinking, strategies for survival, and resources for resistance." (Grossberg, Nelson, and Treichler 2; quoting Hall 22)

This focus on intellectual, activist projects engaged through pragmatic and strategic appropriations of methods and theory spoke directly to my own desire to write from within the social movements that formed and energized me (economic justice, feminist and queer politics). This mode of engagement continued to shape conferences and projects coming out of the University of Illinois and the Unit for Criticism and Interpretive Theory—all brought into being in large part through the efforts of Cary Nelson (see, for instance, Bérubé and Nelson).

The contrast of that moment, 1990 in Urbana-Champaign, with the present moment in the university and the polity is grim. As the US state has moved toward the Right since then, scholarship and politics have tended to fracture and retrench into less expansive and innovative forms. In scholarship, the promiscuous interplay of race, class, gender, sexuality, and nation has been largely, but unevenly, banished from the center of Left projects—labor studies, urban studies, the analysis of corporate globalization—and repositioned at various margins, in transnational feminist and queer scholarship particularly. Though my own work continues the kind of cultural studies practices I learned at the Unit for Criticism (*The Twilight of Equality* focuses on the cultural politics of neoliberalism, with attention to race, gender, and sexuality at its center), I find it increasingly difficult to locate energizing contexts for this kind of work.[1]

At New York University, where I am currently professor of gender and sexuality studies and director of American studies, I am a member of the new Department of Social and Cultural Analysis. This department includes previously autonomous interdisciplinary programs—gender and sexuality studies, American studies, Africana studies, Asian Pacific American studies, metropolitan studies—and one start-up, Latino/a studies. This new conglomeration could be a way forward for democratic Left scholarship, allowing for innovative collaborations and new formations, like the cultural studies of old. Or, this new departmental formation might center forms of urban studies and American studies that effectively marginalize ethnic studies and gender/queer studies as the scholarship of "identity politics" that must be tolerated, though patronized. It could still go either way, but I am not optimistic. A few weeks ago an undergraduate major in metropolitan studies came to me to say that his professor focused on "political economy" but told him he should come to me to talk about "identity politics." I felt myself cast out from the center, as if political economy were not the core of my own work. Somehow, although my recent book analyzes the impact of neoliberalism during the 1990s, my inclusion of feminist and queer perspectives is too often now understood as the scholarship of "identity politics"—a project that can be cordoned off from the center by identifying it solely as "queer studies," therefore separate from, or even irrelevant to, political economy.

One widely circulating paradigm that reinforces the move to remarginalization is the recognition versus distribution divide, derived from the work of Charles Taylor, and most widely circulated by feminist philosopher Nancy Fraser (Taylor; Fraser *Justice*; Fraser "Heterosexism"; see also Butler). Though the differentiation between the politics of "recognition" and "distribution" is presented, in Fraser's work especially, as an analytic distinction and not a hierarchy, its actual deployment is nearly always invidious and pernicious—ultimately evaluating distribution as more important than mere recognition. For instance, Fraser places class and gender politics toward the distribution end of the spectrum, with race and sexuality more toward the recognition end. All might be considered varying mixtures of both distribution and recognition. In order to achieve the placements she posits, Fraser (who as a socialist feminist has always concerned herself more centrally with class and gender than with race or sexuality) must strip the politics of race and sexuality of their political economic analyses. She references the most conservative versions of "equality" politics rather than the long history of political economic analyses of racial formations and sexual arrangements, embedded in histories of imperialism and colonialism, and in the regulation of marriage and the household. In the end, her efforts to assert the importance of the politics of race and sexuality, in the absence of their political economic implications, come off as condescending.

In the arena of national electoral politics, the distinction between "economic" and "cultural" politics also has reappeared with a vengeance, and with no effort to deny a hierarchy the greater relative importance of economic issues is assumed. The best-known example of the current forwarding of this distinction is Thomas Frank's *What's the Matter with Kansas?* (2004). For instance, Frank points out that belonging to a union changes the way workers look at politics—even white male union members voted more for Democrats than Republicans in the 2000 elections. He comments, "Here *values* matter almost least of all, while the economy, health care and education are of paramount importance" (246, emphasis added). But do not unions address cultural values by creating different ways of conceiving of class identity and interests? Is not an emphasis on health and education as much conditioned by cultural values as a stress on gay rights or abortion? Frank's deployment of the distinction between economics and culture is a method for producing a hierarchy of issues, centering some and marginalizing others, not according to some universal and neutral categorization but according to his own values and notions of significance.

Any number of scholars have critiqued the economy/culture distinction, especially through an emphasis on the history of the "household"—particularly scholars of the "household" and of colonialism. In national and global politics, such distinctions have been soundly critiqued for decades as well (see, for example, Moraga and Anzaldua). At the present historical moment, the hierarchy of economics over culture is a dominant mode of thinking and organizing.

Yet the world is full of political survivors who maintain their commitments to more holistic forms of political thought and practice. I recently Googled the Barkan brothers, trying to find out what has become of them since 1970. I found Barry Barkan, currently busy as an activist for humane elder care, running a center in California, where he no doubt organizes the seniors as he did the high schoolers more than thirty years ago. And the last time I saw Nelson, before this conference, he was being arrested in a protest against New York University's efforts to break our graduate student union. As the newly elected president of the AAUP, his presence meant a lot to the embattled pro-union forces.

I wonder now, as we move further into a twenty-first century of neoliberal policy dominance and renewed violent US imperialism, whether we might go Back to the Future, and reinvent Nelson's brand of cultural studies for the world we now must face. I cannot think of a better way of rethinking our intellectual and political world now.

Note

1. Though often identified as a scholar of "queer studies," my work would appropriately be classified as American studies scholarship focusing on the history of capitalism. Within the context of the kind of cultural studies practiced at the Unit for Criticism in the late 1980s and early 1990s, the designation "queer studies" did not carry with it the assumption of "narrowness" that this designation now does. Consequently, I now resist being classified as "merely" a queer studies scholar.

Works Cited

Bérubé, Michael, and Cary Nelson, eds. *Higher Education Under Fire: Politics, Economics, and the Crisis of the Humanities.* New York: Routledge, 1994.

Butler, Judith. "Merely Cultural." *Social Text* 52–53 (1997): 265–77.

Duggan, Lisa. *The Twilight of Equality? Neoliberalism, Cultural Politics, and the Attack on Democracy*. Boston: Beacon, 2003.

Frank, Thomas. *What's the Matter with Kansas? How Conservatives Won the Heart of America*. New York: Metropolitan, 2004.

Fraser, Nancy. "Heterosexism, Misrecognition, and Capitalism." *Social Text* 52–53 (1997): 279–89.

———. *Justice Interruptus: Critical Reflections on the "Postsocialist" Condition*. New York: Routledge, 1997.

Grossberg, Lawrence, Cary Nelson, and Paula Treichler, eds. *Cultural Studies*. New York: Routledge, 1991.

Hall, Stuart. "The Emergence of Cultural Studies and the Crisis of the Humanities." *October* 53 (1990): 11–90.

Moraga, Cherie, and Gloria Anzaldua, eds. *This Bridge Called My Back: Writings from Radical Women of Color*. New York: Kitchen Table, 1983.

Taylor, Charles. *Multiculturalism and the Politics of Recognition: An Essay*. Ed. Amy Gutmann. Princeton: Princeton UP, 1992.

⌁ 12 ⌁

THE RISE OF THE GLOBAL UNIVERSITY

Andrew Ross

I feel obliged to begin this essay with a Cary Nelson anecdote. There is a long list from which to choose, and chances are most of them would get me, and Cary, for that matter, into big trouble if I submitted them to the public page. So this one is about our first meeting—innocuous on the face of it, but prescient in retrospect.

Just after arriving in Urbana to attend the 1983 conference on Marxism and Interpretation of Culture that Cary co-organized, Constance Penley and I ran into him on campus. He was altogether flustered, and with good reason, as it happened. He had just learned that University of Illinois janitors were refusing to clean any of the toilets used by the Marxists who had gathered to diagnose the malaise of late capitalism. One can only imagine the frustration of a conference organizer. "What are you going to do?" we asked Cary in a suitably sympathetic tone, and we waited as he pondered his answer. No doubt some readers of this essay are familiar with this Nelsonian pause. When Cary is processing a response like this, I often have visualized a tug of war in his brain between two departmental authorities. One is called the Department of Mordant Wit, Dedicated to Putting to the Sword all Pieties Known to Humankind. The other is called the Department of Sobriety, Committed to Preserving, in Grudging Good Order, Those Qualities We Associate with Organized Society. As these two angels struggle over the outcome, Cary's eyes are scrutinizing his interlocutor's face for clues to the question: Just how far can I go with this person?

On this occasion I do not recall the exact wording of his response, but I do remember that the more prudent, or Apollonian, department prevailed. On reflection, I realize this was not simply due to the fact that we were still Nelson novitiates, and since Penley and I had come to reside in Urbana, that there would be ample time later to break us in more fully. It also was because we were talking about a highly sensitive labor issue, one of the few subject areas that would come close to being off-limits for the purposes of Cary's pungent wit.

This first encounter seems prescient in light of the time Nelson has devoted in the latter part of his illustrious career to seeing the academic profession from the standpoint of workplace relations. If there does exist an academic labor movement in the United States (a question that is still subject to debate), then it is largely due to his efforts in publishing landmark books such as *Will Teach for Food*, *Manifesto of a Tenured Radical*, and (with Stephen Watt) *Academic Keywords* and *Office Hours*, along with the spate of articles and addresses accompanying these books. We owe a great deal to the formidable combo of his fearless personality and his eye for hypocrisy and corruption on the part of academic employers and their faculty enablers. Without these personal assets, the "academic mystique" we grew up with would not have been debunked with the same militant finality, nor would we have had his lengthy list of constructive theses for reforming the academic institutions and professional practices that have so sorely fallen under the sway of neoliberal restructuring. In these endeavors, Nelson has functioned not unlike I. F. Stone, as the kind of singular voice, aware of its place in time, that has caught the gist of speaking truth to power.

In recent years, his rise to the presidency of the AAUP has been driven by an equally sharp appetite for transforming the culture of the nation's leading organization of academics. With its membership in steady decline since the 1970s, and its general influence on the profession waning, the AAUP had, for some time, been resting on its laurels earned some decades before. Its presidency was a natural office to seek for the reformer in Nelson. The storied pedigree it had acquired in the course of securing and defending basic academic rights no doubt appealed to his own admiration and respect for the historical heyday of progressive institutions (in his own scholarship, the cultural Left of the 1930s is a lodestone). But he also envisaged a renaissance for the organization, if only it could be reanimated by the energies set in motion by the core constituents of the new academic labor movement—part timers and graduate teaching assistants. After all, for the majority of the heavily casualized workforce, the academic freedoms and securities that have traditionally been the raison d'etre of the AAUP are a remote concern, if they are not goals already out of reach.

In order to win a new relevance among contingent faculty and the newest members of the profession, the AAUP might have to confront its "CIO moment," when the privileges of those in the tenure stream (now a minority) can no longer be defended at the expense of those who share their workplace but are excluded from stakeholding rights within it. The analogy with the CIO's challenge to an AFL establishment that only serviced the labor aristocracy does not stand up all that well, and Nelson would be among the first to pick it apart. Nor does the AAUP exactly share the contemporary plight of labor unions with declining membership (membership of its own collective bargaining units has remained steady, or has increased). Nonetheless, a leading edge of Nelson's agenda at the AAUP has been to embrace the concerns of the excluded, in the same spirit as more forward-looking unions have declared their intent to "organize the unorganized."

Whether the outcome of this attention will bear fruit, in either sector, remains to be seen. But it is largely due to Nelson that we are able to speak about the reform of an organization such as the AAUP in the same breath as the internal turmoil of the larger labor movement. In this respect, his efforts (far from over) have made it possible to adopt this interpretation, and to make it resonate among academics who otherwise view their workplace as much too exceptional to bear comparison with those in other occupational sectors.

Yet the landscape of academic labor surveyed by Nelson, and by those of us who are his fellow travelers, has remained, for the most part, national in scope.[1] The time has surely come to expand the orbit of our attention beyond national boundaries to consider the impact on academic labor that is being wrought by patterns of globalization and, correspondingly, by the aspirations of academic institutions to go global. As universities are increasingly exposed to the rough justice of the market, we have seen how their institutional life is distinguished more by the rate of change than by the observance of custom and tradition. Few examples illustrate this better than the rush, in recent years, to establish overseas programs and branch campuses. Since 9/11, the pace of offshoring has surged and is being pursued across the entire spectrum of institutions that populate the higher education landscape—from the ballooning for-profit sectors and online diploma mills to land-grant universities and the most elite, ivied colleges. No single organization has attained the operational status of a global university, after the model of the global corporation, but it is only a matter of time before we see the current infants of that species take their first, unaided steps.

The World Trade Organization (WTO) has been pushing trade services liberalization for several years, of which higher educational services are a highly prized component, with an estimated global market of between $40 and $50 billion (not much less than the market for financial services).[2] Opponents of liberalization argue that higher education cannot and should not be subject to the kind of free-trade agreements that have been applied to commercial goods and other services in the global economy. After all, WTO agreements would guarantee foreign service providers the same rights that apply to domestic providers within any national education system while compromising the sovereignty of national regulatory efforts. Yet the evidence shows that just as corporations did not wait for the WTO to conclude its ministerial rounds before moving their operations offshore, the lack of any international accords has not stopped universities in the leading Anglophone countries from establishing their names and services in a broad range of overseas locations. The formidable projected growth in student enrollment internationally, combined with the expansion of technological capacity and the consolidation of English as a lingua franca, has resulted in a bonanza-style environment for investors in offshore education.

As with any other commodity good or service that is allowed to roam across borders, there also has been much hand-wringing about the potential lack of quality assurance. Critics argue that the caliber of education will surely be jeopardized if the global market for it is deregulated. Much less has been said in this debate about the impact on the working conditions of academics, or on the ethical profile and aspirational identity of institutions. How will globalization affect the security and integrity of livelihoods that are closely tied to liberal educational ideals such as meritocratic access, face-to-face learning, and the disinterested pursuit of knowledge? Will these ideals (and the job base built around them) wither away entirely in the entrepreneurial race to compete for a global market share, or will they survive only in one corner of the market—as the elite preserve of those who are able to pay top dollar for such handcraft attention? This essay profiles some basic preconditions for the rise of the global university, a phenomenon that, for all of its mercurial growth, is not well documented, let alone widely understood.

Lessons from the China Field

While researching my last book, *Fast Boat to China,* I conducted a year of fieldwork in several Yangtze River Delta cities. Once I had wangled a membership in the American Chamber of Commerce in Shanghai, I spent a lot of time attending meetings and functions of that organization. It proved to be a wonderful research site to gather data about the offshore business climate, since almost every roving speculator on the planet eventually shows up there, expecting to make a fast buck. One of the best vantage points to watch this tawdry spectacle was at the chamber's social mixers, usually hosted in one of the city's toniest nightspots, and crafted to ensure a frenzy of networking, promotional pitching, and deal making. Though I was a regular attender at these mixers, I was invariably taken for a musician (no doubt, because I had shoulder-length hair at the time) who was circulating in the crowd before being called upon to perform. How to dispel this perception? As an ethnographer who wanted to clarify his real identity, my opening gambit in conversation often was something along the lines of, "Hello, I'm not here to make money, I just study people who do," but despite all such efforts, my interlocutors found it almost impossible to resist pitching their business models to me, just in case I might want to invest.

Indeed, wherever I went on my research trips in China, I was treated as a potential investor (at least after it was established that I was not in fact a musician). It took me a little while to realize that this treatment had less to do with the fact that I was a foreigner than that I was an academic. My business card, after all, revealed my connection to New York University (NYU), and NYU is a huge brand in China's private sector, much revered because of its Stern Business School, which contributes in no small measure to that country's "MBA fever."

In addition, however, and more significantly, as I discovered after two or three mixers, some of the people most likely to be propping up the bar at these chamber events were representatives of American universities. A few were there for purely social reasons—to make friends and romantic connections—but all of them were ready to pitch their wares as and when the opportunity arose. Desperate for management expertise, the Chinese government, as early as 1991, began to authorize foreign universities to offer MBA and EMBA programs. Shanghai, earmarked for top-drawer development as Asia's new financial capital, became the epicenter for the joint-partnered or wholly transplanted degree programs offered by such universities, with Washington University and the University of Southern California leading the pack. In the last few years, other kinds of academic programs have followed suit, especially in industrial sectors crucial to China's economic growth: engineering, applied science, and tourism management. Skyrocketing tuition fees, long absences from home, the Asian financial crisis of the late 1990s, and, after 9/11, visa restrictions sharply reduced the flow of Asian students to the United States. Consequently, more and more of our revenue-hungry institutions have gone offshore to service these students in their home countries.

After talking to these reps at the bar, and watching them interact with the corporate investors in the room, I came to realize that as a representative of an American university, I was not at all out of place in this environment. My institutional employer and its "brand" were perfectly at home in this watering hole for profit-chasing, cost-cutting investors pursuing a lucrative offshore opportunity. It is one thing to joke in the faculty lounge about our universities going off in pursuit of emerging global markets, and yet another to be handed a business card in such an emerging market by corporate reps who want to do business with you and who assume exactly the same of you. My personal experience in China helped me understand how easy it is, in practice, for our academic culture to meld with the normalizing assumptions and customs of corporate business culture.

Certainly it was easy to see how the academic reps might be influenced by the maverick mentality of these investors, but it is more important to grasp why the investors might feel they have something to learn, and profit materially, from the successes of American higher education in the business of overseas penetration. After all, the history of foreign involvement in China in the nineteenth century was the dual record of missionary educators and businesspeople, the one pursuing a potential harvest of 400 million minds and souls, the other seduced by the lure of 400 million consumer converts, each community providing cover for the other's activities. Arguably, the religious educators were more successful. Many of the colleges that American missionaries established have morphed over the decades into China's top universities; in addition, the lure of American higher education for Chinese students has proven to be quite enduring. Such things are not lost on the keen business mind.

Given the rate at which American universities are setting up shop in China, it is no surprise that NYU opened its own program in Shanghai in September 2006, bringing its list of study abroad locations to eight: the others are in London, Paris, Madrid, Berlin, Prague, Florence, and Accra. At the time of this writing, the Shanghai site is one of several locations being considered as branch campuses of NYU registered to offer degrees to students who will not have attended the domestic US campus.[3] The decision about whether to offer a range of degrees abroad to local nationals is one several universities had already made. It remained to be seen whether this move would be fully debated in light of the experience of these other colleges, and how such a decision would affect the character and resource map of the institution. Open deliberation on this question would surely help address the ailing state of faculty governance at NYU. It also might pressure the administration to observe some measure of transparency in policy decision making. But in practice, NYU, like its peers, had long ago crossed that threshold, and in the larger world of higher education, the distinction between onshore and offshore education—like that between private and public, or nonprofit and for-profit—had become very blurry indeed.

The distinction matters even less when viewed from the perspective of how the export trade in educational services is defined. The WTO, for example, recognizes four categories under this heading. Mode 1 involves arm's-length or cross-border supply, such as distance learning. Mode 2 is consumption abroad, which is primarily covered by international students studying overseas. Mode 3 is commercial presence, basically foreign direct investment in the form of satellite branches of institutions. Mode 4 is movement of natural persons, such as academics teaching abroad.[4] The most rapid growth is in Mode 1 and Mode 3, and much of this is assumed to be linked to a perceived decline in Mode 2 growth. Statisticians justify their own trade as well as the core principles of free trade by showing how these patterns of ebb and flow are interconnected. In response, and as a general fiscal principle, organizations will try to balance their budgets by pushing expansion in one area to compensate for shortfalls in another. This is how global firms have learned to operate, by assessing and equalizing the relative return on their investments in various parts of the world, both in the world of real revenue and in the more speculative realm of brand building for the future. University accounting departments have begun to juggle their budgets in a similar way. A deep revenue stream from a facility in the Middle East will be viewed as a way to subsidize unprofitable humanities programs at home (as is the case at one Midwestern institution where I inquired), just as an onshore science center capable of capturing US federal grant money may be incubated to help fund an Asian venture considered crucial to brand building in the region.

A Balance of Trade

In the interviews I conducted with faculty and administrators at NYU and elsewhere, a clear pattern of talk about this kind of fiscal juggling emerged (though no hard numbers could be accessed with which to match the rhetoric). The global programs of NYU are an eclectic mix of ventures, spread across several schools and divisions, each of which has its own fiscal boat to float. When viewed in their entirety, it is clear that the programs do not hold to any overall rule about the demarcation of onshore from offshore education, let alone any systematic educational philosophy. Though they lack a coherent profile, they show a clear pattern of exponential growth and expansion on every continent—beginning, historically, with the Madrid and Paris study abroad programs in "Old" Europe—and thereafter into each regional market as it was declared open to foreign direct investment.

While its eight study abroad sites are primarily for NYU students to send a semester abroad, places are offered to non-NYU students as and when vacancies open up. In addition, as many as sixty summer study abroad programs are currently offered to non-NYU students in Brazil, Canada, China, Cuba, the Czech Republic, England, France, Germany, Ghana, Greece, Ireland, Italy, Mexico, the Netherlands, Russia, South Africa, Spain, Sweden, and Switzerland. The absence, from New York, during the fall and spring semesters, of a quarter (and, very soon, a half) of its students allows NYU the option of increasing enrollment or reducing the costly expense of providing leased dorm space in downtown Manhattan. Either option has a huge impact on revenue and seems to be a primary motivation not only for university policy in this area but also for other colleges to emulate NYU's successful fiscal example. By 1998, less than a decade after incoming president Jay Oliva pledged to shape a global university to match Ed Koch's global-city aspirations for New York itself, NYU had outstripped all other American universities in the volume of students it sent overseas. It also enrolled the highest number of international students. Oliva was known internationally as the founder and host of the League of World Universities, whose rectors met regularly in New York to discuss how to respond to the challenge of globalization, and his successor, John Sexton, had made his name by pioneering a global law program as dean of the NYU Law School.[5]

In the years since then, NYU has found itself in the forefront of online efforts to offer distance learning abroad (one of which, NYU Online, was a notorious $20 million casualty of the dot-com bust, though its successor has thrived), while each of its schools has been encouraged to make global connections. The Stern Business School entered into partnership with the London School of Economics and the Ecole des Hautes Etudes Commerciales to offer an executive MBA on a global basis, the law school set up a master of law (LLM) program in Singapore for students from the Asia region, and the Tisch School of the Arts also chose Singapore as the location for a new master's program in film production. The scale of the university's newly announced joint venture with the American University in Paris (AUP) has upped the ante. While it is not likely to involve more than a small minority of NYU students, its growth potential is tied to recruiting well beyond the 800 international students currently enrolled by the AUP. As of November 2007, Polytechnic Institute of Brooklyn will soon be joining NYU as its latest "acquisition."

Less conspicuously perhaps, NYU's School of Continuing and Professional Studies (SCPS), which educates more than 50,000 adult learners annually in more than 125 fields, has become widely known for its provision of services abroad. This has even extended to graduate programs, which it has offered online since 1994, first through the Virtual College and now through NYU Online. The SCPS was one of the first university institutions in the United States to register with the Department of Commerce's BUYUSA program, officially described as "an electronic marketplace that connects U.S. exporters with qualified agents, buyers, and partners overseas." In the words of one of the school's assistant deans, this program has helped the SCPS to locate agents and partners in countries that they "never would have considered otherwise" (Moll). Examples of the school's penetration in the China market include instructional seminars offered to executives in that country's publishing industry, and a program in real estate finance designed for brokers and developers active in the People's Republic of China's vast construction boom. The SCPS is a hugely profitable arm of NYU, and its instruction is carried by an almost wholly adjunct workforce whose compensation in no way reflects the lucrative revenue harvested by course offerings in such nonorthodox disciplines as philanthropy and fund-raising, life planning, food and wine, and real estate.

Not surprisingly, the SCPS was one of the first educational institutions in the nation to receive the President's Export Award for its work in promoting US educational services overseas. In the US trade balance, education is the fifth largest export service, totaling $12 billion in 2004, arguably the one with the biggest growth potential. In New Zealand, and Australia, among the other leaders in this field of trade, education is the third and fourth largest export service. Given the intensification of the global competition for high-skill jobs, educational services are increasingly a number-one commodity in fast-developing countries.[6] The Department of Commerce will help any US university develop this trade, here or abroad, in much the same way it helps corporations. For relatively small fees, its commercial service will organize booths at international education fairs, find an international partner for a university's ventures, help with brand recognition in a new market, perform market research, and, through the use of the premium platinum key service, offer six months of expertise on setting up an overseas campus and marketing said campus in one of over eighty countries.

The Race to Deregulate

The Commerce Department's activities are fully aligned with the trade liberalization agenda of the WTO, where higher education falls under the General Agreement on Trade and Services (GATS). Dedicated, like all WTO agencies, to the principle that free trade is the best guarantee of the best quality at the lowest cost, the GATS was formed in 1995, and higher education services were added to its jurisdiction largely as a result of pressure in 2000 from the United States representative to the WTO, backed by representatives from Australia, New Zealand, and Japan. This inclusion has been fiercely opposed by most higher education leaders in WTO member nations, most prominently by a 2001 joint declaration of four large academic organizations in North America and Europe (<http://www.eua.be/eua/>) and by the 2002 Porto Alegre Declaration, signed by Iberian and Latin American associations (<http://www.gatswatch.org/educationoutof gats/PortoAlegre.doc>). The signatories of these two declarations agree that trade liberalization risks weakening governments' commitment to and investment in public higher, that education is not a commodity but a basic human right, and that its reliance on public mandates should make it distinct from other services. Yet the concerted opposition of these professional bodies has made little difference to the forty-five member states (the European Union counts as one) that had already made commitments to the education sector by January 2006 (Knight). Indeed, if the current round of

WTO negotiations, the Doha Round, had not encountered a logjam by acrimonious disagreements over agricultural trade, the GATS would have concluded its work some time ago, imposing severe constraints on individual government's rights to regulate education within its borders.

Such constraints are particularly debilitating to developing countries that will lose valuable domestic regulatory protection from the predatory advances of service providers from rich nations. Indeed, a new ministerial mandate at the GATS allows demandeurs such as the United States, New Zealand, and Australia to band together to put plurilateral pressure on the poorer target countries to accept their education exports (demandeur governments are those doing the asking position under the WTO's request-offer process; see Robinson). Officially, the GATS is supposed to exclude services "supplied in the exercise of governmental authority" (i.e., by nonprofit educational organizations), but most nations that are committed have chosen not to clarify the distinction between nonprofit and for-profit. With good reason, we can expect creeping, if not galloping, liberalization in all sectors if the GATS trade regime proceeds. After all, the free-trade culture of the WTO is one in which public services are automatically seen as unfair government monopolies and should be turned over to private, for-profit providers whenever possible, all in the name of "full market access." From the standpoint of teaching labor, this tendency points in the direction of increasing precarity—an interim environment of job insecurity, deprofessionalization, and ever-eroding faculty governance in institutions stripped of their public service obligations and respect for academic freedom.

Even in the absence of any such formal trade regime, we have seen the clear impact of market liberalization at all levels of higher education: the voluntary introduction of revenue center management models, where every departmental unit has to prove itself as a profit center; the centralization of power upward into managerial bureaucracies; the near abdication of peer review assessment in research units in bed with industry; and the casualization of the majority of the academic workforce, for whom basic professional tenets such as academic freedom are little more than a mirage in a desert. Meanwhile, the gap between the salaries of presidents and senior administrators and the pittance paid to contingent teachers is more and more in line with the spectrum of compensation observed in publicly listed corporations. None of this has occurred as a result of an imposition of formal requirements. Imagine, then, the consequences of a WTO trade regime that legally insists that regulatory standards, affecting procedures of accreditation, licensing, and qualification, might pose barriers to free trade in services.

By the time the GATS negotiations over education were initiated in 2000, the range of educational organizations that had established themselves overseas was already voluminous. These included: (1) corporate spin-offs that offer employee training and degrees, such as Motorola University, McDonald Hamburger University, Microsoft's Certified Technical Education Centers, GE's Crotonville Colleges, Fordstar's programs, and Sun Microsystems' Educational Centers; (2) private, for-profit education providers, such as the Apollo Group, Kaplan, Inc., De Vry, and the mammoth Laureate Education group (which now owns higher education institutions all over South America and Europe, operates in over twenty countries, and teaches a quarter of a million students); (3) virtual universities, such as Walden University and Western Governors Virtual University in the United States, the Learning Agency of Australia, India's Indira Ghandi National Open University, and the United Kingdom's Open University; (4) traditional universities that offer distance learning, especially in countries such as Australia and New Zealand, where governments mandated the marketization of higher educational services in the 1990s; and (5) for-profit arms of traditional universities, such as NYU's SCPS, or the University of Maryland's University College, and eCornell (Sauve).

In the years since then, the volume and scope of overseas ventures has expanded to almost every institution that has found itself in a revenue squeeze, whether from reduced state and federal support or skyrocketing expenses. As a result of market-oriented reforms in Australian higher education, every one of that country's public universities is aggressively involved in offshore education in Asia, creating a whole class of educational entrepreneurs, onshore and offshore, whose pursuit of monetary gain has inspired repeated calls for audits. Since many of these programs carry large fiscal risks, the tendency increasingly is to favor conservative models such as franchising, or producing syllabi in Australia to be taught entirely by local instructors offshore (Rizvi). There is not even a pretense of academic exchange involved in this arrangement in which education is little different from a manufacturing product designed at home, produced and assembled by cheaper labor abroad, and then sold to consumers in emerging markets. In the US for-profit sector, entrepreneurs scrambling to meet overseas demand for degrees ("with no frills") that have an unambiguous market value are taking advantage of notoriously loose accrediting procedures to set up shop and pitch their products. Lax regulation in some southern and western states and offshore diploma mill havens such as St. Kitts and Liberia, or the infamous Sebroga, a small, self-proclaimed principality in Italy, which has granted accreditation to dozens of dubious degree-granting entities, make it easy to license operators who open and close programs overnight to suit market demand.

Most recently, the widespread practice of outsourcing study-abroad education to for-profit intermediaries has attracted investigative scrutiny.

In August 2007, New York Attorney General Andrew Cuomo's probe into the student loan kickback scandal was expanded to assess evidence that universities had received perks from companies that operated their study-abroad programs. These included "free and subsidized travel overseas for officials, back-office services to defray operating expenses, stipends to market the programs to students, unpaid membership on advisory councils and boards, and even cash bonuses and commissions on student-paid fees" (Schemo; also Redden "Study Abroad"; Redden "The Middlemen"). The investigations began to uncover patterns of corruption endemic to the economy of subcontracting and offshore outsourcing.

With China's economy leapfrogging up the technology curve, the jumbo demand for high-value, professional-managerial talent there has sparked a gold rush, with foreign universities scrambling to meet a need that the state (whose professed priority is to fund basic rural education) cannot. There are few US colleges that have not sent prospecting missions to China to scout out offshore opportunities in the last few years. As for their return on investment, many administrators come back from these trips pondering the lesson that foreign companies learned; it is not at all easy to make money in China, let alone break even, and least of all from a joint venture with a Chinese partner, which is the customary arrangement for most colleges (Mooney). Even in the absence of guaranteed revenue, many will set up shop for the same reason that corporations have persevered there—to build their brand in the China market or to establish their name in the region in anticipation of a future windfall.

The United Arab Emirates and neighboring Qatar have been especially successful in attracting foreign colleges with lavish offers and are engaged in a bidding war to outdo each other to add cultural cachet to their portfolio of corporate brands; the Louvre, Sorbonne, and the Guggenheim were all approached at roughly the same time Abu Dhabi government representatives offered to build NYU a brand new branch campus. Dubai hosts a complex called Knowledge Village for offshore branch campuses from Pakistani, Russian, Canadian, and Indian, in addition to select British, Australian, and American universities. In Qatar, several top-brand American universities, including Carnegie Mellon, Cornell, Georgetown, Texas A&M, George Mason University, and Virginia Commonwealth, are already established in Doha's 2,500-acre Education City, with all expenses paid by the royal family's Qatar Foundation.[7]

Students in the Middle East have every reason to feel they may not be welcome in the United States after 9/11, while the philosophical worldview associated with the war on terror has provided administrators with an additional set of arguments to justify their newfound presence in the region. Many of their faculty are no doubt persuaded by Thomas Friedman-style reasoning that aspiring Middle Eastern students would be better served by a Western liberal education than by the curriculum of a glorified madrassah. Never mind that the host countries in question are quasi-feudal monarchies that ruthlessly suppress Islamism, among other belief systems, and are in no small measure responsible, as a result, for the flourishing of terror in the Middle East and beyond. So the debate falls along familiar lines—is it better to try to influence the political climate in illiberal societies by fostering collegial zones of free speech, or is the instinct to engage student elites in such societies a naive or, at worst, a colonial instinct?

Notwithstanding the rhetoric of any university's overseas mission, it is not at all easy to distinguish some of the new offshore academic centers from free-trade industrial zones, where outsourcing corporations are welcomed with a lavish package of tax holidays, virtually free land, and duty-free privileges. Indeed, in many locations, Western universities are physically setting up shop in free-trade zones. In Dubai, the foreign universities are basically there to train knowledge worker recruits in the Free Zone Authority's other complexes—Dubai Internet City, Dubai Media City, Dubai Studio City, DubaiTech, and the Dubai Outsource Zone. In Qatar, the colleges share facilities with the global high-tech companies that enjoy tax- and duty-free investments under that country's free-zone law. Some of China's largest free-trade locations have begun to attract brand-name colleges to relieve the skilled labor shortage that is hampering the rate of the offshore transfer of jobs and technology. The University of Liverpool, first to open a branch campus in Suzhou Industrial Park (which attracts more foreign direct investment than any other zone in the People's Republic of China), advertised entry-level positions at salaries beginning at $750 a month.

Corporate Universities?

Some readers might justifiably say that as long as the quality of education and integrity of research can be maintained, and the lure of monetary gain kept at bay, the push toward internationalization is something of a moral obligation for educators in affluent countries. Surely it is a way of sharing or redistributing the wealth that the reproduction of knowledge capital bestows on the most advanced nations. Surely the domestic hoarding of all this largesse only perpetuates the privileges (not to mention the parochialism) of American students, while it sustains the overdeveloped domestic economy supplied by our universities. At a time when our multinational corporations are plundering the resources of the developing world in the scramble to patent genetic material and copyright indigenous folktales, surely educators are obliged to set a better example.

In response, I would ask whether the spread of Anglophone colleges overseas is really the best way of delivering such goals, especially when

the main impetus for expansion to date has clearly been less philan-
thropic than revenue driven, and when the crisis of domestic student
debt is more likely to be exported in the form of a new "debt trap" for
students in developing countries to bear. Is there not a more direct way
for universities to make globally available the knowledge and research
they generate?

One obvious alternative is to give it away, with no intellectual property
strings attached. In the Massachusetts Institute of Technology's (MIT) pio-
neer OpenCourseWare project, the university makes its courses accessible
online for self-learning and nondegree-granting purposes. Other colleges,
like Tufts, Utah State, and Carnegie Mellon University have followed suit.
To date, MIT's courses are being translated in China and other Asian countries. While laudable in inspiration, the content that is being imported has
a clear cultural standpoint. If it is not absorbed alongside teachings from a
local standpoint, it remains to be seen how this export model will differ, in
the long run, from the tradition of colonial educations. All over the developing world governments, desperate to attract foreign investment, global
firms, and now global universities, are channeling scarce public educational
resources into programs tailored to the skill sets of a "knowledge society" at
the expense of all other definitions of knowledge, including indigenous
knowledge traditions. Under these conditions, higher education is increasingly regarded as an instrumental training for knowledge workers in tune
with capitalist rationality as it is lived within one of the urban footprints of
corporate globalization.

If universities were to closely follow the corporate offshoring model,
then what would we expect to see next? In a labor-intensive industry
(a characteristic that education shares with the garment industry—75%
of education costs go to teaching labor), the instructional budget is where
one's employer will seek to minimize costs first, usually by introducing
distance learning or by hiring local offshore instructors at large salary dis-
counts. Expatriate employees, employed to set up an offshore facility and
train locals, will be a fiscal liability to be offloaded at the first opportunity.
If one's satellite campus is located in the same industrial park as Fortune
500 firms, then it will almost certainly be invited to produce customized
research for these companies, again at discount prices. It will only be a
matter of time before an administrator decides it will be cost-effective to
move some domestic research operations to the overseas branch to save
money. And once the local instructors have proved themselves over there,
they may be the ones asked to produce the syllabi, and, ultimately, even
teach remote programs for onshore students in the United States.

Inevitably, in a university with global operations, administrators who
have to make decisions about where to allocate budgets will favor locations
where the return on investment is relatively higher. Why build expensive

additions at home when a foreign government or free-trade zone authority is offering free land and infrastructure? Why bother recruiting overseas students when they can be taught more profitably in their countries of origin? If a costly program can only be saved by outsourcing the teaching of it, then surely that is the decision that will be made.

Along the way, there will be much high-minded talk about meeting the educational needs of developing countries, and some pragmatic talk about reducing the cost of education for domestic students. Substandard academic conditions will be blamed on foreign intermediaries or partners, or on "unfair" competition. Legislators and top administrators will grandstand in public and play along in private. Clerical functions and data-dense research will be the first to go offshore. As for teaching instructors, those in the weakest positions or the most vulnerable disciplines will feel the impact first, and faculty with the most clout—tenured full timers in elite universities—will be the last and the least to be affected.

As far as the domestic record goes, higher education institutions have followed much the same trail as subcontracting in industry—first, the outsourcing of all nonacademic campus personnel, then the casualization of routine instruction, followed by the creation of a permatemp class on short-term contracts, and the preservation of an ever-smaller core of full timers, those who are crucial to the brand prestige of the collegiate name. Downward salary pressure and eroded job security are the inevitable upshot. How do we expect offshore education to produce a different result?

From the perspective of academic labor, I do not believe we should expect an altogether dissimilar outcome. But the offshoring of higher education, if and when it occurs, will not resemble the hollowing out of manufacturing economies, with full-scale employer flight to cheaper locations, or even the more recent select outsourcing of white-collar services, where knowledge transfer involves the uploading and downloading of skills and know-how from and to human brains on different sides of the planet. The scenario for education will be significantly different, given the nature and traditions of the services being delivered, the vested commitment of national governments to the goals of public education, and the complexity of relationships between various stakeholders.

Moreover, for all of the zealous efforts to steer higher education into the rapids of enterprise culture, it would not be hard to demonstrate that with the exception of the burgeoning for-profit sector most universities do not and cannot, for the most part, function fiscally like a traditional marketplace, and that the principles of collaboration and sharing that sustain teaching, learning, and research are inimical or irreducible, in the long run, to financialization after the model of the global corporation. Yet one could say much the same about the organizational culture of the knowledge industries. High-tech firms depend increasingly on internationally available knowledge in specialized fields; they collaborate with each other on research that is either too expensive or too multisided to undertake individually; and they depend, through high turnover, on a pool of top engineers to circulate brainpower throughout the industry. So too the management of knowledge workers has diverged appreciably from the traditions of Taylorism and is increasingly modeled after the work mentality of the modern academic, whose job is not bounded by the physical workplace or by a set period of hours clocked there. Modern knowledge workers no longer know when they are on or off the job, and their ideas—the stock-in-trade of their industrial livelihoods—come to them at any waking moment of their day, often in their most free moments. From this perspective, talk about the "corporate university" is a lazy shorthand. The migration of our own academic customs and work mentalities onto corporate campuses and into knowledge industry workplaces is just as important a part of the story of the rise of knowledge capitalism as the importation of business rationality into the academy, but the traffic in the other direction is all too often neglected because of our own siege mentality.

In all likelihood, we are living through the formative stages of a mode of production marked by a quasiconvergence of the academy and the knowledge corporation. Neither is what it used to be; both are mutating into new species that share and trade many characteristics. These changes are part and parcel of the economic environment in which they function—where, on the one side, a public commons unobtrusively segues into a marketplace of ideas, and a career secured by stable professional norms morphs into a contract-driven livelihood hedged by entrepreneurial risks; and, on the other side, the busy hustle for a lucrative patent or a copyright gets dressed up as a protection for creative workers, and the restless hunt for emerging markets masquerades as a quest to further international exchange or democratization.

It may be all too easy for us to conclude that the global university, as it takes shape, will emulate some of the conduct of multinational corporations. It is much more of a challenge to grasp the consequences of the *co-evolution* of knowledge-based firms and academic institutions. Yet understanding the latter may be more important if we are to imagine practical educational alternatives in a civilization that relies on mental labor to enrich its economic lifeblood.

Notes

1. One notable exception is Slaughter and Leslie's *Academic Capitalism.* While they survey higher education in the United States, United Kingdom, Canada, and Australia, the authors focus more on how institutions have

responded domestically to global changes in each of these national systems rather on how they have internationalized their operations.

2. Organization for Economic Co-operation and Development (OECD) figures, which only covered students studying abroad, were $30 billion for 1999 (Fuller). Estimates of the global market for educational services vary wildly. For example, Richard T. Hezel, president of Hezel Associates, a research company focused on e-learning, valued the market at around $2.5 trillion in 2005 (Redden "No Risk").

3. The first two branch campuses are to be established in Paris and Abu Dhabi, the first in conjunction with the American University in Paris at a site on the Isle Seguin and the second as a freestanding NYU campus in the United Arab Emirates.

4. These basic GATS definitions can be found at <http://www.wto.int/english/tratop_e/serv_e/cbt_course_e/c1s3p1_e.htm>. Mode 3, in particular, has seen intense plurilateral pressure on developing countries from OECD states to open up their services sectors.

5. The philosophical drive beyond NYU's global aspirations in the Oliva years is summarized in "NYU: The Global Vision" (NYU: 1995). In that document, Duncan C. Rice, vice chancellor at the time, argued that NYU had a "unique obligation among colleges to become internationalized," because "it serves the greatest international entrepôt in the world." The university's history of fulfilling the educational aspirations of the "sons and daughters of working Americans and waves of succeeding immigrants" made it an especially appropriate mission to undertake.

6. For an ultimately enthusiastic, though broad-ranging, summary of some of the salient issues in the GATS debate over educational services, see Pierre Sauve, of the OECD Trade Directorate.

7. Knowledge Village's official Web site is <http://www.kv.ae/en/>. For the Qatar Foundation, see <http://www.qf.edu.qa/>.

Works Cited

Fuller, Thomas. "Education Exporters Take Case to WTO." *International Herald Tribune* 18 Feb. 2003: 15.

Knight, Jane. "GATS: The Way Forward after Hong Kong." *International Higher Education* 43 (Spring 2006): 12–14.

Moll, Jennifer. "Trade in Education and Training Services: Excellent Opportunities for U.S. Providers." *Export America: The Federal Source for Your Global Business Needs.* 22 Feb. 2008 <http://www.ita.doc.gov/exportamerica/New Opportunities/no_edu_0902.html>.

Mooney, Paul. "The Wild, Wild East." *Chronicle of Higher Education* 17 Feb. 2006: A46.

Nelson, Cary. *Manifesto of a Tenured Radical.* New York: New York UP, 1997.

———, ed. *Will Teach for Food: Academic Labor in Crisis.* Minneapolis: U of Minnesota P, 1997.

Nelson, Cary, and Stephen Watt. *Academic Keywords: A Devil's Dictionary for Higher Education.* New York: Routledge, 1999.

————. *Office Hours: Activism and Change in the Academy.* New York: Routledge, 2004.

New York University. "NYU: The Global Vision." New York: New York UP, 1995.

Redden, Elizabeth. "The Middlemen of Study Abroad." *Inside Higher Ed* 20 Aug. 2007 <http://www.insidehighered.com/layout/set/print/news/2007/08/20/abroad>.

————. "No Risk, No Reward." *Inside Higher Ed* 7 Dec. 2006 <http://www.inside highered.com/news/2006/12/07/for_profit>.

————. "Study Abroad under Scrutiny." *Inside Higher Ed* 14 Aug. 2007 <http://www.insidehighered.com/layout/set/print/news/2007/08/14/abroad>.

Rizvi, Fazal. "Offshore Australian Higher Education." *International Higher Education* 37 (Fall 2004): 7–9.

Robinson, David. "GATS and Education Services: The Fallout from Hong Kong." *International Higher Education* 43 (Spring 2006): 14–15.

Ross, Andrew. *Fast Boat to China: Corporate Flight and the Consequences of Free Trade: Lessons from Shanghai.* New York: Random, 2006.

Sauve, Pierre. "Trade Education and the GATS: What's In, What's Out, What's All the Fuss About?" <http://www.oecd.org/dataoecd/50/50/2088515.pdf>.

Schemo, Diana Jean. "In Study Abroad, Gifts and Money for Universities." *New York Times* 13 Aug. 2007: 1+.

Slaughter, Sheila, and Larry Leslie. *Academic Capitalism: Politics, Policies, and the Entrepreneurial University.* Baltimore: Johns Hopkins UP, 1997.

PART 3

PEDAGOGY AND THE
POLITICS OF MENTORING

✌ 13 ✌

Graduate Mentoring

A Poetics

Marsha Bryant

I am tempted to consult modern poetry in addressing the issue of graduate mentoring, given this essay's appearance in a volume dedicated to one of the field's most prominent critics (who also happens to be an inspirational mentor). We would start with Stein (dissertation as explanation: a chapter is a chapter is a chapter), hook with Brooks (write first, then fiddle), sample some Stevens (it must change, it must give pleasure), and infuse with Hughes (what happens to a dissertation deferred?). And yet the issue of graduate mentoring is too important, indeed, too urgent, to approach in anything less than a systematic fashion. So I offer instead a *poetics* of mentoring that considers its key elements and dynamics within the rules of our profession. While much of my discussion focuses on ABD students, many of its principles also apply to graduate students pursuing course and thesis work. A poetics of mentoring is not an instruction manual but a topography of its processes and relationships, its logic and emotions. Such a poetics invites us to reflect on what and how mentoring means.

Calibration

Faculty cannot mentor graduate students unless we calibrate with our fields and the job market. In other words, we must perform a continual adjustment of how we read the profession across the course of our careers. Incorrect advice can prove more damaging than insufficient advice. It simply will not do to endorse theses and dissertations that are mere "forms of homage or duplication," as Jennifer Wicke puts it (56), or to write short reference letters with large signatures. Failure to calibrate often signals generational bias. It is neither useful nor ethical to transport the days of clubbish job placements into advising candidates for the contemporary market. One

187

way to calibrate is by participating in our departments' searches—even if
we are not on the search committee. I was fortunate to have a mentor who
tracked trends among the applications to my graduate institution; for
example, he saw the growing importance of dissertation abstracts in the
job market of the late 1980s. Although I have considerable mentoring experience, I wrote this essay after calibrating my perspective with those of recent graduate coordinators and placement officers from my department:
Pamela Gilbert, Susan Hegeman, Kenneth Kidd, and Phillip Wegner. I also
consulted with current and former graduate students in our program. Just
as scientists must calibrate their instruments to perform research, we must
calibrate our professional awareness if graduate mentoring is to succeed.

Project

Perhaps the first adjustment we must help graduate students make is the
move from *papers* to *projects*. While papers are end products tied to the requirements of a particular professor and course, *projects* are more open-
ended because of personal investment, rich cultural and/or theoretical
contexts, and ambitious framing. Put another way, a paper is a stopping
point, but a project expands into future writing (a conference paper, another seminar paper, a thesis, a dissertation chapter, a publication). Ideally the move toward projects begins with one's first graduate seminar,
because a project's forward propulsion is crucial to successful graduate
work. As one of our students put it, "If the dissertation doesn't materialize
from the course work, the mooring lines are cut." When I was in graduate school in the 1980s—the twilight period for securing tenure-track jobs
without publication—some faculty still clung to the view that graduate
writing was mere apprentice work. They gave end-stopped assignments
more suitable for undergraduates, and we performed them merely to pass
the class. Ultimately, both graduate students and faculty have the responsibility to insist on *projects*. As Gilbert told me, dissertation students "must
have a strong sense of topic, one they find on their own" rather than
"Rorschach" ideas on which faculty will inevitably impose their own interests. And faculty must learn to say "come back and see me when you have
a project," as Hegeman noted. The dynamics of mentoring become a
strategic interplay of distances and proximities.

Director

Except for our own research, being primary mentor for a dissertation is
the most intimate relationship to a project that faculty will have. And yet
good directors never impose ideas but elicit them. "Mini-me" mentors do
students a tremendous disservice, because "you can place only so many
people who do what you do," as Gilbert explains. I have known of failed

tenure cases resulting from disinterest in the dissertation work, often because it was never really the candidate's own. Thus the director's role should be, in Cary Nelson's words, "to help students to recognize and define their own interests; then, to draw the best work out of them, shaping it to assure that it is realistically achievable and that it will be recognized as important and interesting by others" (163–64). The first group this project must interest is the student's doctoral committee, so directors must play an active role in assembling the best faculty for each project. It is irresponsible to let graduate students pick committee members on their own, as faculty have a better sense of their colleagues' full range of expertise, of who works well with whom, of who tends to hijack or stymie students' projects. Directors also push students to engage a larger audience through publishing. As Wegner noted, "A good mentor is somebody who from the beginning says to get things in submission." In addition, good directors integrate their students into the larger profession through personal contacts. This kind of mentoring takes many forms: urging your student to participate in the graduate lunch or colloquium with a visiting speaker, inviting your student to introduce a speaker in his or her field, including a student on your conference panel, introducing your student to people at conferences, telling peers about your student's project. Finally, directors must direct. They do not cede their responsibilities to the committee, the graduate coordinator, and the placement officer—although directors consult with these colleagues to calibrate their sense of how the project fits into particular fields. As a guide and an advocate, the director enters into one of the most potentially rewarding professional relationships.

Professionalization

While the director is the prime mover, the process of professionalization is the responsibility of the entire graduate faculty. It should begin in the seminar room. And yet "professionalization is still an embarrassing word," as Wegner noted. Every year I tell my seminar students to get business cards for conferences, and every year I see discomfited faces and down-turned eyes as I look around the suddenly hushed room. (Think about it: How often have you seen conferees fumbling for scraps of paper to jot down contact information that will likely be lost? How helpful, indeed, how *professional*, is that?) After regaining my students' attention by revealing how one of my publications resulted from an exchange of business cards, I continue the seminar's work of professionalization. I require seminar paper proposals that are addressed to a particular conference or panel organizer. Several of my students have ended up presenting their seminar work at conferences, and they tend to make a quicker "paper-to-project" transition than their peers. I also talk openly about such things as the submission and selection process, conferencing 101, types of journals, and productive strategies for dealing with rejection. (As a former student told me, a rejection letter with *no* feedback prompts a different emotional response than one with a treatise of criticisms.) With the group of graduate students that I direct, I talk about such professional matters in more depth. I hold additional meetings for the ABD students to review cover letters for journal submissions and to prepare application materials for the next year's market. All of these gatherings begin with each of us telling the group what we are *working on*. As Wicke points out, "For graduate students to reproduce the profession, they must be inducted into it as professionals" (53). Demystifying the profession is one of the most important things we can do for our graduate students. (It is not helpful to give the impression that cv's spring full-blown like Athena from bulging faculty foreheads.) Indeed, I find that those of us who were blessed with good mentors often perform the vital work of professionalization for our colleagues who lacked them.

Writing

Besides demystifying our profession, good mentors "humanize the process" of academic writing for our graduate students, as Kidd put it. For most of them, writing becomes a tremendous source of anxiety as well as the determining factor for graduation and placement. One student told me that seminars may "foster an advanced thinker but not necessarily an advanced writer," so that even students completing their course work feel "that gap between where you are and the articles you read." Perhaps the best way to humanize the act of writing is telling our students about our own writing processes: its moments of clarity and ambivalence, "its frustrations as well as its pleasures," to borrow from Kidd again. He gives himself an assignment in his seminars, writing "alongside the students" and using part of the class to discuss how everyone's work is going. Besides sharing our writing processes with individual students and seminars, faculty also can form writing groups with the students they direct. Some of my colleagues use this kind of collective mentoring to share conference and seminar papers, as well as dissertation chapters. Discussing our own strategies for common problems like positioning arguments offers students reassurance as well as guidance. I shared during one seminar an especially difficult experience I had in rewriting the introduction to an early article—even showing students the editor's initial markup (in red ink!) and waving in the air the three subsequent versions. Such humanizing needs to continue when our former students are revising their dissertations into their first books—when the stakes are even higher. How liberating it was when my mentor told me that after all he had published, each book in progress yielded days when it felt like the best book in the world and days when it felt like the worst. Of course students must do the writing alone and on their own, but they need not think they are the only ones who experience doubts and detours.

Commitment

All projects require some level of commitment, but the dissertation presents a special case because, as Gilbert notes, there is "no incremental transition between modes of work" as doctoral students move into the long form. They have been told to write more professional papers, and now they are told to go and write something akin to a book. However committed mentors may be to these projects, dissertations will not happen if students are "unable to commit to the work," as one student told me. Nelson characterizes the dissertation as "an exercise in intellectual concentration and focus, the deepest long-term investment in individual research that many Ph.D.'s will ever make" (163). While faculty cannot force commitment on the part of our students, we can foster it. One way of doing this is to encourage *public* forms of intellectual commitment outside the private space of writing, the personal relationship with a mentor, and the local institution. Publication, which Wicke calls "professionalism's public face" (54), effects this kind of commitment. As Wegner notes, "Students who get publications don't have problems completing the dissertation writing." One also commits publicly by presenting parts of the dissertation at conferences. As a graduate student, I sought out calls for papers that would enforce my dissertation deadlines, using proposals to get started on individual chapters. And because I could not stand before an audience with nothing to say, I wrote the requisite chapter. One of my recent graduate students had tremendous success generating chapters and publications through conferencing, forming a peer group that will carry her into future projects. These commitments that students have made on their own, outside their local institutions, can provide a motivation free from the emotional entanglements of a particular program or department.

Confidence

When I discuss mentoring with Nelson, he often tells me that the greatest thing we can give our graduate students is confidence. It begins, I think, with the director's belief in the student's work. A director's endorsement proves crucial in getting through the doubts that arise in completing dissertations, and in facing a highly competitive job market (and eventually, in earning tenure). During this fraught time in their lives, graduate students often will find themselves unable to perceive our confidence in them, so it bears repeating in different registers. Recently I told a student that I would not have put him on my conference panel had I not considered his project timely and sophisticated. To another I noted that innovative interdisciplinary work often does take more time to synthesize, and would be well worth the difficulties. I shared with another student the good impression she had made on a conference colleague. I am not invoking the model of the doting parent here but, rather, the professional coach who can gauge benchmarks in ways that students cannot. Paradoxically, we also instill confidence when we *cannot* perceive the project's final destination but know the student will take it where it needs to go. Hegeman recalled her director's "extraordinarily open gesture" after she presented an early draft of her dissertation prospectus: "Well, I'm completely confused, but I trust you." Ideally, examinations and defenses will communicate this vital sense that a student has the resources to succeed. Like a project, these gatherings with the director and the committee should inspire in our students a sense of new beginnings, for as Hegeman explains, mentoring is ultimately "a transferential relationship because the student to some degree identifies with the mentor, but then must move beyond the mentor." This distance gained through confidence does not necessarily end the relationship, even when the student is "**Ph**inally **D**one." Rather, the interplay of distance and proximity continues, as "mentoring blurs into collegial equality," to borrow from Nelson again (165). Over time, the mentor and former student may collaborate, or turn to one another for advice.

So why a poetics? To consider graduate mentoring as a *text* is to acknowledge its system and components, its requirements and nuances, its productive tensions and strategic balances. Mentoring is "incredibly improvisational," as Hegeman notes, so that we assemble its components differently with each student and project. There is no fixed formula for good mentoring, but there are clear responsibilities. One of these is to reflect on our mentoring and discuss it with our colleagues, for ultimately graduate mentoring is so much more than marching our students through the hooding ceremony. It is a way in which we renew our own commitment to the profession by ushering in its future.

Acknowledgments: I would like to thank my colleagues Pamela Gilbert, Susan Hegeman, Kenneth Kidd, and Phillip Wegner for consulting with me on this essay. I also am grateful to the graduate students I cite, who prefer to remain anonymous.

Works Cited

Nelson, Cary. "Mentoring." *Academic Keywords: A Devil's Dictionary for Higher Education.* Ed. Cary Nelson and Stephen Watt. New York: Routledge, 1999. 162–66.
Wicke, Jennifer. "I Profess: Another View of Professionalization." *Profession 2001.* New York: MLA, 2001. 52–57.

⌁ 14 ⌁

EMPIRE AND THE ANXIETY OF INFLUENCE

Brady Harrison

Any progressive social change must be imagined first, and that vision must find its most eloquent possible expression to move from vision to reality.
—Martín Espada, "Poetry Like Bread"

For much of my career, to date, I have researched and written about the literatures and cultures of American imperialism, and, for the most part, I know why I have written about the conjoined twins of continental expansionism and overseas adventurism. At the most visceral level, catastrophic violence and avarice appall and anger me as they appall and anger many Americans, and the often glaring contradictions between what we say we believe in—say, democracy, freedom, equality, fair play, honesty—and what we do—say, justify invasions and wars in the Philippines, Vietnam, Nicaragua, or Iraq with lies, collude with dictators and tyrants, permit transnational corporations to conspire with US security forces to topple (or seek to topple) democratically elected governments, and so on—makes matters worse. Less viscerally, perhaps, I can say that as a blue-collar kid raised in northern Canada, I very early on identified with labor and the Left and have, like many Canadians, always been fearful and suspicious of American power and—to be wholly pejorative—arrogance. More, if I could not, as a child, have cared less about 1968 (I turned five that august year), I was deeply affected by 1977: as odd as it sounds, even to me, the Clash had as much impact on my sense of politics (and appropriate targets and willingness to tilt at windmills) as being the son of a butcher.

If growing up, at least in part, in trailer parks and working in meatpacking plants through high school and college shaped some of the values that persist in my work, then I can say, too, that by the time I arrived at graduate school at the University of Illinois at Urbana-Champaign, I was a pretty inchoate mess of ideas and beliefs—some reliable, some ridiculous, and some in need of a five- or ten-year plan. Although I have been fortunate enough to have a handful of excellent mentors along the way—Bill Connor, Shirley Neuman, Bruce Greenfield, Bob Parker, Gerry Brenner, Beverly Chin, and others—my dissertation chair and steady advisor all these years, Cary Nelson, has, as no other, helped shape not only my intellectual concerns and commitments but also my sense of what it means to be a scholar and teacher in twenty-first-century America. Yet this is not hagiography: we learn the hard lessons in all sorts of ways.

In matters of mentorship, one should always begin with talk of murder. In his famous study, *The Anxiety of Influence* (1973), Harold Bloom famously argues that the "belated" poet (or, in my case, scholar), faced with the achievement of his precursors, experiences a range of emotions, including envy and fear of the earlier writer's dominance, and responds in his own writing by distorting the work of the earlier writer beyond conscious recognition. If my relationship with Cary has been nowhere near as dramatic or strange as Oedipus's struggle with his father—grad school is tough enough without going to the bother of murdering one's chair on the road, say, to Kankakee, or gouging out one's own eyes, or worrying about the cornfields around Urbana-Champaign opening up to swallow one whole—I have thought of myself as his somewhat cow-handed student (for those non-baseball types, a person who holds the bat one way, say, left-handed, but bats as if right-handed). In almost all ways, my work has been an obverse elaboration and revision of Cary's: Where he has focused—in at least one of the major strands of his career—on poetry, I have concentrated on prose; where he has been a recoverer and champion of writers and intellectuals on the Left, I have—with exceptions, of course—most often researched and written about authors, politicians, and soldiers of fortune on the Right (and even the far, whacked-out, truly frightening Right)[1]; where he has written about the marginalized and the forgotten, I have written about those who, in very real, very material ways, have occupied the centers of American power and prestige; where he has written about, say, Eddie Rolfe, poet, worker, communist, and combatant in the Spanish Civil War, I have written about Richard Harding Davis, best-selling novelist, travel writer, dandy, model for the escort to the Gibson Girl, and celebrator of nascent American imperial power. Cow-handed though I may be, however, it turns out that I have tried to build upon our shared values and commitments to intellectual and human freedom and dignity. It turns out, fantasies of ascending the throne aside, that I have tried to build outward from such groundbreaking solo and collaborative works as *Marxism and the Interpretation of Culture* (1988), *Repression and Recovery* (1989), *Cultural Studies* (1992), *Academic Keywords* (1999), and others.

Adhering to Fredric Jameson's exhortation, "Always historicize!" (9), most of us can probably say that we are scholars of our eras. I began at Illinois in 1988, too late for the Marxist summer of 1983, but just in time for the publication of *Marxism and the Interpretation of Culture*, the landmark volume growing from the courses and international conference organized by Cary and Lawrence Grossberg through the Unit for Criticism and Interpretive Theory at the University of Illinois at Urbana-Champaign. What days those must have been, and I regret not being there; still, my cohorts were the inheritors of that legacy, and in the process of reading this vast and challenging collection as a new doctoral student—could not Spivak or Jameson make a little more effort to communicate with mere mortals? Did all missives need to appear to have been written in prison?—and in the process of reading for Cary's seminars on critical theory and cultural studies, I began, for the first time in any serious way, to ask a series of interrelated questions: What was the purpose of literary studies? What was the purpose of theory? What was the purpose of Marxist (and poststructuralist) theory? What, as a would-be scholar and teacher, was the purpose of my work? Marxist theory was in the air (and the corn), and through Cary's influence, I began to read and record what I have taken, even after all these years, as statements of purpose.

First, from Marx himself: "But if the designing of the future and the proclamation of ready-made solutions for all time is not our affair, then we realize all the more clearly what we have to accomplish in the present—I am speaking of a *ruthless criticism of everything existing*, ruthless in two senses: The criticism must not be afraid of its own conclusions, nor of conflict with the powers that be" (13, emphasis in original). For a young man fresh from what Canadians somewhat unironically call "the bush"—I had been working north of Lesser Slave Lake on Métis settlements before moving to Illinois—these were staggering, heady, albeit impossible, words. No way was I that fearless—or that visionary—but this passage also was incredibly liberating: one could try. Then, once again via Cary's seminar, enter Antonio Gramsci, the hero of cultural studies: "The starting-point of critical elaboration is the consciousness of what one really is, and is 'knowing thyself' as a product of the historical process to date which has deposited in you an infinity of traces, without leaving an inventory. Such an inventory must therefore be made at the outset" (326). Once again, impossible words, an impossible call-to-(intellectual) arms, but one could still try, could try to sift the countless shards within. And why? What was the purpose of all this (self-reflexive) study, this reading, this writing, this trying to say that the world is not as it should be? According to Edward Said, "For in the main—and here I shall be explicit—criticism must think of itself as life-enhancing and constitutively opposed to every form of tyranny, domination, and abuse; its social goals are noncoercive knowledge produced in the interests of human freedom" (29). Yet more impossible words—too lofty, too grand, too hopelessly romantic—I was grading freshman comp essays by the gross. Still, one could try, and one could keep interrogating power, methods, assumptions, and more.

If my generation was not around for the Marxist shindig, then perhaps the institutional highlight of our graduate career was the Cultural Studies Conference of 1990, once again organized by the Unit for Criticism and Interpretative Theory and co-chaired by Cary, Grossberg, and Paula Treichler. Over the course of a few days, we heard Homi Bhabha (who danced when the sound system hiccuped and broadcast somebody, somewhere, running scales on some kind of horn) on "Postcolonial Authority and Postmodern Guilt," Simon Frith on "The Cultural Study of Popular Music," Stuart Hall on "Cultural Studies and Its Theoretical Legacies," Janice Radway on "Mail-Order Culture and Its Critics: The Book-of-the-Month Club, Commodification and Consumption, and the Problem of Cultural Authority," and dozens of other landmark speakers and papers. The most immediately memorable slide show/video/paper had to be Constance Penley's study of slash fiction and its practitioners and consumers, "Feminism, Psychoanalysis, and the Study of Popular Culture."

The conference—and the seminar Cary ran in conjunction— performed its mind-altering work, freeing many of us to think about all sorts of texts and practices, to think critically, self-reflexively, and creatively about our methodologies: "For cultural studies has no guarantees about what questions are important to ask within given contexts or how to answer them; hence no methodology can be privileged or even temporarily employed with total security and confidence, yet none can be eliminated out of hand" ("Cultural Studies: An Introduction" 2). More, the conference and course asked us to think diligently about the past, present, and future of literary studies. For a moment or two, cultural studies, as Lata Mani writes, seemed to promise "respite to those weary from disciplinarily inflected ideological skirmishes. It will offer hospitality, if not centrality, to practitioners of postmodern, postcolonial, transnational historiography and ethnography, and provide a location where the new politics of difference—racial, sexual, cultural, transnational—can combine and be articulated in their dazzling plurality" (392). At the time, whether or not the field could transform English (and other) Departments into pocket utopias was beside the point for me: the transnational and pop culture energies of cultural studies were just what I was looking for. I wanted to research American writing about Central America (and especially about William Walker's forays into Nicaragua and Honduras), and that meant reading and writing about scores of "non-" and "sub-" literary works such as mercenary romances, potboilers, jingoist best sellers, rabid expansionist editorials, policy statements, neutrality laws, and more. Here, then, was the flexible methodology and the intellectual freedom to pursue writers and subjects well beyond the canonical. The conference was, of course, a landmark "intervention" in literary and cultural studies, but it was also, for Cary's students, an exemplary educational happening.

If Illinois' venture into cultural studies informed in countless ways my own critical interests and practices, then the work that ultimately had the most influence on my own—yet once again in a cow-handed fashion—was Cary's landmark study *Repression and Recovery*. For me, no work, aside from Jameson's *The Political Unconscious*, spoke more about the processes of forgetting or not wanting to remember writers, moments, and forms of knowledge. As Cary puts it:

> The focus for this reflection on how we do literary history is my contention that we no longer know the history of the poetry of the first half of this century; most of us, moreover, do not know that the knowledge is gone. Indeed, we tend to be unaware of how or why such a process of literary forgetfulness occurs, let alone why it occurs among the very people who consider themselves the custodians of our literary heritage. (4)

Whole worlds of poetry and knowledge were forgotten or repressed because Americans (including professors) did not want to hear voices that engaged in cultural critique, that belonged to leftists and blacks and women, that put the lie to authorized representations of life and values in America, that refuted the public discourses of capital and the dominance of the few over the many, that did not conform to narrow and conventional (and depoliticized) definitions of the modern, of poetry, of modern poetry.

In my obverse way, Cary's questions about memory and forgetting became central to my study of the literatures and cultures of US imperialism. In particular, why did no one remember Walker, the American soldier of fortune who seized control of Nicaragua in 1856? If known to historians, Walker was almost totally unknown among most literary scholars (and Americans in general), despite the fact that he had resurfaced in songs, poems, plays, short stories, novels, and films repeatedly since his death by firing squad in Honduras in 1860. Why did he keep coming back, only to be forgotten again and again? Here is what I came to argue in the book that grew out of my dissertation:

> Walker keeps returning to popular culture because his narrative continues to resonate within the broader history of U.S. interventionism; historical events (such as the rise of imperial furors, for example, before the Spanish-American War, or after the Korean War, or in advance of renewed U.S. interventions in Central America following defeat in Vietnam) keep calling him back to

mind, and whatever a particular author's intentions or ideology, Walker's story—a tale of conquest, colonization, grand visions, rapacity, and defeat—lays bare many of the fantasies and desires for power that run beneath the rhetoric of the good neighbor and American exceptionalism. (197)

Walker keeps reappearing only to be forgotten again and again, because his story lays too bare the truths of imperial desire and violence; he keeps ratting on his latter-day peers, yet nobody really wants to hear it. If literary historians (and nearly everybody else) were reluctant to hear voices of cultural critique, then they were just as unwilling to pay attention to tales that showed the nation to be rapacious, imperial, and less than advertised. Building upon Cary's work, I could argue that while many speak, only a few (middling, reasonably safe) voices can be heard: the bounds of acceptable, understandable speech appear remarkably—even frighteningly—narrow.

From the specter of Walker, we return to the specter of Oedipus; we turn, in other words, from the subject of intellectual mentorship to the subject of professional mentorship: it is time for throwing a few punches at poppa.[2] Working with Cary was not the easiest thing in the world for me. I do not think I am exaggerating when I say that he is a rather intimidating presence: smart as hell, the tallest English professor ever, and gifted with a way of looking at a person that pins her or him to the floor, just as one would pin a live bug to a display case, he stands, literally and figuratively, head and shoulders above most of us. Add to that a tight job market and my instinctual (Canadian) tendency to be self-effacing and polite no matter what, and you have what remains perhaps the most unequal professional relationship of my life. Although I sensed and observed that most of my peers proceeded with much more confidence and élan than I did, I was unnerved by Cary's presence and the stakes: I was not just doing this for fun; I wanted a job. The only solution—and Cary positively radiates this notion—was to get tough (and smart).

In the end, I can say that Cary mentors best by example. As I observed firsthand as his student and sometime research assistant—and as his publication and professional record amply demonstrates—Cary works incredibly hard. No lesson has ever sunk in more with me, and that means showing up for work every day, thinking as hard and as well as I can, and putting in the hours. I learned from Cary what it means to be a professional: research and write diligently; present one's work at the right places at the right times; publish a wide range of projects; teach well and put pressure on one's students; keep track of one's people and the mentorship continues well after they have moved on; and invest one's time and energy not only in one's own work but in the greater profession as well. It sounds too easy to say, but I try to instill the same values in my own students.

Notes

1. Cary has written extensively, of course, about the Right and its impact on higher education. See, for example, Michael Bérubé and Cary Nelson, eds., *Higher Education Under Fire: Politics, Economics, and the Crisis of the Humanities* (1994), Cary Nelson, ed., *Will Teach for Food: Academic Labor in Crisis* (1997), and Cary Nelson and Stephen Watt, eds., *Academic Keywords: A Devil's Dictionary for Higher Education* (1999).

2. The phrase comes from the title of Norman Mailer's review of Morley Callaghan's memoir *That Summer in Paris* (1963), where Callaghan recounts his "memories of tangled friendships with Hemingway, Fitzgerald, and some others." Mailer objected to Callaghan's portrait of Hemingway, particularly the story of his beating Hemingway in a boxing match while Fitzgerald kept inexpert time. To Mailer's taste, Callaghan was "punching poppa" unfairly; the great man could not, from the grave, punch back. See *The New York Review of Books* 1.1, 1 Feb. 1963.

Works Cited

Bérubé, Michael, and Cary Nelson, eds. *Higher Education Under Fire: Politics, Economics, and the Crisis of the Humanities.* New York: Routledge, 1994.

Callaghan, Morley. *That Summer in Paris: Memories of Tangled Friendships with Hemingway, Fitzgerald, and Some Others.* New York: Coward, 1963.

Espada, Martín. "Poetry Like Bread: Poets of the Political Imagination." *Zapata's Disciple.* Cambridge: South End, 1998. 99–106.

Gramsci, Antonio. *An Antonio Gramsci Reader.* Ed. David Forgacs. New York: Schocken, 1988.

Grossberg, Lawrence, and Cary Nelson, eds. *Marxism and the Interpretation of Culture.* Urbana: U of Illinois P, 1988.

Grossberg, Lawrence, Cary Nelson, and Paula Treichler. "Cultural Studies: An Introduction." *Cultural Studies.* Ed. Lawrence Grossberg, Cary Nelson, and Paula Treichler. New York: Routledge, 1992. 1–16.

Harrison, Brady. *Agent of Empire: William Walker and the Imperial Self in American Literature.* Athens: U of Georgia P, 2004.

Jameson, Fredric. *The Political Unconscious.* Ithaca: Cornell UP, 1981.

Mani, Lati. "Cultural Theory, Colonial Texts: Reading Eyewitness Accounts of Widow Burning." *Cultural Studies.* Ed. Lawrence Grossberg, Cary Nelson, and Paula Treichler. New York: Routledge, 1992. 392–405.

Marx, Karl. "For a Ruthless Criticism of Everything Existing" (Marx to Arnold Ruge, September 1843). *The Marx-Engels Reader.* 2nd ed. Ed. Robert C. Tucker. New York: Norton, 1978. 12–15.

Nelson, Cary. *Repression and Recovery: Modern American Poetry and the Politics of Cultural Memory, 1910–1945.* Madison: U of Wisconsin P, 1989.

———, ed. *Will Teach for Food: Academic Labor in Crisis.* Minneapolis: U of Minnesota P, 1997.

Nelson, Cary, and Stephen Watt. *Academic Keywords: A Devil's Dictionary for Higher Education.* New York: Routledge, 1999.

Said, Edward W. *The World, the Text, and the Critic.* Cambridge: Harvard UP, 1983.

~: 15 :~

Learning My
Professional Responsibilities

James D. Sullivan

My memory cannot be accurate. Cary Nelson cannot have been actually skipping down the second-floor hallway of the University of Illinois English building. Lightly tripping, anyway, and as happy as I have ever seen him, straight toward me with a cheery, "I've got something you need to do today!"

"Oh? What's that, Cary?"

"Buy my book!"

Nelson's *Repression and Recovery* had appeared on the bookstore shelves that day, and he was right. I did need to buy it. And I have needed to read it and reread it several times over the years since then. But at that time, I needed to buy and read it because I was writing a dissertation on nontraditional ways of publishing American poetry in the 1960s: broadsides, posters, pamphlets, postcards, art prints, and so on. I needed to read it for a model of how to look at those objects. That new book, besides arguing for an expansion of the canon—broader, fuller attention to African American poets, to women, and to writers on the political Left—explored also what people have done with poems: what Americans in the first half of the twentieth century thought poetry was for, and what they thought they could accomplish by writing and distributing poetry. A poem is not only an abstract linguistic construct but something material, something accessible through the senses rather than accessible directly to the mind, something that specific people have used on specific occasions for specific purposes. So Cary has looked at old magazines, newspapers, and posters, old book jackets and postcards to find traces of what poetry has meant to people and how they have used it. I learned from him to look at the object in my hand rather than to ignore it and to look through it toward the words alone. I learned from him to ask, "What have people done with this?" and to find cultural meaning in answers to that question.

201

Without Cary's role as an intellectual model and without his encouragement as a mentor, the book that came out of that dissertation never
would have seen print. I am grateful that he had me, from the beginning,
think of it as a book rather than just an exercise on the way toward a degree.

But I must confess, when that book came out in 1997, I felt, unfortunately, only anticlimax. After finishing my PhD in 1991, I spent the 1990s
in the adjunct wilderness: temp jobs here and there for a year or two at a
time, part-time gigs to fill the years in between them. During my years of
professional exile, I learned, from the bottom, a lot about how the academy works. I learned, among other things, that the profession does not,
after all, value the things my education had taught me to value: teaching,
service, collegiality, or publication—even book publication. None of
those, in the saturated job market of the 1990s, actually mattered at all.
Sure, for people who landed tenure-line jobs, those things matter a great
deal in the progress toward tenure. But my ever-growing frustration that
nothing I did would get me anywhere professionally—or would get me
nothing but another turn on the low-status, low-pay adjunct treadmill—
stripped away my naivete. I lost my faith that the accumulation of merit
would win me a place in the Paradise of the Assistant Professors.

Cary encouraged me again, this time to write about the issues, problems, and experiences that were crushing the professional life out of me.
And so I have had a small second emphasis as a critic of the profession,
writing some articles and book reviews that I hope others have found enlightening, but that I know have been therapeutic for me.

Once again, with his encouragement, I was following the lead of my
mentor. Beginning in the 1990s, I would read articles in *Profession, PMLA,*
or *The Chronicle of Higher Education* by great professors who suffered from
the terrible disease of Prestige-Induced Blindness (PIB), a disease we have
yet to eradicate—an AAUP-sponsored telethon is in order. Correlations
have been found between PIB and professional altitude, with those most
likely to be offered a public forum for bloviation most likely also to contract the disease. It makes sufferers unable to see with any clarity the working conditions and career prospects of graduate students and adjuncts. I
have in recent years learned that it also makes community colleges invisible. Cary's long habit, however, of looking at what is actually there at hand
had immunized him from this epidemic among the higher tiers of the
profession. Education does not happen irrespective of any material context any more than poetry does. Just as Cary attends, as a critic, to the specific poem-bearing objects that real people have used to circulate poems
in specific situations, he has also looked at the labor conditions and economic underpinnings of contemporary higher education.

As a critic and a scholar, he has made himself one of the most influential figures in the study of modern American poetry. The Oxford *Anthol-*

ogy of American Poetry and, on the Web, the *Modern American Poetry Site* have reshaped the way modern American poetry is taught. The conferences he has organized and the anthologies he has coedited have markedly influenced the direction of American cultural studies and cultural criticism. Such prestige unused, unexercised, results typically in a bad case of PIB. But this is what I most admire about him now: rather than let achievement and prestige cloud his vision, Cary has used them toward practical goals.

As a man of influence within his academic field, he has the status to be heard when he speaks. So he speaks and writes about what happens to the lower tiers of the profession: what happens to the graduate students, especially in English, but in all fields, lured in by the intellectual pleasure of advanced study of the things that fascinate them, only to find that the main occupiers of their time are the labor-intensive intro classes (composition, basic math, 100-level language courses, etc.) that form the bulk of the department's offerings but that fall beneath the dignity of the professors to teach; what happens to them when they object to the meagerness of their compensation, then get smacked down by both the university and the National Labor Relations Board (NLRB) for daring to speak of unions; what happens to them at the end of the grad school road when they find they have apprenticed themselves all those years of their youth to a labor market of colleges and universities that do not want them, have no room for them, do not care about their training and their skills; what happens to them when they work practically pro bono and without security as cheap and expendable adjuncts; what happens to those who give up. He speaks and writes about the economic, social, and cultural history of the modern university to illuminate what has made it so indifferent to its own young. As Cary used his disciplinary prestige to make himself into a high-profile activist for the rights of the academic underclass, I would see articles by and about him, and I would feel so proud of him.

In 2000, the gods of raw chance finally handed me a tenure-track job at a community college in Peoria: scholarship there a nice hobby but nothing the institution really cares about, the teaching load five courses a semester, mostly composition. And I daily kiss the dust off my office carpet and mutter a morning hosanna over the department coffee pot in gratitude that at last, at last, I have a real college job! (Here is one virtue of the professional wilderness: out there, I learned humility. With every semester possibly my last, I became a better teacher. Scholarship and writing, leading toward no professional reward, became pleasurable ends in themselves.) I teach mostly first-generation college students looking for the associate degree in a technical field that will give them a secure blue-collar job, as well as some others who plan to transfer on for the bachelor degree—lots of nontraditional students, a thoroughly mixed bag of abilities.

This semester, fall 2006, my department of English and language studies (an omnibus that includes literature, composition, film, journalism, foreign languages, and sign language interpretation, among other things) has 137 faculty, 19 of whom are full time. The foreign language division offers courses in Spanish, French, German, and Chinese, but it has only one full timer, teaching Spanish. This is not unusual. I get paid for the work I do, my family gets medical care, I get an office of my own, and I get a convenient parking space. The part timers get none of these. The tuition their students pay, added to the subsidies the state sends us for those students, far more than pays the cost of setting a part timer in front of a room. Those part-time instructors bring in the money that the college uses to pay my salary. I owe them.

University full timers owe them too. The professors hand off to graduate students and adjuncts the low-pay, low-prestige, labor-intensive introductory level classes that make up the bulk of academic labor at universities. There would be even more of it at the universities if the job were not, to such a large extent, outsourced to community colleges. This level of exploitation is utterly invisible to many at the top of the profession because it occurs off the university campus.

Anyway, I owe them. So I write, I make noises, and I serve on a committee called the Adjunct Advisory Committee that oversees policies regarding lower-tier faculty. Some committee members see it as their role to work for small gains in the pay, privileges, and dignity of part-time colleagues, as well as to fend off new, petty indignities and still pettier takeaways of the small privileges and benefits available to them. Struggles that are more than just marginal are not possible right now, but to do less would offend my conscience.

Again, Cary's example is critical for me. I may not have the wide professional standing of someone who can become president of a national organization, but as a tenured full timer, I have professional standing within my college. The measure of my professionalism is not books published but what I do for the underprepared student who wants to be a respiratory therapist and who finds college (and standard punctuation) a bewildering foreign world, or what I do for the sucker in the adjunct office who has loved Flannery O'Connor so much that he, as a direct consequence, finds himself starving in a room full of half-graded bad prose. I remember my responsibilities, and Cary is still there, skipping toward me saying, "I've got something you need to do today."

❧ 16 ❧

LET US NOW
PRAISE FAMOUS MEN

Jim Finnegan

I have seen myself anonymously represented in Cary Nelson's writings on the politics of the profession of English.

And it was not pretty. But it was accurate. So I accept these truths, and I embrace them, and now, when it is appropriate, I pay tribute to the profound influence that Cary's work has had on me so far in my life's journey toward historical and ideological awakening—as a teacher and a scholar certainly but also more generally as a damaged-but-persistent, working, thinking, loving human being in all my immortal and sacred, historically specific existence [*Agee-ian Catholicism mine*]. I was one of those smart but socially inept and "quirky" graduate students "less inclined to interact with faculty" who Cary describes in his essay "Mentoring" in *Academic Keywords*. I was one of those students likely to be "overlooked when fellowships are awarded," who might then "begin to lose confidence and be impeded in his or her progress toward the degree" (164). In *Manifesto of a Tenured Radical*, when Cary once again expounds on the problem of graduate student debt, I was one of those improvident graduate students who raised a family on credit card debt, part-time jobs (to supplement my instructor's pay), and student loans, only to "talk about celebrating their Ph.D.s by declaring bankruptcy" (173).

While I struggle professionally against both imaginary and real, personal and institutional demons, reading Cary Nelson (and Raymond Carver) has helped me cope with, confront, and, ultimately, claim ownership of my experiences of failure. Cary helped me parse out the "intersection of the psychic and the social, the material and the discursive, the extreme and the everyday" (Rothberg 6) of my protracted career as a graduate student and an adjunct lecturer here at the University of Illinois—a flawed, dysfunctional state research university and a flawed, dysfunctional English Department if ever there was one. If you imagine yourself as a scholar or a teacher of social conscience and you have not learned to value personal, social, and historical meanings of failure, then you are probably missing something substantial in Cary Nelson's cultural studies theory, his literary history, his pedagogy, and his contemporaneous political commentary.

One thing you also may be missing is his humility. Let us pause now for those skeptical guffaws. But attentive readers will hear a soft-spoken, humble voice in the deliberativeness of Cary's prose when he speaks truth to power, even when he engages the sport of "strategic rudeness," even when he is relating one of those juicy insider anecdotes naming the names of some of the profession's grossest abusers of power and privilege, and even when he is shining a humorous spotlight on some of the profession's most hypocritical, preening-and-posturing frauds.

One of Cary's more profound moments of humility occurs when, using his own stellar career as his example, he challenges his readers to accept the proposition that getting a full-time job makes and shapes one's career and, therefore (instances of nepotism aside), luck or chance plays a role for *everyone* who lands on their feet in this profession. Amongst ourselves, here in these conference rooms, here within this profession so warped by class-inflected neuroses and elitism, I wonder how many accept the validity of this proposition. How many feel it at the core of their being, how many carry it with them in the dailiness of their lived experiences as scholars and teachers, how many hold it close to their heart when speaking, casually or formally, from *their* positions of power and privilege? It is a working-class thing. (Go back and reread "Cohorts—The Diaspora of the Teachers" now.)

In the fall of 2003, I came back to the University of Illinois to teach as an adjunct lecturer after spending a miserable four months driving a semitruck for an over-the-road company, and then, after that did not work out, loading trucks at the local FedEx Ground hub here in Champaign— another of my many ill-conceived schemes to (selfishly) secure some time of my own to read and write while at the same time hoping to get my family "caught up" financially. (Did I mention already that I really, really "get" Raymond Carver?) Anyway, late one Friday afternoon in November, my good friend Gardner Rogers and I were relaxing in my grad-adjunct office discussing *Revolutionary Memory* and speculating about why some of Cary's disciples tend to historicize 1930s' Popular Front culture in reductively binary, ultimately idealized and reified terms, when a very young, first-year graduate student interrupted us to ask, somewhat embarrassedly and apologetically, "What does Cary Nelson look like?" She of course had heard of him, she said, and she knew a little of his work, but would not know him if he walked right past her in the hall. "You can't miss him,"

Gardner replied, deadpan. "He's about six-feet, five-inches tall and looks like a cross between Karl Marx and Santa Claus." What a compliment, really! For, like Karl Marx, Nelson's words will no doubt reverberate and inspire revolutionary change, not only for those of us whose careers have already been shaped (if not made possible) by *his* career and *his* life's work, but also for future generations of scholars and teachers who will only know him through his published work. And, like Santa Claus, Cary's paternal benevolence toward his student-children knows no bounds.

Works Cited

Nelson, Cary. *Manifesto of a Tenured Radical.* New York: NYU Press, 1998.

Nelson, Cary, and Stephen Watt. *Academic Keywords: A Devil's Dictionary for Higher Education.* New York: Routledge, 1999.

Rothberg, Michael. *Traumatic Realism: The Demands of Holocaust Representation.* Minneapolis: U of Minnesota P, 2000.

ᴠ: 17 ᴠ

Cary Nelson at the
Naval Academy

Jeff Sychterz

I first met Cary Nelson in 2001 when I was a student in his "Modern American Poetry" class. He had published the Oxford *Anthology of Modern American Poetry* a year earlier, and our class represented his first use of the completed text in the classroom. At that time, I had recently returned to school after eight years as a naval officer. Neither the literature education I received at my alma mater, the United States Naval Academy (USNA), nor my own self-directed reading had quite prepared me for the theoretical direction that the humanities had taken in the previous two decades. Most of the graduate classes I took at the University of Illinois adopted such distinctly theoretical approaches that we rarely ever discussed the primary literary texts. Yet despite his reputation as a fierce cultural critic and political advocate, Cary's poetry class was much different; the only texts he assigned were the anthology and the accompanying Web site. In that class we discussed only the poems, but those discussions often took us through great swaths of historical, sociological, theoretical, and even biographical context—sometimes we got through only two poems in three hours. Cary did not need to assign Marxist or feminist theoretical texts, because the poets we read were their own political advocates. Through them, I learned a great deal about American history and forms of literature. Subsequently, I asked Cary to chair my dissertation on twentieth-century Anglo-American war poetry. In 2005 I graduated, and after an unsuccessful bid on the tenure-track job market, I accepted a three-year recall to military service to teach English at the USNA. This institution at times seems very foreign to Nelson's classroom—for one, his ubiquitous Hawaiian shirts and sandals would never fly in this place, where even the tenured professors are required to wear coats and ties—but nevertheless I use his socially engaged model of poetry in my own classroom every day.

Nelson has dedicated himself to the recovery of American labor and the leftist poetry of the 1920s and 1930s in order to keep alive not only certain social possibilities of poetry but also the possibility of socially conscious resistance and change. In that time of history, poetry "had the power to help people not only come to understand the material conditions of their existence but also to envision ways of changing them" (*Repression and Recovery* 124). Although the formation of the canon during the McCarthy years severely blunted that power by repressing leftist poetry and labor history, Nelson has suggested that poetry can have that transformational power again, as it indeed did in the 1960s. Meanwhile, we must recover and keep in circulation instances of poetry as an "oppositional language" that can offer "socially critical perspectives of anger and idealization" in answer to the rarified definition canonized in the classroom. This more agile social definition of poetry keeps alive possibilities for both marginalized and nonmarginalized citizens. Certainly when a culture represses political poetry, in both the public and personal sense, it silences the dispossessed, be they black, poor, woman, leftist, or transsexual. But it also deprives itself of their hard-fought lessons, thus narrowing the field of possible actions; workers who have never heard of a strike will be less likely to mobilize one to protect their rights. The more a culture limits the public contestation of voices, the more it lapses into autocracy, shifting authority from the governed to a centralized power, be it the state, a religion, a gender, or an ethnicity.

Nelson has gone so far as to suggest that because of poetry's "inscaped language" it "embodies all you need to know on earth" (Interview). From one point of view, therefore, the canonical reification of poetry marginalizes poetry and the special form of knowledge it represents. If poetry offers some form of comprehensive knowledge, then we deny it a certain use value when we limit its definition to the universal, the transcendental, and the transhistorical, because it has little to say to the real conditions of our everyday lives. But such a demarcation of epistemological realms works the other way to cheapen nonpoetic discourses as well. By separating off poetry as a higher form of knowledge and limiting the scope of subjects and rhetorical modes considered properly poetic, we mark those discourses that fall outside of the "poetic," and the subject positions defined by them, as inherently meaningless. If we repress inconvenient voices, whether too quotidian or too exotic, then we quite literally limit our own knowledge and understanding. This circumscription reaches down to the most personal level, for "poetry offers us subject positions we can take up consciously and with a paradoxically self-conscious sense of personal identification" (*Repres-*

sion 124). By narrowing the field of validated voices, we rule out potential human identities and communities and restrict the very boundaries of our own egos. By recovering lost poetic voices, whether lost to time or actively repressed, we gain a better perspective on not only our history—who we were—but also our present—who we are. The more voices we listen to and learn from, the more we resist the ossification of identity, whether personal, national, or human.

As I write this from my office at the USNA, I wonder how I can apply Nelson's recovery model in the classroom here. Does a decentered, non-canonical approach to knowledge fundamentally conflict with the mission of a military academy? Here the students, as well as many of the instructors, wear a uniform and are bound by law to a central military bureaucracy. They are trained to respect that centralized authority, and one of the tacit, but central, tenets of that respect is to not question it. Not asking questions plays such a hallowed role in a midshipman's education that there is a special term for it, "Message to Garcia." The term comes from the title of an inspirational essay published in 1899 by Elbert Hubbard, that all midshipmen must learn as plebes (freshmen initiates). Hubbard relates the tale of "a fellow named Rowan," who during the Spanish-American War was asked by President McKinley to carry a message to an insurgent leader "somewhere in the mountain fastnesses of Cuba" (5). Nobody knew where he was or how to locate him, but Rowan completed the task. Literally, "Message to Garcia" means "don't ask me, go figure it out for yourself," and as such it teaches a laudatory self-sufficiency and ingenuity—something I personally know Nelson tries to develop in his students. Yet midshipmen apply "Message to Garcia" so broadly that it often acts as a bar to institutional memory and the productive interchange of ideas. I hear it in the classroom after I have asked for the purpose behind one of the many idiosyncratic events that make up their lives, and a plebe replies, "It's just tradition, sir." Citing tradition encourages students to accept the status quo simply because it is the status quo. United States military personnel are proud of their traditions and broadly consider them the bulwarks of their identities. To question them is to threaten that identity, both institutionally and personally.

But the US military certainly does not want mindless automatons as officers. Each commissioning source, whether ROTC or academy, requires recruits to take a series of discussion-based classes in areas such as ethics, leadership, and literature to ensure that they develop into bright, thoughtful, and even agile thinkers. But that same military hierarchy prefers its leaders to narrowly apply their intellect, curiosity, and talents to new and more efficient ways of carrying out the will of their superiors. The lesson of "Message to Garcia," and a respect for tradition, delimits the scope of subjects open for questioning. The young officer understands that she has a duty to disobey an immoral order but must rely on a higher authority to

define exactly the limits of morality, something Nelson refers to as "a simu-
lacra of agency." Many times that higher authority will be the same one
issuing the questionable order. To produce such a narrowly fixated intelligence requires contorted mental gymnastics reminiscent of Orwell's
doublethink—all in the name of relieving young officers of the authority to
speak, or, more properly, ensuring that they speak only as mouthpieces of
a higher authority.

Yet does this essentialized model of authority taught in a military
academy differ that greatly from the educational model of other US universities? Nelson's almost decade-long critique of the corporate direction
of higher education highlights some troubling similarities. Increasingly,
universities regard their mission as producing a workforce for corporate
America rather than developing democratic citizens. Thus curricula
focus more and more on a narrow set of skills directly applicable to the
workplace and less on giving students access to subject positions from
which to question and evaluate the corporate hegemony. Meanwhile, the
shift to part-time faculty, whether graduate student or adjunct, gives the
university more power to silence dissenting voices in the increasingly diminishing liberal education classes. In a 2002 interview, Nelson explained that the university not only had the means but also the will to
broadly exercise that power, affirming that "the corporate university
wants complete loyalty across the board." Such a statement sounds more
characteristic of a military command than a university boardroom. But
what, after all, is a military academy but an institution dedicated to a narrow form of occupational training? Military terms such as discipline, dedication, and tradition all enforce a fundamentally military concept of
"complete loyalty." To a certain degree, therefore, we can locate the difference between civilian and military institutions in the greater length of
time that military academies have worked under a "Message to Garcia"
model, as well as how thoroughly they have applied it.

Of course, we tend to associate such blind loyalty with the military, but
the consequences of producing yes-men in their ranks can be much more
immediate and shocking than in the corporate world. The average business
student will not find himself soon after graduation having to weigh the lives
of his soldiers against those of Iraqi civilians, or be asked to carry out an "extreme interrogation" order. However, although less sensational than these
headlines from a war zone, the aggregate loss of oppositional voices in educational institutions throughout the United States is far more troubling:
"The world's only superpower," explains Nelson, "should be training its citizens to be critical members of democracy. You don't want a vast power
that's willing to use that power across the world to have citizens that can't
think and talk and intervene in public life. That's really dangerous" (Interview). The military is only the forward most extension of that power. Even

considering its specialized training in harnessing and directing violence, it moves and acts within patterns of behavior legitimized at home. If we produce graduates who do not know or care how that power is used, or how and why to contest its abuse, then our country will place few constraints on the use of violence to forward national ambition. Atrocities abroad begin with acquiescence at home.

That internally uncontested power is not only dangerous but also profoundly un-American. The lesson of Nelson's poetry recovery project is that the triumph of a corporate hegemony has been constructed precisely through a complex repression of national and institutional memory. Current military identities rely on just such repression as well. In the classroom and through my research I attempt to fill in some of those holes for my students. I teach them about the history of military resistance from World War I to the first Gulf War. We discuss the Vietnam Veterans against the War and the widespread and organized revolt of soldiers during the Vietnam era, correcting misconceptions that hippies and draft dodgers sapped our national will, or that only draftees resisted. We read texts, such as Tim O'Brien's "On the Rainy River," that suggest that it takes more courage to resist than to go to war. I teach them about post-traumatic stress disorder (PTSD), and we watch John Huston's *Let There Be Light*, a 1945 Army training film on battle fatigue that was officially suppressed because it normalized PTSD as an inevitable consequence of combat. And, of course, we read the poetry of combat veterans from World War I to the current Iraq War, all of which powerfully dispels the lies of nationalism and the myths of battlefield glory and honor that had attracted many of them to the academy in the first place.

More importantly, though, we weigh their military obligations against their duties as democratic citizens. We read texts, such as Thoreau's "Resistance to Civil Government," that offer alternate modes of citizenship and that consider skepticism and resistance necessary components of a healthy democracy. Thoreau's text also introduces a more skeptical view of militarism to students who think that the military represents the most hallowed form of public service. Situating Thoreau within a historical distrust of militarism shows that he is far from a lone voice—only for the last fifty years have Americans accepted a standing army without question; prior to World War II, such a prospect was considered dangerously unconstitutional. And, of course, we read a range of texts offering points of view on more immediate aspects of their lives, from racism, misogyny, and poverty to gender construction, because after graduation they will find themselves responsible for subordinates who often come from very different socioeconomic backgrounds from themselves. Learning in the classroom to hear and empathize with others' voices can only help them become better leaders.

Not once do I advocate a particular ideology, because I certainly do not intend to turn my students into revolutionaries. Even if I did, recent studies suggest that teachers can do little to change a college student's ideology. I do, however, introduce texts that offer students a range of skeptical positions from which to more meaningfully assess their duties as officers and citizens. I want them to think seriously about the oath they take "to support and defend the constitution of the United States." They do not swear allegiance to the president, to Congress, to their superior officers, or to a political party, but to an ideal of democracy. Skepticism is profoundly American, because the US Constitution disperses authority broadly through the citizenry, at least in ideal if not in practice, charging each of us with determining the direction of the country. My students need to know that many citizens and servicemen and servicewomen who have gone before them fundamentally believed that resistance to centralized authority can be profoundly patriotic and is sometimes necessary to the health of a democratic system. If today's senior military leadership had access to this repressed notion of citizenship, would we have invaded Iraq? Only after the fact have several retired generals come forward to testify to their misgivings in the run up to the war. Can we imagine a situation in which these same generals would have felt compelled by their oath to speak out *publicly* against the official half-truths and flagrant misconceptions?

Like Nelson, I am pessimistic about the direction of higher education, both generally and in the specific case of the USNA. Recently, the academy has undergone a number of institutional changes designed to focus midshipmen training on a particularly instrumentalized model of naval officer as technocrat. In 2006, a board of senior officers recommended replacing freshman "Introduction to Literature" classes with "Navy Writing." That recommendation went unheeded, but such calls will become only more frequent and more insistent in the future, especially as petitions to produce a more technically proficient workforce become more frequent. Most recently, the chief of naval operations mandated that the academy graduate at least 65% technical majors. To make that a reality, the class of 2011 may be forced to sign up 72% of its class as engineers. Meanwhile, in an apparently unrelated development, the new superintendent (the vice admiral who heads the academy) stresses that since 2001 America has been a nation at war, therefore, midshipmen must reduce "distractions" in order to focus on training themselves as "warriors." The distractions that he suggests eliminating or reducing include alternative educational models, such as field trips and lectures, and outreach programs, such as building houses for Habitat for Humanity. These may seem like developments unique to the academy, but they reflect a nationwide trend of narrowing the scope of a university education to job training. These changes ensure an erosion of the classic liberal education, the production of students less able and willing to publicly engage in shaping democracy, and less exposure to voices that contest traditional notions of community, citizenship, and, in the case of the academy, military duty.

But even if these trends were reversed, can a military academy ever be an agent of change? I have at least one student who thinks so. When I taught my first majors' course, I developed a rapport with a particularly bright and socially engaged English major. He comes by frequently to talk about current events, the military, politics, ethics, or whatever. He inevitably steers our discussions toward a question that he takes very seriously: How can he effect a social revolution—one that gives the people more voice in their government, gives workers more control over their workplace, and transforms our cultural aspirations from wealth and power to compassion and justice? Some may be surprised that a young man with such high-minded goals would pursue a military career. To those, I suggest they read the poetry of Thomas McGrath, US Army Air Force officer and communist organizer, or even the British officer-poet Siegfried Sassoon, who believed that World War I soldiers would return from the front to lead a socialist revolution. Like these predecessors, my student does not consider military service antithetical to this larger goal. On the contrary, he reminds me that at certain moments in our history the military has been in the vanguard of social change—integrating almost two decades before the civil rights movement and placing women in leadership roles well before corporate America did. He considers that progressive potential as something innate in military service: "After all," he says, "onboard ship, people from vastly different backgrounds all eat and sleep together, while working toward a common goal, which doesn't involve earning someone more money." He is attracted to the communal elements of that military life, socialized housing, meals, health care, child care, and so on. Most importantly, he wants to pursue a naval career so that someone like him will be in a position to say no the next time a president wants to use the military as a tool for naked empire building. These aspects, he contends, are embodied in the officer's oath, which he finds "beautiful and breathtaking," for it places him in service to a democratic ideal.

Overly idealistic? Certainly. But that form of idealism can keep alive alternate forms of identity formation, encouraging other midshipmen to approach their military and civil obligations with a healthy skepticism, and hopefully a clearer notion of social justice. Besides, his idealism includes a practical commitment to action: working to build a community of like-minded midshipmen as a forum where notions of duty, service, and citizenship can be debated and contested. In the classroom, I endeavor to keep alive this same sense of social contestation at the heart of American identity for him and others, so that when faced with tough decisions, which

I have been lucky enough to avoid in my peacetime service, they recognize options that previously they may never have considered possible. This is the legacy of Cary Nelson that I carry forward into the English classroom at the United States Naval Academy.

Works Cited

Hubbard, Elbert. *A Message to Garcia.* East Aurora: Roycrofters, 1899.

Nelson, Cary. Interview with Marc Bousquet. "An Intellectual of the Movement: An Interview with Cary Nelson." *Workplace: A Journal for Academic Labor* 5.1 (2002) 29 Sept. 2006 <http://www.louisville.edu/journal/workplace/issue5p1/bousquetnelson.html>.

———. *Repression and Recovery: Modern American Poetry and the Politics of Cultural Memory, 1910–1945.* Madison: U of Wisconsin P, 1989.

∾ 18 ∾

WITHOUT SHAME

ON CARY NELSON'S LEGACY

John Marsh

Else, to-morrow a stranger will say with masterly good sense precisely what we have thought and felt all the time, and we shall be forced to take with shame our own opinion from another.

—Ralph Waldo Emerson, "Self-Reliance"

During my first or second year of graduate school at the University of Illinois at Urbana-Champaign—this would have been 2000 or thereabouts—I was reading some history of the late-nineteenth and early twentieth-century United States that briefly mentioned "The Man with the Hoe," Edwin Markham's frequently reprinted poem full of sympathy for the farmer, "the slave to the wheel of labor" and outrage at the "masters, lords and rulers in all lands," whom Markham charges with having made and kept this "thing"—that is, the farmer—in abject, ignorant bondage. Intrigued, I wondered if anyone had studied or written about the poem or poet, and if not, someone (that someone was me) certainly should. Later that week, browsing in the university bookstore, I came across Cary Nelson's recently published *Anthology of Modern American Poetry* and found Markham's poem. Worse yet, the head note revealed that "the original"— that is, the original illustrated version of the poem published in the *San Francisco Examiner*—was "in the editor's collection." Oh well, I said, and moved on.

Not long after, I became actively involved in the campaign at Illinois to form a graduate student union. Desperate for more information on labor in the university, particularly the humanities, I wondered if anyone had studied or written about how the university was beginning to act in ways more becoming a corporation than a university, and if not, someone (again, that someone was me) certainly should. Sure enough, Nelson, together with Stephen Watt, had just published *Academic Keywords: A*

Devil's Dictionary for Higher Education, which made good on Marc Bousquet's blurb on the back cover that it was "an utterly frank, witty, and thoroughly engrossing portrait of the appalling experience of today's students and educators."

I began to worry. Had Nelson already had every good idea that might manage to burrow its way into my young academic head? I decided that I had to test the phenomenon by embarking on an act of scholarship so unpredictable, so impossibly obscure, that no one, not even Nelson, could have known about it or written about it beforehand. What was my unpredictable, impossible idea? In the course of doing some other research, I stumbled onto the fact that throughout the twentieth century people oftentimes wrote poems on postcards or circulated postcards with poems already printed on them.

That last paragraph is a lie. Of course I learned about the postcards from Cary, and the thought never crossed my mind before then, but my larger point stands. For a while, it seemed that as I became interested in a topic—Marxism, cultural studies, radical poets, the Spanish Civil War—Cary had already published a book on the subject. On the one hand, and as a graduate student, it felt good to have a senior and respected scholar like Cary confirm that your scholarly and research hunches were good ones, even if they arrived anywhere from six months to six years too late. On the other hand, and also as a graduate student, I wanted to do original research, to contribute to the field in some new and uncharted way, and recycling Cary's work clearly would not do. Feeling more like a latecomer than ever, I had had about all the anxiety of influence I could stand. It was time for some serious misprision.[1]

Eventually, of course, I moved on to projects that not even Cary had thought to do. Or maybe he had but had not gotten around to doing them. I did not ask, and I do not want to know. Still, and the point I want to make here, those projects may well have never happened without his earlier efforts. Cary never told me to start digging around in union newspapers from the 1930s for the remarkable poems that workers published there, or to start thinking and writing about how many of our most canonical modern American poets invented themselves as modernists largely by incorporating the poor and working class into their poetry. But Cary, whether in seminars, in conversation, or just in his published work, did provide reassurance that the poems I spent months digging up or that the critical and interpretive work I was doing had merit. He encouraged me to believe that these were poems worth recovering, and that these were arguments worth making, even if at times it felt like others in the discipline did not always think so and were even less likely to say so.

As my examples of Markham and *Academic Keywords* might suggest, I have been principally influenced—and relatively free of anxiety regarding that influence—by the attention Cary has given to questions of labor, aca-

demic and otherwise. I come from a working-class family, and poetry—
and, even more so, the study of poetry—oftentimes seemed to lie on the
opposite end of the class spectrum. I was interested in poetry despite this,
or perhaps because it was a way to escape my class background, but I remember the thrill I experienced when I learned from reading Cary that
labor and poetry were not mutually exclusive areas of inquiry. But the fact
that people, including me, for so long believed that they were meant that
much work remained to be done, and not even Cary had exhausted all of
the questions worth asking about these subjects.

Cary was interested in labor not just as it appeared in modern American poetry but also as it appears on campuses. Just as I began to understand that one did not have to disavow labor (or one's background) to
study poetry, I also realized that one did not—could not—escape the
question of labor when one taught poetry (or anything else) either. During the graduate student union campaign at the University of Illinois,
Nelson was required reading—or required listening since he frequently
spoke at our meetings, rallies, and direct actions. Of all of Cary's contributions, it is easily this one that I admire most: his capacity, and also
his willingness, to bring questions of labor into our scholarship and
onto our campuses. A sentence from his recent book, *Revolutionary Memory*, makes the point. In discussing, as it happens, Markham's "The Man
with the Hoe" and a particularly asinine comment by a Yale English professor during that campus's strike, Cary writes, "Contempt for workers
might be less easily mustered if we had sustained our awareness of their
place in literary history" (55). I do not know whether that is true, but I
hope it is, and that hope, at any rate, is above all else what I have taken
from Cary.

In summation, in reflecting on and celebrating Cary Nelson's legacy
as a teacher, a mentor, a scholar, and an activist, I want to say that while
he may have preempted some of our best ideas, he also has enabled our
even better ones. In this, then, as in so much else, Emerson—and the
passage from "Self-Reliance," which begins this essay—is wrong. There is
no shame in taking our opinion from another, if only because opinions
are not, as Emerson would have it, a finite or fixed resource. We build
upon opinions and ideas, adapt them to new situations, and in the adapting we generate new opinions, new ideas. Cary's opinions—and his work
more generally—constitute a remarkable legacy, as will the opinions and
work generated from them. We can all be shamelessly in his debt.

Note

1. As Harold Bloom makes clear, critics too are subject to the anxiety of influence. "There are no interpretations but only misinterpretations," Bloom oracularly
writes, "and so all criticism is prose poetry" (95).

Works Cited

Bloom, Harold. *The Anxiety of Influence: A Theory of Poetry.* 2nd ed. New York: Oxford UP, 1997.

Emerson, Ralph Waldo. "Self-Reliance." 1841. *The Essential Writings of Ralph Waldo Emerson.* Ed. Brooks Atkinson. New York: Modern Library, 2000. 132–53.

Markham, Edwin. "The Man with the Hoe." *Anthology of Modern American Poetry.* Ed. Cary Nelson. New York: Oxford UP, 2000. 18–20.

Nelson, Cary. *Revolutionary Memory: Recovering the Poetry of the American Left.* New York: Routledge, 2001.

Nelson, Cary, and Stephen Watt. *Academic Keywords: A Devil's Dictionary for Higher Education.* New York: Routledge, 1999.

☙ 19 ❧

AFTERWORD

ACTIVISM AND COMMUNITY IN THE ACADEMY

Cary Nelson

Not long ago I was talking to students in a graduate seminar in poetry about what I would do differently were I writing *Repression and Recovery: Modern American Poetry and the Politics of Cultural Memory, 1910–1945* (1989) now. Not for a minute would I consider altering the structure of the book, but there are a number of textual/cultural episodes I would be eager to add. These additions would not be sufficient to turn the book's account of modern poetry into a continuous narrative. We will never arrive at such a construction of the past except by emulating the false disciplinary confidences of the 1950s and 1960s. As literary historians have increasingly learned over the last generation, the past is never fixed and settled. It is always being reconceived and rearticulated; it is subject to continual modification; and it has no final destination, no certain teleology.

Historians have perhaps always known that. Literary critics, long in thrall to the illusions promulgated by faith in the canon of masterpieces, resisted such knowledge until major efforts to open up the canon gained force in the 1980s. The general public, unfortunately, still largely believes the humanities as a whole serve to transmit and preserve an unchanging heritage. If that were the case, then neither academic freedom nor faculty members themselves would be so necessary. As long as the past remains inherently discontinuous and unresolved, as long as its encapsulation in current memory needs to be challenged again and again, we need new research and we need faculty with the freedom to confront received and revered truths.

It is such canonized truths that *Repression and Recovery* sought to challenge. Yet further challenges have emerged since the book was published. I have since done enough work, for example, to realize that—despite its absence from literary histories—a significant body of anti-McCarthy poetry was written in the 1950s. The turning point for me was recovering the unpublished work of Edwin Rolfe, adding it to the privately published anti-McCarthy poems in his posthumous *Permit Me Refuge* (1955), then editing his *Collected Poems* with my former graduate student Jefferson Hendricks. Later I would find Alvah Bessie's anti-McCarthy poems, also existing only as unpublished manuscripts. Adding Rolfe's and Bessie's poems to the fiercely anti-McCarthy poems of Aaron Kramer, once again privately published in 1954, makes such apparently isolated poems as Langston Hughes's "Un-American Investigators," first published posthumously in 1967, part of a much longer and broader political movement.

Doing justice to this body of work would necessitate adding a decade to *Repression and Recovery's* chronology. That would also let me address Kramer's twenty-six-poem sequence "Denmark Vesey," perhaps the best poem on African American history ever written by a white American, which uses a South Carolina slave revolt to address 1950s racism and repression. "Denmark Vesey," in consequence, would be my first choice for an addition to my *Anthology of Modern American Poetry*. I would not, however, have learned to appreciate the special music of Kramer's rhymed politics without Alan Wald's prompting. Expanding *Repression and Recovery's* reach to 1955 also would enable me to cover Melvin Tolson's "Libretto for the Republic of Liberia," a masterpiece made accessible for the first time by Ed Brunner's wonderful annotations in the *Anthology of Modern American Poetry*. The importance of Tolson's career gets its best treatment in Michael Bérubé's *Marginal Forces*, but I could not represent the 1950s in an anthology without rethinking the decade in light of Brunner's groundbreaking scholarly study *Cold War Poetry*.

A new edition of *Repression and Recovery* also would need to give space to some of the work I did in *Revolutionary Memory: Recovering the Poetry of the American Left* (2001). I did not realize before then how prescient were the poems written in protest of the 1899 war in the Philippines, especially those that indict the fundamentally racist character of imperialism. Nor did I realize how extensive, how long lasting, and how widely international was the continuing tradition of American poems written in response to the 1936–1939 Spanish Civil War, a tradition that began in 1936 and that continues to the present day. Nor did I quite understand in the 1980s how thoroughly choral and intertexual the poetry of social movements can be. Authorship is, in truth, not always central to poetry's signifying effects.

Yet there are many potential additions to *Repression and Recovery* that neither I nor any other scholars are yet ready to make. Among these would be an account of the newspaper poems, anthologies, and individually authored books of poems that immigrants in the United States produced in other languages, especially in the late nineteenth and early twentieth centuries. Few of us are ready to master all the languages at issue, ranging from Yiddish to Finnish, but the poems are out there waiting to be recovered. Another vast domain is represented by all the kinds of popular poetry largely ignored by literary scholars. I have collected several thousand advertising poems from the late nineteenth and early twentieth centuries, ranging from a long poem in imitation of Walt Whitman advertising a New York newspaper, to an equally long poem in imitation of Oscar Wilde promoting a Boston department store, to a twenty-six poem sonnet sequence on behalf of a Philadelphia shoe manufacturer. These are not the jingles of more recent memory but, rather, substantial poems with elaborate cultural references.

At the same time *Repression and Recovery* would be enriched by more recent work by other scholars. I never thought of giving any space to Sara Teasdale, whom I dismissed as hopelessly sentimental. But now my student Melissa Girard has recovered Teasdale's uncollected and unpublished antiwar poems written on the eve of the US entry into World War I, and Teasdale thereby becomes a different and newly powerful poet. Her work thus must be added to the wonderful work my former student Mark Van Wienen has done in recovering a major body of forgotten American antiwar poetry written before we entered World War I. My colleague and former student John Marsh has researched the poems published in modern union newspapers and given us an anthology of those forgotten texts. And no summary of the recovery work linked to Champaign-Urbana could omit mention of research projects by two University of Illinois faculty—William Maxwell's immensely important and unsettling discovery of Claude McKay's late, unpublished anticommunist sonnets or Robert Parker's recovery of scores of forgotten and unknown Native American poems. Parker has identified 128 Native American poets writing before 1930, 52 of them prior to 1900, an immense expansion of the literary record, and one to be embodied in an anthology that he is editing.

The present book exists in part to celebrate the scholarship done by members of this extended community. The work done by one department's students and faculty—a group whose Illinois PhDs include several highly productive poetry scholars included in this book, among them Karen Jackson Ford, Walter Kalaidjian, and Michael Thurston—suggests how critical continuing humanities scholarship is to our knowledge of American history, culture, and political life. Would any of us prefer to keep disseminating the false claim that American poets did not address the subject of McCarthyism? Are we comfortable now with the image of Teasdale that prevailed for a century, the image indeed that she herself promoted by excluding her antiwar poems from her books? Would we rather be ignorant of the Japanese-American haikus composed in America's World

War II concentration camps, poems only recently recovered and now, for the first time, ably analyzed in Ford's essay? This evolving story will never be complete. It will always be riddled with gaps and erasures. But it is the continuing work of revising and supplementing the past that sustains its presence and keeps it vital.

We thus owe humanities scholars the resources to continue the search for better truths about our cultural heritage. At the very least, such research requires funds for travel and hotel costs, along with the free time to do the work. Yet such resources are seriously threatened. My own university considered eliminating all funds for humanities research in 2007, all in service to the logic that research that does not turn a financial profit is not worth supporting. We could argue, of course, that there is likewise no profit in cultural and political blindness and ignorance. That is the alternative held out to us by the emerging corporate university, an entity I described in *Academic Keywords: A Devil's Dictionary for Higher Education* (1999), and one that, as Andrew Ross shows us here, continues to morph into new, more international incarnations.

In order to sustain the humanities and enable them to enrich American culture—a culture otherwise destined to be set in fascist stone, sustained by uncontested platitudes—we need to redefine the communities dedicated to humanities research. This book is a modest example of such a community, one embracing all those who produce, interpret, and disseminate ongoing humanities research. The work these scholars do extends well beyond major publication to include teaching graduate and undergraduate students, reviewing and evaluating the scholarship of others, and interrogating the state of the university, a field of scholarship, and the discipline as a whole.

Put simply, humanities research would be worth little if it were not disseminated to new generations of students. It would have much less chance for impact if it were not evaluated in book reviews or in the much longer career overview essays that Edward Brunner and Kalaidjian contribute here. The meaning and impact of a book, the cultural work a book can hope to do, can be transformed by the kind of in-depth reflection that Grant Farred offers for *Repression and Recovery*. It is a book deeply influenced by Jacques Derrida's work, but Farred extends its Derridean implications substantially by linking *Repression and Recovery's* reflections on canonicity to Derrida's own analysis of the law and of the archive.

What I am suggesting is that we need a level, nonhierarchical model of subdisciplinary and interdisciplinary research communities that encompasses the whole range of teaching and research activities and the whole range of academic institutions. We need to find ways of honoring and recognizing all the kinds of contributions people make to their particular research communities. Peer review and recognition of teaching, for example, should include an evaluation of how faculty incorporate and interpret recent research in their teaching. In order to protect the humanities from administrative aggression and public indifference, they need the solidarity and sense of shared mission that broad-based research communities could promote.

These research communities also would necessarily embrace the whole range of academic teaching and research positions—part-time faculty, full-time faculty ineligible for tenure, academic professionals, and the tenured and tenure-track faculty who were once the bedrock of the teaching staff. No more. In 1975, tenured and tenure-track faculty made up 56.8% of the professoriate. As AAUP figures show, by 2005, thirty years later, their combined proportion of the professoriate had fallen to 31.9%.

Promoting research communities is one critical way to unify this diverse group of academics, something that must happen if diverging interests are not to divide these constituencies still further and turn them against one another. Those who wish to suppress humanities research to diminish its influence on current and future generations—and to curtail enhancing critical citizenship as a central goal of higher education—will welcome the primary identification of research with elite institutions. The notion of research communities can demonstrate that the combined production and dissemination of research unifies all of higher education, from Harvard University to Dade County Community College.

Disciplinary associations usually have defined divisions or interest groups that accurately name potential research communities, but their meaningful activities often are limited to planning convention sessions or editing a journal. They may do little else to unify their membership. And they do not typically make outreach efforts to contingent faculty or to the two-year sector. Much more would need to be done, not only to broaden membership but also to recognize, promote, coordinate, and publicize all of the teaching and writing that research communities do. Such communities also would need to confront the special pressures that contingent faculty face. Jane Juffer's cautionary account here of student needs would have still greater force in community colleges.

Publication itself often blurs the line between teaching and research, since not only publishing unknown or forgotten primary texts but also disseminating interpretations of texts often will have a direct classroom impact. Research communities also would need to give more full recognition (and more serious evaluation) to the impact that major textbooks have on the culture. Kalaidjian is an immensely distinguished scholar, but he also happens to be the author of the single best textbook introduction to poetry.

One way the local wing of the modern American poetry research community has built itself and has had international impact is by contributing to the large Web site I describe in *Office Hours: Activism and Change in the Academy* (2004). Since the Modern American Poetry Site (MAPS) (<http://www.english.uiuc.edu/maps/>) was established in 2000, among the new essays found online have been several hundred written by University of Illinois graduate students, offering interpretations of twentieth-century poems. Many of these essays have been devoted to poets for whom no other published analyses exist. The poems themselves are reprinted in the Oxford *Anthology of Modern American Poetry* (2000). The hundreds of thousands of students and faculty worldwide who visit the site are able to access close readings that help stimulate their own thinking. Meanwhile, as time goes on, and new additions to the site commenting on earlier readings are added, a dialogue among generations of readers and critics takes place in a single communal space. Among the results is a palimpsest of local graduate students commenting on each other's work through the years.

The need for a sense of community in higher education is in fact still more pressing than even the multiple assaults on humanities research might suggest. Just as power in higher education once flowed centrifugally toward departments, it has reversed course over a generation and begun to flow centripetally toward central administrations. Two generations of faculty—obsessed with their careers and identified almost exclusively with their academic disciplines—have been distracted and inattentive as the character of campus decision making has been gradually transformed. This trend has been accelerated by the growing number of contingent faculty lacking the job security that undergirds academic freedom. Shared governance as a consequence is being undermined. Faculty control over the curriculum and over faculty hiring is on the decline. Faculty input on shaping their institutions' educational mission is seriously threatened.

These developments need to be resisted, but we cannot do so without visible models of community-oriented subject positions for faculty to emulate. A number of the contributors to this book have found ways of combining commitments to scholarship and teaching with substantial forms of community service, whether it has been directing the Unit for Criticism and Interpretive Theory at Illinois or rebuilding the New York University AAUP chapter and supporting NYU graduate employees in their struggle to regain their collective bargaining rights. I, along with Michael Bérubé and Marc Bousquet, am currently active in the national AAUP. The three of us also worked for long years trying to turn the Modern Language Association (MLA) into an organization that would take some responsibility for the destructive behavior of its constituent departments, especially their exploitation of contingent faculty and graduate employees. Others have combined writing about their disciplinary interests with writing either about national politics or about the politics of higher education. I have been particularly proud that several of my graduate students have gone that route and developed that sort of dual publishing career.

As the previous paragraph suggests, writing alone can be an important form of activism. I would not want to say that activist writing has to be supplemented by organizational work or commitment to contemporary causes. Yet the profession has discursively and psychologically awarded activist credentials to far too many publications that do not merit the honor, just as it has idolized scholars for the political impact that they often have not had. Merely opening intellectual opportunities for other scholars to add to their vitae does not amount to groundbreaking political work. One should not have to add, but I have found it necessary to do so repeatedly, that academic political heroes who actively subvert progressive political movements, among them faculty who refuse to support employee group collective bargaining rights, do not deserve our adulation. At the very least, then, activist writing needs to be integrated with a personal political ethic, with credible reflection on contemporary cultural and political choices.

Though the number of faculty members adopting such double consciousness—simultaneously looking after their own interests and the interests of a local or national community—is dwarfed by the number who count self-interest as their main priority, the lives of many of the contributors to this book prove that such multiple commitments are possible. Bousquet's groundbreaking *How the University Works* is matched by continuing activism. It is increasingly clear that higher education needs more people like him. The national AAUP includes hundreds of people devoted both to their own careers and to the common good, typically with a dedication that is generous and selfless.

Yet much in the acculturation of current faculty militates against this model. Whether local or national, community commitment often entails tolerance for acting collectively. Faculty's faith in their absolute independence of mind and will has helped instill a revulsion for collective action. Of course that faith in self-sufficiency requires suppression of awareness of one's self-subjection to disciplinary norms, but faculty seem skilled at such self-deception.

Nor has modern history altogether made collective action or mass movements appealing to American academics. As the major mass movements of the 1930s—communism and fascism—came to be deceptively identified with one another in the 1950s, the postwar model of faculty identity settled into the illusion of self-sufficiency. Yet history soon provided new counter-opportunities for collective action in the civil rights movement, the anti-war movement, and the feminist movement. Many faculty who came of age in those group causes willingly adopted dual identities within the university, including those who pioneered the principled university unionization movement of the 1970s, a movement that emulated earlier labor history by looking beyond bread-and-butter issues and embracing both community social responsibility and appropriate principles of campus governance. Unfortunately, a number of those unions failed to recruit new leaders from the next generation of faculty. Some locals lost their broader commitments and hired staff to take over from faculty and run the union, often thereafter focusing exclusively on salary and benefits. The pendulum had swung back again; faculty identity once again embraced subjective isolationism.

Historical opportunity and individual experience typically combine to shape an academic life that eschews or embraces some version of community. I would most likely not have taken the route I did without a series of formative experiences. In the late 1950s my family began attending antinuclear and peace rallies in Bucks County, Pennsylvania. There I repeatedly heard speakers like Norman Thomas and Linus Pauling. I heard firsthand about passionate and eloquent political advocacy. I also experienced the special excitement of being in a crowd of like-minded people. All of that culminated when we joined the demonstrators on the Washington Mall to hear Martin Luther King deliver his most famous speech.

Meanwhile, in my other life, in high school, I was writing long term papers on Franz Kafka and William Faulkner. At Antioch College, I mixed papers on William Butler Yeats and Ranier Maria Rilke with regular antiwar activism. A secret service agent wrestled me to the ground after a dozen of us interrupted a Lyndon Johnson speech in Columbus, Ohio. In Washington, D.C., I would hear Allen Ginsberg read his "Pentagon Exorcism Chant" on a flatbed truck facing thousands of armed troops. I ended my undergraduate career with a paid job as a college draft counselor, which at Antioch meant being a draft avoidance counselor, helping to coordinate access to psychiatrists willing to write letters for young men desperate to avoid Vietnam. Neither my publication history nor my activism could be said to break with this past. In 2006, about to become AAUP president, my predecessor Jane Buck and I were arrested on a New York street for civil disobedience in protest of the NYU administration's withdrawal of graduate employee collective bargaining rights. Later that year I was on a picket line supporting faculty on strike at Eastern Michigan University. Edwin Rolfe, cultural studies, and academic freedom had replaced Kafka and Faulkner as paper topics.

Of course these are the affirmative continuities that brought me where I am today. There were also the discontinuities, which sometimes amount to a dystopian continuity. Until becoming a faculty member, I was either let go—or on the verge of being dismissed—from every job I had. Though I can work long hours on my own, I found myself constitutionally incapable of working in an office from 9 to 5. Nor was I very good at following orders. Problems also arose with political work. Meetings dominated by fruitless speculation about improbable political effects, among them Students for a

Democratic Society (SDS) meetings in the 1960s, I found intolerable. Even worse were MLA Executive Council meetings devoted to ceremonial trivialities, elitist self-indulgence, and parochial interests.

To my astonishment, I discovered that AAUP meetings often were devoted to accomplishing something. Even with principled issues, to be sure, all the power dynamics of interpersonal relations were in play, but the AAUP likes to end a meeting with a goal achieved. Like all voluntary organizations, it has—contrary to all reason—a few leaders focused on personal gain, but it also has a remarkable number of faculty activists who are selflessly devoted to the common good.

I could add to this narrative, but there is no need. My point is that many faculty activists have some comparable intersections of history and biography enabling them. It is far more difficult simply to create the circumstances that lead to faculty activism. Happily, we do not need a majority of faculty to lead their lives this way. It would make a considerable difference if most faculty simply joined the AAUP and paid their dues to the one organization dedicated to defining the key principles that should govern higher education. But we also need a core of effective leaders committed to maintaining shared governance and academic freedom on every campus, and many campuses seem not to have even that core critical mass of community-oriented faculty leaders.

At the moment, the main social movement currently producing future faculty who combine personal intellectual commitments with a sense of broad professional responsibility is graduate employee unionization. Beyond that, we have only the implicit mentoring done by the example of faculty personal practice, the lives committed faculty lead and their capacity to inspire graduate students to find their own ways to construct identities that interweave ambition with service. My own long support for graduate employee unionization no doubt helped encourage several of my own graduate students to assume leadership roles in their local American Federation of Teachers (AFT). The example faculty members set does help inspire the next generation. Best of all is the tendency that devoted faculty have to exceed their mentors' reach. While I have been close to many graduate students, the mentoring that Ford and Marsha Bryant now do as faculty members—exemplified in Bryant's compelling essay here—encompasses more than I either did or imagined.

Although I have faith in the power of exemplary lives, I realize that artificial calls for change can fall on no ears more deaf than those of tenured faculty. Effective change has to be rooted in material conditions. We could wait for history to provide us with the impetus to reform faculty identities, but so far recent history is not treating shared governance and academic freedom well. We must at least prepare the ground for a resurgence of higher education focused on critical citizenship, for which we need more than humanities disciplines that are thoroughly housebroken and corporatized. We need to act before everyone forgets there were alternatives to higher education slavishly devoted to job training and income generation.

The conference on which this book was based was a wonderful opportunity to see how some very special people from multiple generations have embodied these commitments. It was an unforgettable gift.

Works Cited

Bérubé, Michael. *Marginal Forces/Cultural Centers: Tolson, Pynchon, and the Politics of the Canon.* Ithaca: Cornell UP, 1992.

Bousquet, Marc. *How the University Works: Higher Education and the Low-Wage Nation.* New York: New York UP, 2008.

Brunner, Edward. *Cold War Poetry: The Social Text in the Fifties Poem.* Urbana: U of Illinois P, 2004.

Hughes, Langston. *The Collected Poems of Langston Hughes.* Ed. Arnold Rampersad and David Roessel. New York: Knopf, 1994.

Kalaidjian, Walter. *Understanding Poetry.* Boston: Houghton, 2004.

Kramer, Aaron. "Denmark Vesey." *Wicked Times: Selected Poems of Aaron Kramer.* Ed. Cary Nelson and Donald Gilzinger. Urbana: U of Illinois P, 2004. 44–65.

Marsh, John. *You Work Tomorrow: An Anthology of American Labor Poetry, 1929–41.* Ann Arbor: U of Michigan P, 2008.

McKay, Claude. *Complete Poems.* Ed. William Maxwell. Urbana: U of Illinois P, 2004.

Nelson, Cary, ed. *Anthology of Modern American Poetry.* New York: Oxford UP, 2000.

———. *Repression and Recovery: Modern American Poetry and the Politics of Cultural Memory, 1910–1945.* Madison: U of Wisconsin P, 1989.

———. *Revolutionary Memory: Recovering the Poetry of the American Left.* New York: Routledge, 2001.

———, and Stephen Watt. *Academic Keywords: A Devil's Dictionary for Higher Education.* New York: Routledge, 1999.

———, and Stephen Watt. *Office Hours: Activism and Change in the Academy.* New York: Routledge, 2004.

Rolfe, Edwin. *Collected Poems.* Ed. Cary Nelson and Jefferson Hendricks. Urbana: U of Illinois P, 1993.

———. *Permit Me Refuge.* Los Angeles: California Quarterly, 1955.

CONTRIBUTORS

Editors

Peter K. Garrett is professor of English and former director of the Unit for Criticism and Interpretive Theory at the University of Illinois at Urbana-Champaign. He is the author of several studies of nineteenth- and twentieth-century fiction, including *Scene and Symbol from George Eliot to James Joyce*, *The Victorian Multiplot Novel*, and *Gothic Reflections*. He is currently working on a book tentatively entitled *Little Wars*, which traces the trope of model warfare from eighteenth-century to late-twentieth-century versions and explores its role as a site of reflection on narrative representation and play.

Michael Rothberg is associate professor of English and director of the Unit for Criticism and Interpretive Theory at the University of Illinois at Urbana-Champaign. He is the author of *Traumatic Realism: The Demands of Holocaust Representation* and coeditor, with Neil Levi, of *The Holocaust: Theoretical Readings*. He has published many articles on American, French, and German literature, film, and critical theory, and he is completing a book tentatively entitled *Multidirectional Memory: Remembering the Holocaust in the Age of Decolonization*. Chapters from that book have appeared in the *Yale Journal of Criticism*, *PMLA*, and *Critical Inquiry*.

Authors

Michael Bérubé is the Paterno Family Chair of English at Penn State University. He is the author of *Marginal Forces/Cultural Centers: Tolson, Pynchon, and the Politics of the Canon*, *Public Access: Literary Theory and American Cultural Politics*, *Life As We Know It: A Father, a Family, and an Exceptional Child*, and *The Employment of English: Theory, Jobs, and the Future of Literary Studies*. He is also the editor, with Cary Nelson, of *Higher Education under Fire: Politics, Economics, and the Crisis of the Humanities*. His most recent

231

books are *What's Liberal about the Liberal Arts?: Classroom Politics and "Bias" in Higher Education* and *Rhetorical Occasions: Essays on Humans and the Humanities.*

Marc Bousquet is the author of *How the University Works: Higher Education and the Low-Wage Nation.* Active in the graduate student caucus throughout the 1990s, he was the founding editor of *Workplace: A Journal for Academic Labor,* and he serves on the AAUP national council. He is working on two new books, *Tom Sawyer, Temperance Cadet* and *Child Labor Campus,* and he keeps a video Weblog at <http://www.howtheuniversity works.com>.

Edward Brunner is a professor of twentieth-century literature at Southern Illinois University. His previous publications include books on Hart Crane, W. S. Merwin, and on cold war poetry. Recent essays discuss "cultural front comics" on either side of World War II, particularly the artists and writers who used the adult-adventure comic strip as a form of dissent.

Marsha Bryant is an associate professor of English at the University of Florida and a recent recipient of a fellowship from the National Endowment for the Humanities. She is the author of *Auden and Documentary in the 1930s* and the editor of *Photo-Textualities: Reading Photographs and Literature.* Her recent work on women's poetry has appeared in *American Literature, Modernism/Modernity, Tulsa Studies in Women's Literature,* and the anthology *The Unraveling Archive: Essays on Sylvia Plath.*

Lisa Duggan is a professor of gender and sexuality studies, and director of the American studies program in the Department of Social and Cultural Analysis at New York University. She is the author of *Twilight of Equality: Neoliberalism, Cultural Politics, and the Attack on Democracy, Sapphic Slashers: Sex, Violence, and American Modernity,* and *Sex Wars: Essays in Sexual Dissent and American Politics.* She also has edited *Our Monica, Ourselves, the Clinton Affair and National Interest.* In addition, she writes frequently for newspapers and magazines such as *The Nation* and *The Village Voice,* and she is currently at work on *The End of Marriage: The War over the Future of State-Sponsored Love.*

Grant Farred is the author of, most recently, *What's My Name? Black Vernacular Intellectuals, Phantom Calls: Race and the Globalization of the NBA,* and *Long Distance Love: A Passion for Football.* He is the general editor of the journal *The South Atlantic Quarterly* and has taught at Duke University and Cornell University.

Jim Finnegan is an assistant professor of English at Anne Arundel Community College. His publications include "Edwin Rolfe's Historical Witness to the Spectacle of McCarthyism" in *College Literature* and "Theoretical Tailspins: Reading 'Alternative' Performance in *Spin* Magazine" in *Postmodern Culture.*

Karen Jackson Ford is a professor of English at the University of Oregon, where she teaches poetry and poetics. She also is director of the creative writing program. She has published *Gender and the Poetics of Excess, Split-Gut Song: Jean Toomer and the Poetics of Modernity*, and essays on American poetry. She is currently working on a book about race and poetic form in the United States.

Brady Harrison is a professor of English at the University of Montana. He is the author of *Agent of Empire* and the editor of a Broadview Literary Texts edition of Richard Harding Davis's *Soldiers of Fortune* and of a forthcoming collection of critical essays on Montana literature. He is currently at work on *Abysmal Folly: Negation in Late Modernist Narratives of Empire.*

Jane Juffer is an associate professor of English and feminist, gender, and sexuality studies at Cornell University. She is the author of *Single Mother: The Emergence of the Domestic Intellectual* and *At Home with Pornography: Women, Sex, and Everyday Life* and the editor of the *South Atlantic Quarterly* issue, *"The Last Frontier? Contemporary Configurations of the U.S.-Mexico Border.* She has written articles on mothering, lingerie, Latinos in baseball, Latina/o studies at the corporate university, and various aspects of the US-Mexico border. She was codirector and then director of Latina/o studies at Pennsylvania State University from 1999 to 2007.

Walter Kalaidjian is a professor of English and director of graduate studies at Emory University. He is the author of four books, *The Edge of Modernism: American Poetry and the Traumatic Past, American Culture between the Wars: Revisionary Modernism and Postmodern Critique, Languages of Liberation: The Social Text in Contemporary American Poetry*, and *Understanding Theodore Roethke.*

John Marsh is an assistant professor of English at the University of Illinois at Urbana-Champaign and the coordinator of the Odyssey Project, a year-long, college-accredited course in the humanities offered at no cost to adults living below or slightly above the federal poverty level. He is the editor of *You Work Tomorrow: An Anthology of American Labor Poetry, 1929–1941*, and he is currently at work on a book that reconstructs the role of the poor and working class in the development of modern American poetry.

Andrew Ross is a professor of social and cultural analysis at New York University. A regular contributor to *The Nation, The Village Voice*, and *Artforum*, he is the author of nine books, including *Fast Boat to China: Corporate Flight and the Consequences of Free Trade–Lessons from Shanghai: Low Pay, High Profile: The Global Push for Fair Labor, No-Collar: The Humane Workplace and Its Hidden Costs*; and *The Celebration Chronicles: Life, Liberty, and the Pursuit of Property Value in Disney's New Town*. He also has edited several books, including *No Sweat: Fashion, Free Trade, and the Rights of Garment Workers*, and, most recently, *Anti-Americanism*.

James D. Sullivan is an instructor of English at Illinois Central College, Peoria. His book, *On the Walls and in the Streets: American Poetry Broadsides from the 1960s*, was lauded as "a major contribution to modern print culture."

Jeff Sychterz graduated in 2005 with a PhD in English from the University of Illinois at Urbana-Champaign. He has published on Walt Whitman and has articles forthcoming on E. E. Cummings's sonnets and American Vietnam War poetry. He will complete in 2008 a three-year postdoc at the United States Naval Academy. He specializes in poetry and poetics, American literature, Anglo-American modernisms, and twentieth-century war literature.

Michael Thurston is an associate professor of English at Smith College. He is the author of *Making Something Happen: American Political Poetry between the World Wars* and the coeditor of *Modernism, Inc.* He has published numerous essays on modern and contemporary poetry and recently finished his manuscript, *Going to Hell: The Underworld Descent in Modern Poetry*.

Stephen Watt is a professor and chair of English at Indiana University, Bloomington. A frequent collaborator with Cary Nelson, he is the coauthor of *Academic Keywords: A Devil's Dictionary for Higher Education* and *Office Hours: Activism and Change in the Academy*. A specialist in American and Irish drama, he also is the author/editor of such books as *Postmodern/Drama: Reading the Contemporary Stage, Marketing Modernisms, American Drama: Colonial to Contemporary*, and *Joyce, O'Casey, and the Irish Popular Theater*.

INDEX